Carve-out M&A Transactions

A Practical Guide

Consulting Editor **Robbie McLaren**

Consulting editor
Robbie McLaren

Managing director
Sian O'Neill

Carve-out M&A Transactions: A Practical Guide
is published by

Globe Law and Business Ltd
3 Mylor Close
Horsell
Woking
Surrey GU21 4DD
United Kingdom
Tel: +44 20 3745 4770
www.globelawandbusiness.com

Printed and bound by CPI Group (UK) Ltd, Croydon CR0 4YY

Carve-out M&A Transactions: A Practical Guide

ISBN 9781787422407
EPUB ISBN 9781787422414
Adobe PDF ISBN 9781787422421
Mobi ISBN 9781787422438

Table of contents

Introduction

Robbie McLaren
Latham & Watkins

Cross-border carve-out transactions have been a recurring theme throughout my career. From the first transaction I led at the very start of my career to the most recent deal prior to this publication, each and every transaction has brought its own unique factual challenges. Such deals involve legal issues and risks that need to be understood, managed and apportioned, frequently bringing together a range of advisers and specialisms. I am hugely grateful to all of the specialist contributors to this volume for the giving of their time and expertise, without which this book would not exist.

While carve-out transactions are not new, what has changed in recent years is the increasing complexity and cross-border nature of these deals. This shift is largely due to:

- the greater sophistication and number of regulatory regimes, including national and regional antitrust bodies, national security bodies and other supervisors of regulated businesses; and
- the myriad of structuring solutions available to multinationals and the increasing globalisation of many industries and sectors.

Further, carve-out transactions are becoming more prevalent, with four key trends driving this growth.

- *Activist investors.* The increasing involvement of activist investors in US companies and the growing number of activists focusing on non-US markets has required boards worldwide to look more critically at their portfolio and product mix, as well as their geographical spread, either to avoid attention from activists or as a result of activist activity. If a board ultimately decides to divest non-core products or geographies, it is rare that this does not involve some kind of carve-out or separation.
- *Regulatory divestments.* In the current environment of shifting business models and the creation of new industries,

regulators have to work hard to catch up or keep up. This environment, combined with the trend towards heightened national scrutiny of transactions in sectors that were formerly not considered 'sensitive', has led to a growing number of transactions that are cleared subject to some kind of remedy. Scepticism amongst antitrust authorities regarding the effectiveness of behavioural remedies is leading to a renewed regulator focus on undertakings to divest product lines or business units, in order to secure necessary approvals.
- *Private equity*. In the recent era of easy liquidity and record amounts of available dry powder, private equity buyers are taking an expanding share of merger and acquisition (M&A) activity. This shift has increased the number of buyers chasing assets, thereby putting greater pressure on sponsors to originate primary deals internally and, ideally, away from an auction process. Many of these deals are developed through existing relationships with family-owned businesses, but also through proposing divestment ideas to large corporates – which also take the form of carve-outs.
- *Transformational mergers*. Truly transformational mergers bring together the themes of activist intervention, regulatory requirements and private equity acquisitions. For example, an activist investor will typically lobby for a merger of the target business with a competitor, in order to drive synergies etc, which leads to regulators requiring divestment of Y business division or business in X territory, that business is then acquired by a private equity purchaser. Alternatively, the purchaser may need to de-lever its balance sheet post-closing to maintain its investment grade rating or in order to persuade its shareholders to approve the transaction. The process to undertake such divestments, whether mandated by a regulator or as part of portfolio rationalisation post-closing, most often takes the form of a carve-out transaction.

Whilst these trends reflect current global dynamics, I expect that carve-out transactions will continue to play a role in M&A activity through all parts of the economic cycle – during times of distress (fire-sales), disruption (disposal of non-core or old-tech businesses), or booming M&A cycles (all of the above).

Regardless of the factors that facilitated any given carve-out, certain themes must remain at the forefront of practitioners and deal teams' minds throughout the carve-out process. Locating, protecting and acquiring the key assets and revenue drivers of the carved-out business is the core concern and focus of the buyer. Deeply integrated businesses can pose challenges, but understanding how the business operates (which may also require the seller's transaction team to be educated as to how it operates) and how the business will continue to operate in the future will mean that both buyers and sellers can achieve their goals.

In writing and editing this book, my goal has been to produce practical and usable guidance. The book contains contributions from specialists on subjects linked to the structuring and execution of carve-out transactions, providing an invaluable insight into the legal, regulatory and practical elements in play. Topics include documentary provisions, separation pitfalls, diligence matters, transitional services, employment risks, antitrust concerns and private equity financing challenges. The appendices include short guides to help counsel prepare for and implement a carve-out; from the preparatory steps and considerations through to thoughts on how to assess the buyer landscape and, ultimately, achieve closing and then manage a smooth and pain-free separation.

Given the complexity involved in structuring and managing carve-out transactions, this book is not intended as a guide for more straightforward M&A transactions. Instead, it seeks to assist M&A practitioners engaged in complex M&A transactions, both in-house and those in private practice. The guidance focuses not only on the key differences in negotiating and drafting transaction documents, and the various legal risks practitioners must manage, but also assesses the role of in-house counsel and separation advisers. I hope that you find this book enjoyable and instructive as you navigate your next carve-out transaction.

Purchase price mechanics

Farah O'Brien
Niall Quinn
Latham & Watkins

1. Introduction

The question of how much do I need to pay and how much will I receive, whether you are buying or selling, is critical for any mergers and acquisitions (M&A) transaction. In this chapter, we will consider the mechanisms used to answer this question and the relative merits of applying these on a carve-out. Carve-outs are complex transactions – it is often more challenging to work out how to get from the headline valuation to the purchase price in a carve-out compared to the sale of an existing stand-alone business.

A buyer values a business using various metrics to arrive at the 'enterprise value'. The enterprise value is a measure of the target's economic value as a whole and is important to a buyer because it represents the amount of cash required to acquire the equity of the target, on the assumption that the target has a normalised level of working capital, and has no cash or debt (often referred to as on a 'cash-free, debt-free' basis). A buyer will make certain assumptions in deriving the equity value of a target from its enterprise value, including as to the amount of net debt in the business, and as to what is a 'normal' level of working capital for that particular business.

The enterprise value and the assumptions on which it is based are typically agreed between the parties in principle at the outset of a transaction – in a competitive auction process, it can be helpful to have the highest 'headline price' to make the bid appear as attractive as possible to the seller.

As such, a mechanism is required in order to get from the enterprise value to the equity value. The two main mechanisms used to get there are:

- completion accounts; and
- locked box.[1]

---

1 While the majority of transactions use either a completion accounts or locked-box mechanism, the parties may also agree a fixed purchase price. The L&W Study shows that 18% of transactions surveyed had a fixed purchase price (ie, no adjustment); this is often the case in a restructuring scenario/sale out of administration or where a particular asset class (eg, real estate) means that a fixed price is more appropriate.

Figure 1. Enterprise to equity value

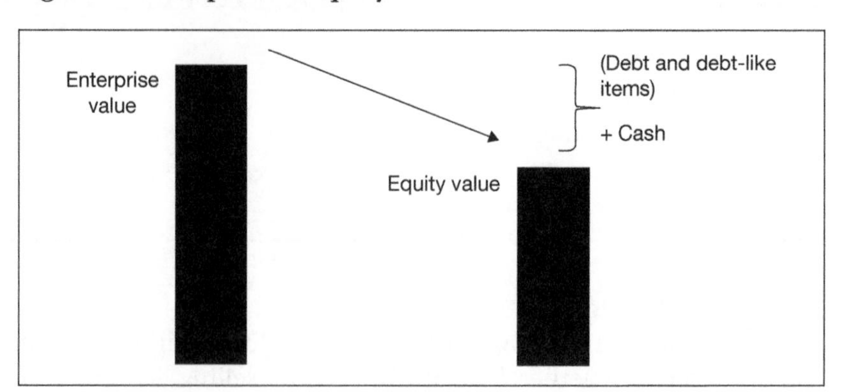

In principle, if the assumptions bridging the gap between enterprise value and equity value are the same, the completion accounts process and the locked-box mechanism should result in the same equity value. In practice, the choice between the two can have a major impact and result in cash coming out of the buyer's pocket and into that of the seller's (and vice versa). In a carve-out scenario, the choice between employing a completion accounts mechanism or a locked-box mechanism is particularly important – the target business may not operate on a stand-alone basis or have its own set of financial accounts; the seller may need to separate the target business from the seller's retained business before completion.

In this chapter, we will consider the basic principles of each of a locked-box mechanism and a completion accounts mechanism – how each works and their relative advantages and disadvantages. We will also consider why a locked-box mechanism is often not appropriate for a carve-out transaction and why completion accounts are the most commonly used mechanism for carve-outs.

2. Locked box

2.1 What is a locked box?

The locked-box mechanism is the most commonly used purchase price mechanic on European M&A transactions. According to the 2018 Latham & Watkins European Private M&A Market Study (the

L&W Study), 49%[2] of transactions surveyed[3] included a locked-box purchase price mechanic, up from 45% in the previous two-year period surveyed, a trend we have observed since the L&W Study began in 2013.[4]

So, what is a locked box? Under a locked-box mechanism, the equity value (being the cash paid to the seller) is agreed at signing by reference to a balance sheet (which is referred to as the 'locked-box accounts') as at an effective date prior to signing (known as the 'locked-box date'). The buyer, with the help of its accounting and financial advisers, has the opportunity before signing to diligence the locked-box accounts, in order to confirm the items, such as debt, cash and working capital, in order to reduce the enterprise value by the net amount of such items to derive the equity value of the target as at the locked-box date.

Having determined the enterprise value and equity value as at the locked-box date, the parties agree that from that point on:

- As the seller's equity value is fixed, the seller is unable to extract any further value from the target (commonly known as 'leakage'), in whatever form that may take. The starting point is that any payment to the seller(s) should constitute leakage, but as we will see in the context of a carve-out transaction this needs to be considered carefully depending upon the relationship between the target group and the seller. The classic example of leakage is a dividend but, in addition to dividends, leakage may also include (depending on the target business):
    - management fees;
    - the transfer of assets to the seller (unless, perhaps it is at a fair market value and occurs in the ordinary course);
    - the provision by the target of a guarantee or indemnity in favour of the seller;

---

2 In the United States, the position remains very different. According to the 2017 American Bar Association M&A Deal Points Study for private targets acquired by listed entities (the ABA Study), 86% of such deals in 2016–17 feature completion accounts, although anecdotally there has been increased interest in locked-box mechanisms in the United States in the last 12 months. In Asia, the market is somewhere between the United States and Europe with completion accounts used on around half of deals.

3 The L&W Study analysed over 210 deals that either signed or closed between July 2016 and June 2018 on which a Latham & Watkins European office advised.

4 The use of a locked-box mechanism on European deals has increased from approximately 46% to 49% over the five years that we have conducted the L&W Study.

  - the forgiveness of any debt or claim outstanding against the seller;
  - transaction costs; and
  - transaction bonuses.
- The buyer takes effective economic ownership of the target business as at the locked-box date – so, to put this another way, the buyer takes the risk or reward of performance of the target in the period between the locked-box date and completion. Whether or not levels of debt, cash or working capital increase or decrease between the locked-box date and completion, absent any leakage to the seller, the price payable (ie, the equity value which is determined as at the locked-box date) will remain the same (subject to the seller agreeing to compensate the buyer for the net cash profits generated between signing and closing – see below).

It is clear to see therefore that there is a certain amount of risk at play for both the seller and the buyer. Why would the buyer take effective economic ownership of a business before it has legal ownership and control, and why would the seller risk not benefiting from any upside in the business right up until completion?

There is a commonly held view that the locked-box mechanism favours sellers – and given the continued seller-friendly market, the results of the L&W Study showing the prevalence of the locked box across Europe support this view. The price is fixed at a point in time when the seller controls the business and the seller typically fixes the locked-box date and is better able to foresee (based on prior year trends) how the business is likely to perform from the locked-box date to completion. The seller has access to all of the information and essentially controls the flow of financial information to the buyer before signing when the price is agreed. The onus is therefore on the buyer, with access only to information provided by the seller, to diligence the locked-box accounts. Ideally the locked-box accounts would be audited to provide extra comfort as to their accuracy, but often this may not be the case (for example, if the latest audited accounts are stale, a buyer may wish to use a more recent set of accounts). The buyer is often therefore limited to seeking warranties on the accuracy of the locked-box accounts albeit that the buyer is likely to have to settle for warranties more akin to those given with respect to a set of management accounts.

Given the buyer has taken effective economic ownership of the business from the locked-box date but does not yet have legal control, the buyer will try to reduce its risk by requiring that the seller takes or refrains from taking certain actions that might impact on the economic performance of the business or the amount of debt that is to be repaid at completion (eg, by requiring that the seller does not enter into any new financing facilities). The buyer's ability to request these types of undertakings from the seller is, however, restricted by a number of factors including the risk of 'gun-jumping' where merger control clearance must be obtained before the deal completes, the competitive nature of an auction process, or simply the risk of hampering the business from operating in the ordinary course by having to seek consents from the buyer.

In addition, market practice has developed such that the seller would typically expect to be paid an additional amount (commonly known as a 'ticker') between the locked-box date and completion, calculated either as a fixed daily amount or as a percentage of the equity value, to compensate the seller for the fact that it has passed economic ownership to the buyer as at the locked-box date but will not receive its cash for transferring the ownership of the target until completion. Typically the ticker is calculated either by determining the amount of net cash expected to be generated (ie, taking into account any cash that is required to service debt) by the target between the locked-box date and completion, or the interest rate the seller would receive should it be able to put an amount of cash equal to the target's equity value to use as at the locked-box date – clearly in the case of the former, the seller is being compensated for not benefiting in the rewards of the business after the locked-box date.

The locked-box mechanism was devised in the early 2000s in the United Kingdom by the private-equity industry in frustration at the complexity of the completion accounts process. As we will see in further detail later in this chapter, a completion accounts process can take a very long time to resolve (sometimes many years) at substantial cost, both financially and in terms of management time for the buyer and the seller.

By contrast, the locked box was created as a simpler, faster and cheaper purchase price adjustment mechanism. As we saw above, the seller agrees with the buyer that it will not 'leak' any value out of the business between the locked-box date and completion. The buyer's only claim in respect of the purchase price post-completion is therefore to the extent there has been any value leakage to the

Figure 2. Timeline of a locked box

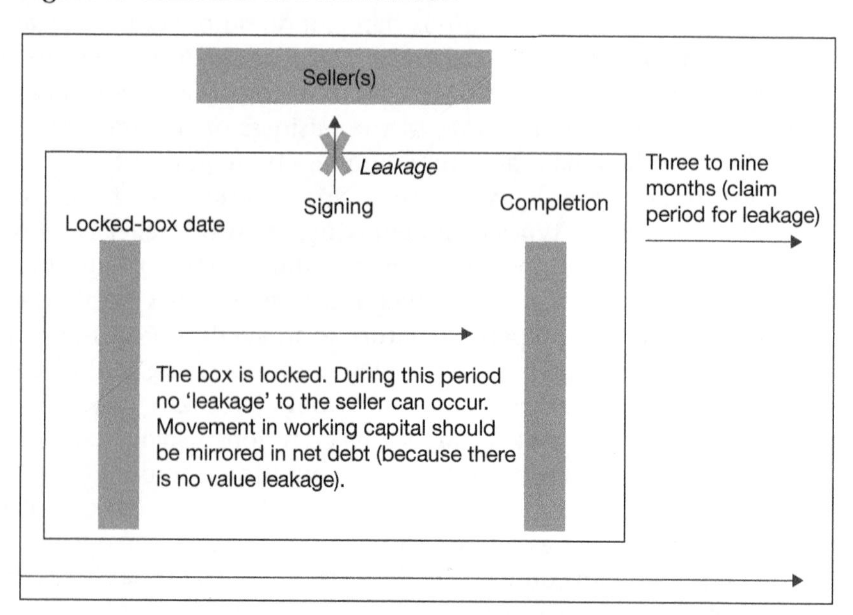

seller or its affiliates. In practice, the buyer typically pays the equity price at completion with no further claims relating to the purchase price between the parties after completion. It is very appealing, particularly for a private-equity seller who must distribute funds to its limited partner investors post-completion, to receive a final sum on completion which is not subject to adjustment in the same way as it would be with a completion accounts mechanism. Similarly for a private-equity buyer, it would need to consider how it can pay for a post-completion price adjustment which doesn't go in its favour – does it have the ability to draw down additional funds from its limited partners or under its acquisition financing facility? A locked-box mechanism avoids the time, energy and resources post-completion that a completion accounts mechanism requires and is less likely to result in a dispute post-completion.

2.2 Advantages/disadvantages of a locked box in a carve-out

To determine whether a locked-box mechanism is appropriate for a deal, you must ask yourself two key questions:

- Do you have a 'box' (ie, a legally and operationally separate business)?
- Can you 'lock' it (ie, are payments back and forth between the target business and the seller easy to determine)?

When asking these questions in respect of a carve-out, the answer is likely to be no.

As discussed earlier, ideally the 'box' is a nicely-contained stand-alone business under a single holding company with very little or no trading between it and the seller, the constituent parts of which are represented by a recent set of (audited) accounts which can be compared against a good history of like-for-like financial reporting (eg, three years of historical financials).

By definition, a target business which needs to be carved out of a larger business will not be standalone – it is true that there are varying degrees of integration within businesses undergoing carve-outs – for example, a target business may have few synergies with the larger retained business, or have been recently acquired and never fully integrated. It would be rare in even these circumstances however for the target business to be truly 'standalone'. For example, it may still benefit from a group-wide insurance policy or be subject to cash-pooling arrangements, or there may be liabilities outstanding under guarantees provided to guarantee obligations of the seller's group. It is unlikely too that a set of audited accounts will have been prepared for the target business as it is unlikely that it would report financially on a stand-alone basis. While the seller can of course prepare a set of *pro forma* financial statements for the target business, in an M&A process, it is unlikely however that any such *pro forma* accounts would be audited and so the buyer will be limited to undertaking its own diligence with limited historical information to compare against the *pro forma* accounts.

The second question of whether you can lock the box at the locked-box date is particularly challenging in the context of a carve-out. As between the seller's retained group and the target group, there may be many transactions occurring on a regular basis which would otherwise constitute leakage. For example, there may be payments passing between the two groups because there is significant intra-group trading; services such as payroll and procurement (for which fees and expenses may be due) may be provided, there may be intra-group debt and, assets may need to be transferred in order to ensure they are in the correct group at completion, and some assets may genuinely be shared between the two groups. It is unlikely to be in the interests of either group for all of these relationships to be terminated at the locked-box date. What if the transaction ultimately does not complete because of failure to secure merger control approvals? How does the target group carry on its business without these services provided by the seller's group? The more integrated the target business is into the seller's business, the more difficult it will be to 'lock the box' and therefore more difficult for the buyer to be comfortable that none of the transactions occurring between the seller and the target group constitute leakage. For example, in a situation where there is significant trading between the target and the seller, how can the buyer diligence whether payments made by the target to the seller are for goods or services genuinely provided by the seller and on arms' length terms? Conducting diligence on past practice may be helpful but might not provide the full picture. Is the seller happy with this or does it genuinely need flexibility to increase such payments between signing and completion in order to cover increases in its own costs? So the issue is, either leakage is tightly defined and the seller takes the risk of the continuing trading arrangements constituting leakage (for which the buyer would be indemnified), or, the buyer requires an extensive list of permitted actions (for example, daily cash pooling), which will be almost impossible to audit or police.

From a seller's perspective, using a locked box on a carve-out is challenging for similar reasons. Given the seller will typically agree to reimburse the buyer for leakage, in a complex carve-out scenario where there are trading relationships between the target business and the seller which are difficult to define, the seller is potentially opening itself up to the risk of leakage claims post-completion. For example, in the event that not all of the trading relationships between the seller and the company are provided for in permitted leakage, the buyer would have a claim against the seller to recover any such leakage.

3. Completion accounts

Despite the prevalence of the locked-box mechanism in European M&A, completion accounts continue to be used in a large number of transactions in Europe: 33% of transactions surveyed in the L&W Study included a completion accounts mechanism. Interestingly, the L&W Study showed that completion accounts are more commonly used on what we term English law transactions (being 42%) whereas they are much less common on French and German law deals (22% in each respectively). This may be because of the number of US buyers acquiring UK assets (following the recent decline in the value of sterling relative to the US dollar) where such US buyers will require the transaction to have a completion accounts mechanism because they are more familiar with it. It may also however be because English law is a popular governing law for transactions involving a large complex carve-out of a business located in a number of jurisdictions – and such a transaction is likely to use completion accounts rather than a locked-box mechanism.

3.1 What are completion accounts?

Completion accounts are a post-completion price adjustment mechanism. Under a completion accounts mechanism, the buyer and the seller agree a mechanism and a set of assumptions to enable an estimated equity value to be generated prior to completion to establish the amount paid at completion, such an estimate itself being based on estimated net debt as at completion, and the difference (if any) between the estimated level of working capital as at completion and a pre-agreed level of normalised working capital. The equity value will, however, be adjusted post-completion according to the actual value of certain of the target's assets and/or liabilities, and the actual level of working capital in the target, in each case, as at completion. Such assets and/or liabilities and working capital can only be determined once the completion accounts are drawn up after completion; the completion accounts are based on agreed criteria and principles, which are typically reflected in *pro forma* accounts attached to the share purchase agreement (SPA). The fundamental difference between completion accounts and a locked-box mechanism is the timing of the passing of risk and reward in the target business. For completion accounts, the risk and reward passes to the buyer at completion of the transaction, when the assets and/or liabilities of the business are calculated and feed into the equity value. This is in contrast to a locked-box deal, where the risk and reward passes to the buyer on the locked-box date (which, as discussed earlier, is the date of the reference accounts used to determine the equity value prior to signing).

Completion accounts and the purchase price adjustments that flow from them can take a number of forms depending on the target's business, assets, operations and the impact of seasonality on the business. For example, it is generally market standard to make adjustments based on net assets where the target business is in the real estate or financial institution sectors, or net debt for a leveraged business. The most common types of post-completion price adjustments are with respect to net-debt and working capital. The mechanism for determining the equity value as agreed before signing typically assume a normalised level of working capital – something which may be difficult to determine for a seasonal business or when the timing of completion is uncertain. The equity value also assumes an estimated amount of indebtedness. The equity price paid at completion will be based on the estimated levels of net debt and either the normalised or sometimes the estimated working capital at completion.

After completion has taken place, completion accounts will be prepared to determine the actual levels (depending upon the adjustments agreed in the completion accounts) of net debt and working capital as at the completion date. The equity price paid at completion will then be adjusted up or down based on the actual amounts at completion. This means the buyer could be required to 'top up' the amount of consideration it paid at completion or receive a 'refund' if it paid too much at completion. Similarly, the seller could be required to repay part of the consideration it received at completion or be entitled to receive additional consideration at completion. As explained above, this may be particularly unattractive for a private-equity sponsor, whether acting as seller or buyer because of its obligations to its limited partner investors.

(a) Process for preparing completion accounts

The SPA will provide for the preparation, review and agreement of the completion accounts within an agreed timeframe following completion. Typically, one party will prepare the first draft of the completion accounts, while the other party will review and potentially dispute items that it disagrees with. There is a perceived advantage in being the party which prepares the first draft of the accounts as that party's draft naturally frames the discussion around any disagreements/issues, and it falls on the other party to rebut the presumption that these accounts are correct. In practice, the buyer will control the financial records of the target after completion and, whilst the point is up for negotiation, the buyer will therefore generally prepare the first draft of the completion accounts.

To minimise the potential for disputes (as far as is possible), it is important for the SPA to clearly prescribe how the completion accounts are to be prepared. The SPA should provide for a set of accounting definitions to be used, a hierarchy of accounting policies with an appropriate order of precedence and a prescribed format for the accounts. There may be relative advantages and disadvantages of using a particular set of accounting policies over another depending on the type of business and the form of historic reporting. A clearly defined and detailed set of policies (for example, adopting the existing accounting policies used by the target) gives more certainty. However, a seller may have issues if there is a new item not dealt with in the previous accounts and it is hard to plan for every eventuality. Alternatively, general cooperation obligations (and less rigidly defined accounting policies) give the parties flexibility to pick any one of a number of policies but this may also lead to disagreement between the parties. Unlike a set of locked-box accounts where the definitions for leakage and permitted leakage are fairly standard and tightly defined, where completion accounts are used, there are likely to be extensive negotiations between the parties, their lawyers and accountants as to how to define the various assets and liabilities within the completion accounts. For example, if there is a net debt adjustment, the buyer will want 'third party indebtedness' to be drafted as widely as possible so as to catch not just third-party loans and bonds that are to be refinanced as part of the transaction, but (depending on the business) potentially also finance leases, operating and capitalised leases, and so-called 'debt-like items' such as pension liabilities, liabilities in respect of litigation or other claims against the business, unpaid deferred consideration or revenues, accrued but unpaid dividends, unpaid tax liabilities, transaction bonuses owing to employees and costs and expenses payable by the business in connection with the transaction.

If the buyer and the seller fail to agree the completion accounts within a certain period of time, a dispute resolution mechanism will be triggered, with disputes typically being referred to an independent accountant. In our experience, completion accounts provisions are frequently the subject of dispute between the parties; this is one of the drawbacks of using a completion accounts mechanism. Even where the parties have detailed provisions regarding what constitutes net debt and working capital, and the hierarchy of accounting policies, ultimately the adjustments are subjective in nature and the parties will often disagree on how to provide for them in the completion accounts. There is a tendency for post-completion price adjustments to result in a payment from the seller to the buyer – usually the quantum of any such adjustments is less than 5% of the purchase price, although in significant disputes, the value of the contested adjustment can be much higher.

(b) *Advantages/disadvantages of completion accounts in a carve-out*

One of the main drawbacks of the completion accounts mechanism is that it can take significant time to determine the final equity value. With this comes significant uncertainty because neither party knows for certain what the final purchase price will be until the post-completion price adjustment process has been completed. A typical completion accounts process might take anywhere between three months to a year to determine whether any adjustments are required. The parties rarely agree first hand and disputes often arise which prolong the process further. This is a particular issue for financial sponsors who need to ensure financing availability in order to pay any increase in consideration (when acting as buyer) or have obligations to return funds to their investors after exit (when acting as seller). Additional expense and risk is incurred by the buyer in connection with maintaining financing availability. From a seller's perspective, there may be costs associated with retaining (a portion of) the proceeds it received on completion to make any refund back to the buyer if necessary (and it may also affect the return on investment that a financial sponsor can report prior to finalisation of the completion accounts process). It is possible for the parties to agree a cap and/or a collar to the completion accounts adjustments, which would mean the buyer and seller can take comfort that they are only potentially liable up to the limits of the relevant cap and/or collar (although we note this is not common). Depending on the type of transaction and the parties involved, an escrow or retention account may also be used to give comfort to both parties that funds are available to fund adjustments. An 18-month completion accounts process, prolonged by a dispute which ultimately requires a financial sponsor seller to make a 'refund' to the buyer as a result of an adjustment down of the purchase price can be a real headache. The process of preparing, negotiating and settling completion accounts can also be expensive; particularly if there is a dispute between the parties. It can also serve to distract management from their day job of actually running the business.

A number of challenges are also presented when determining the correct level of working capital for completion accounts; in a carve-out transaction this is made more complex because the target business may not yet operate on a stand-alone basis. On a carve-out, one of the key challenges is the quality of financial information available in relation to the target business (eg, monthly, intra-month, historical and forecast financials) – in particular, easily identified historical accounting information for comparison purposes may not be available. As such, on a carve-out it may be even more difficult for the parties to agree on a set of accounting definitions, a hierarchy of accounting policies with an appropriate order of precedence and a prescribed format for the completion accounts (ie, the items we discussed above). It may be that the accounting standards used historically are appropriate only for the seller's retained business, and are less appropriate in the context of the target business (for example, where the target is a European operation and the seller's group was US based and so reported based on US GAAP). The accounting policies and methodology used should as far as possible be unambiguous and set out clearly the treatment of judgemental areas with the aim of minimising any element of subjectivity. Disputes are more likely to arise where there is ambiguity in the accounting principles which would allow for accounting judgement to be applied which could drive bigger adjustments (classic examples being long-term contract accounting judgement and environmental provisions). When both parties seek to address as far as possible every potential scenario or outcome to deal with this uncertainty, this can result in protracted negotiations. Despite the efforts of the parties, their lawyers and their accountants to identify those issues that are likely to prove contentious in practice and deal with them appropriately in the SPA, it becomes even more difficult to resolve such issues after completion when there is less incentive for either party to compromise. Contentious issues may very well result in a dispute between the parties further down the line.

As discussed before, in order to have completion accounts, you typically agree a format for the accounts (which can include relevant line items), and agree (so far as possible), a set of accounting policies. You also need to agree what constitutes net debt and a normalised level of working capital for a business which doesn't yet exist – and that assumes there is clarity as to the transaction perimeter – there is of course added complexity where the scope of the carve-out is either somewhat unclear at signing, or is subject to change between signing and completion. Customer contracts may be held with particular contracting entities but those entities may not hold any employees or incur other costs in relation to the running of the business (which instead may be shared across the wider group as a whole). Furthermore, to the extent that the carved-out business continues to transact with the seller's group going forward, it may not benefit from the same terms on a stand-alone basis as it did when part of the seller's group (at the more extreme end of the scale, this could mean that working capital needs to be remodelled). There may be separation costs involved with the carve-out itself, and potential for disagreement as to who should economically bear these costs. It should also be determined whether the buyer or the seller should bear any costs in excess of agreed estimates for such separation costs. In a carve-out, there are often significant intercompany balances/positions with the retained seller group which may need to be unwound, and in respect of which structuring and tax implications can arise. Similarly, the target business may not ever have been financed/funded on a stand-alone basis so there will be a need to consider cash requirements and foreign exchange considerations. All of these matters need to be agreed prior to signing so far as possible, which requires substantial time, cost and effort, and to the extent not determined prior to signing, the risk of a post-completion dispute increases materially.

Ultimately, however, the key advantage of using a completion accounts mechanism is that it gives both parties the ability to check they agree with the price at completion. In a carve-out, the target business and the existing group are often connected on many levels and the target group may have little or no track record of trading on a stand-alone basis. The buyer can take significant comfort from the fact that it can finalise the actual purchase price after completion when it can better understand how the business operates on a stand-alone basis. This is particularly relevant, where most of the carve-out may not be complete until completion and in fact at signing, the parties may only have a draft transaction perimeter that needs to be agreed before completion. Another plus point is that the seller does not need to spend the time (and incur the associated costs) involved with creating a suitable set of locked-box accounts for the carve-out business (which, given the complexities of carve-outs that we have discussed above, may prove to be inaccurate anyway). The relative speed of execution (assuming the parties do not get into protracted negotiations on the accounting policies) can be attractive for the parties to a large, complex carve-out where the transaction is sensitive or particularly confidential.

4. Conclusion

In summary, while a locked-box mechanism is the most commonly used purchase price mechanic on European transactions generally, it can often be difficult to define the box and lock it in a carve-out transaction. However, there are varying degrees of carve-out transactions, and so for a less complex carve-out, the parties may decide that the risk of relying on the locked-box accounts is worth avoiding a lengthy, complex and drawn out completion accounts process. For this reason, as a starting point, it is typically more appropriate to use completion accounts on a carve-out. Ultimately, completion accounts provide the parties with more comfort that the value of the assets and liabilities transferred at completion is accurately determined (because these are calculated after completion has occurred) – but it can take significant time (and expense) to actually finalise this process.

Conditionality

Jennifer Cadet
Nick Cline
Emily Cridland
Latham & Watkins

---

1. Introduction

This chapter provides an overview of several of the possible conditions to completion that the parties may agree to include in the documentation for a carve-out transaction. The precise conditions will vary from one deal to another and will depend on an array of factors, including the bargaining power of the parties and the relationship between the seller and the business and/or assets to be sold. Customary conditions also vary between European and US transactions.

Uniquely to carve-out deals, buyers will look to include conditions which will put the target business in the best position to operate independently of the seller upon completion in addition to the customary conditions. In a competitive bid process, and this is true whether or not the sale is a carve-out, the terms of the deal will be more seller-favourable and the sale agreement will therefore usually have fewer conditions.

Carve-out transactions tend to have more conditions than a typical mergers and acquisitions (M&A) transaction, not least because of the additional steps and potential complications caused by the mechanics of the separation of the business and/or assets being sold from the rest of the seller's business. Depending on the level of integration between the target assets and the seller's retained business, the completion of the carve-out can be one of the more complex conditions to completion.

2. The carve-out/reorganisation

A driving factor in the success of carve-out transactions is ensuring that the target business is set up in such a manner that it will be able to operate as independently as possible upon completion. In its simplest terms, a carve-out may be a neat acquisition of part of a corporate structure that already operates almost wholly independently and will only need minimal post-completion support from the seller's group. However, the target business may also be fully integrated within the seller's business, sharing, among other things, contracts, licences, support functions, employees, premises, intellectual property (IP) and customers. The completion of a complex group reorganisation to separate the businesses may be required to ensure that everything that's needed to run the target business is owned by the entity or entities being acquired, or that such entities have the rights to such assets prior to the completion date.

Depending on how amalgamated the target business is with the rest of the seller's business, the parties may want to include one general condition on the completion of the reorganisation in line with an agreed plan or target end structure, and/or include separate conditions related to specific parts of the reorganisation. The completion of the reorganisation as a condition is beneficial for both parties, so that the seller is able to deliver on its obligation to sell the relevant assets, and the buyer is able to track the creation of the stand-alone business that it wants to buy.

Monitoring satisfaction of the reorganisation condition can be complicated, especially as the buyer will have limited access to, and knowledge of, the inner workings of the target business in the interim period, but will want to have sufficient oversight to give the buyer comfort on the timeline and the satisfaction of the condition. The seller, on the other hand, will be (and will want to remain) in control of the reorganisation and will want to avoid an overly prescriptive plan to allow for necessary changes whilst it is still in control of the business. The parties will also want to avoid 'gun jumping' concerns arising as result of the buyer taking control prior to completion if there are anti-trust approvals required.

One of the most helpful deliverables for all parties is the structure paper, or step plan, typically prepared by the seller's tax advisers. The paper will detail the steps required in order to transfer the target business and/or assets to the buyer including what and how any assets, shares, people, cash and debt will move, timings, what new entities may need to be created and if any tax elections need to be made. This can range from a few simple steps to complex manoeuvring involving multiple jurisdictions over the course of several months.

If satisfaction of the reorganisation condition is tied to the completion of the steps as set out in an agreed form structure paper, the parties will want the ability to make any necessary amendments to the plan during the implementation. The buyer will be led by its own tax planning goals (which may not tie in with the seller's), but the seller will want to minimise the buyer's involvement. The seller will also be obliged to comply with its interim covenant obligations (eg, operation of the target business in the ordinary course) and the language in the sale agreement will need to be reviewed carefully to ensure that there is no inadvertent breach of either the covenants or the reorganisation condition by the seller's compliance with the other.

The buyer will usually want to be provided with written, documentary evidence of the completion of each aspect of the reorganisation, the form of which will depend on the nature of the relevant step, and it will be important to maintain regular dialogue during the course of the reorganisation to discuss the progress and any proposed changes. For actions that do not readily come with confirmations from third parties, for example the migration of internal payroll or other information technology (IT) systems, it will be important for the parties to be clear upfront how evidence of the satisfaction of such elements of the condition will be communicated. Depending on the complexity of the reorganisation, it may be prudent to establish a 'separation committee' of representatives from each party's operational and legal teams so that regular calls or meetings can take place to monitor the progress of the reorganisation and determine when each aspect has been completed.

Set out below are some of the key categories that the parties will need to consider when dealing with the pre-sale reorganisation, each of which will require diligence by both parties' advisers:

- *Entities.* The corporate bodies (be they companies, partnerships or other legal entities) that make up the target business may be spread throughout the seller's existing group and transfers may be required to move all of the target business's entities underneath one or more direct target companies, and to move out entities that are not to be sold to the buyer. If a share of any joint venture entities will be transferred, then consents from the other joint venture party may be required, which could also be requested as a condition to close by the buyer if the joint venture is material to the business. In a study on US carve-out transactions, 55% had the receipt of third-party consents as a condition to completion.[1]
- *Employees.* The parties should assess which employees are required to operate the target business post-completion

1 2017 American Bar Association M&A Carve-out Transactions Deal Points Study, which analysed 126 carve-out transactions announced in 2015 and 2016.

and whether any employment arrangements they have with the seller's retained group should be transferred to the target business, and vice versa. For target businesses which are particularly reliant on the input and know-how of their employees, sellers may look to include a separate condition that the workforce, or more likely specific key employees, are employed by the target business in advance of completion, potentially on new terms that the buyer has agreed to. In addition, the seller may be obliged to hire new employees where someone is in a split role and will be retained by the seller. There may also need to be redundancies and/or an employee or works council consultation process. A carve-out transaction may more readily trigger a works council or employee notification or consent requirement if it includes direct employee transfers rather than an indirect share sale.[2]

- *Contracts*. The parties will need to determine how to handle each of the contracts with the target business's customers and suppliers, especially if no entity in the target business is a party to such agreements or the contract contains a right for the other party to terminate on a change of control. Certain contracts may need to be transferred out by the target entities if they relate solely to the seller's business, and some contracts may need to be split if they relate to both. In the event that the target business has any material contracts which require third-party consents or notifications in advance of completion, the buyer may request a separate condition to completion that these are obtained or completed. The seller will likely only agree to this as a condition where the target business cannot be run without the relevant contract, as in most cases a commercial contract can be terminated (usually with notice) by the other party in any event.
- *IP/IT*. The parties should also evaluate what intellectual property (IP) and IT assets, including any licences for the same, are held by the seller and should be transferred to the target business and whether any such licences have consent requirements. The parties will also need to determine whether any such assets held by the target business should be transferred to the seller prior to completion, and possibly licensed back to the target group, or whether the target group

2 See the "Employment and pensions aspects of carve-out transactions" chapter for further information.

will need to license any IP or IT that it will hold following completion to the seller (such license may be included in a transitional services agreement).[3] With respect to transfers of registered IP, the parties will need to assess carefully the transfer requirements to determine whether separate transfer or assignment documents and filings are needed, in which jurisdictions and when.

- *Regulatory.* In regulated businesses there are likely to be licences and permits required to be held by the target group, and the parties will need to assess whether any will need, and are able, to be transferred to the target business and if the buyer needs to submit any applications for their transfer, or the grant of new licences or permits, in advance of completion. The grant of any such new or transferred material licences or permits to the buyer may be requested as a separate condition to completion.
- *Property.* To the extent any real property or other physical assets need to be transferred to the target business, thought should be given to any filing or consent requirements, how and when physical assets will be delivered to their new location or if access to third-party property (eg, storage facilities for stock) is required. If the buyer is granted access to the target business's sites in the interim period between signing and completion to monitor compliance with interim covenants, evidence of the physical delivery of any assets could be provided then.
- *Financing.* The carve-out of the target business may also include the need to settle inter-company debts, move cash to or from the target business as well as open or close bank accounts. If the business is being acquired on a cash-free, debt-free basis, then the seller will likely need to terminate all inter-company and third-party indebtedness prior to completion in any event, but evidence of such transfer or termination may be requested in the context of the reorganisation as well. The buyer may also need to obtain new insurance coverage for the business or assets that it will acquire.

3 This is discussed in more detail in the "Transitional services" chapter.

3. Other conditions

The parties may agree to include other conditions in the sale agreement in addition to the completion of the carve-out of the target business and/or assets from the seller's group.

3.1 Antitrust

While European deals do not usually include as many conditions as are found in US deals, antitrust and certain regulatory clearances are often mandatory across all jurisdictions because many merger control regimes are suspensory, meaning that approval is required prior to the merger/carve-out acquisition being completed. The seller and buyer will need to cooperate to complete both analyses and filings, potentially in multiple jurisdictions, and the condition to completion will be the receipt of any applicable clearances needed from a particular government or regulatory body or the expiration of any relevant waiting periods. Obtaining antitrust and regulatory clearances may require the parties to enter into certain side arrangements or require the buyer to divest certain assets to limit the restriction on competition caused by the proposed transaction.[4]

3.2 Shareholder approval

The parties would usually require that all shareholder/board approvals are obtained prior to signing so that no such conditions (which could give the relevant party a walk right) are required. If the transaction involves a public company and the transaction is significant then it may be necessary to obtain shareholder approval after the transaction has been announced but prior to completion in which case a condition that relevant shareholder approval has been obtained will need to be included. On the sell-side, shareholder approval might be necessary if the transaction involves all or substantially all of a seller's business. For buyers, the issuance of shares as consideration could trigger approval rights for their shareholders.

3.3 Financing

While buyers may wish to include a condition that it will not be obliged to complete the transaction without its debt or equity financing being in place, it is rare to see such a condition in European transactions. The 2018 Latham & Watkins European Private M&A

---

4 This is discussed in greater detail in the "Antitrust" chapter.

Market Study (the L&W Study)[5] found that only 3% of private M&A transactions in Europe between July 2016 and June 2018 contained a financing condition. Rather than agree to conditionality around buyer financing, the seller will want the buyer, if it is obtaining external funding, to rely on its commitments from lenders/investors and if such funding is withdrawn for any reason, the seller will want the buyer to still be obliged to close even if it has to procure expensive last minute financing.

3.4 Material adverse change

Material adverse change (MAC) conditions also remain relatively uncommon in European transactions – with the L&W Study noting that only 15% of such deals had such a clause. This percentage has increased from 10% in 2012,[6] but still remains well behind US transactions where, overall, 88% included a stand-alone MAC clause,[7] and when only carve-out transactions were surveyed, the figure was 66%.[8] In Asia, a mixture of US and English law style documentation is used and the approach to MACs tends to follow the style of the sale agreement.

A buyer may request a MAC condition with respect to the whole or only a particular part of a business being acquired on a carve-out, and such a condition can take various forms. They can also refer to events that have a detrimental impact on the market generally, events that relate to the target business specifically, or a mixture of both.

3.5 Accounts information

Where the financial information that has been prepared on the target business is not of sufficiently high quality (whether due to time constraints or the complexities involved in preparing it), a buyer will seek some form of contractual protection with respect to such information, usually in some form of warranty. However, where the buyer is a public company and/or is raising cash through the issue of public securities (whether equity or debt), there will

---

5 The L&W Study (2018), which analysed over 210 deals which were signed or closed between July 2016 and June 2018 and on which a European office of Latham & Watkins was an adviser.

6 The L&W Study (2018).

7 2018 SRS Acquiom MarketStandard Deal Terms Study, which analysed 925 private-target acquisitions that closed from 2014–2017.

8 2017 American Bar Association M&A Carve-out Transactions Deal Points Study, which analysed 126 carve-out transactions announced in 2015 and 2016.

likely be an obligation on the seller to prepare audit-quality historical financial information with respect to the carved-out business after the transaction has signed. It may be possible for the buyer, if they are in a strong negotiating position to require some right to terminate the transaction prior to closing in the event that the subsequently prepared audited financial information materially deviates from the financial information provided at signing.

Naturally, the seller will want to avoid giving the buyer a walk-away right, especially one which may be more easily triggered given the complexities in pulling together the financial information prior to signing a deal and the limited history the target business has of producing such financials.

This type of condition is not that common although it did appear in the 2014 acquisition by Mylan Inc of the non-US businesses of Abbott Laboratories, where there was a complex completion condition that the audited financial statements delivered following execution of the transfer agreement contained no material differences compared to the reference performance financial statements provided at the time of signing.

3.6 Breach of warranty/covenant

Where there is likely to be a significant gap between signing and completion, a buyer may request a condition that there has been no (material) breach of any covenant or warranty. If agreed to, a seller may request a cure period, or the ability to delay completion, before the buyer has the right to terminate the sale agreement. Such conditions are also relatively unusual in European deals, with only 12% of transactions studied in the L&W Study containing one. Comparatively, 99% of US acquisitions studied contained a provision that the seller's representations and warranties should be accurate on the completion date, though in 97% of transactions this is qualified by some level of materiality.[9]

4. Details of conditionality

As noted above, with respect to the reorganisation, in addition to agreeing the specific conditions to completion, the seller and buyer should also consider how they will verify and, if necessary, vary the requirements imposed in the sale agreement.

---

9 2018 SRS Acquiom MarketStandard Deal Terms Study, which analysed 925 private-target acquisitions that closed from 2014–2017.

If the parties include very detailed conditions in the sale agreement, they should also consider including the obligation to allow immaterial deviations from such conditions. For example, if the buyer has a prescribed list of each contract which must be novated in favour of the target group as part of the defined reorganisation condition, there should likely be an exception in the event any of those contracts terminates in the ordinary course of business during the time between signing and completion of the transaction.

The parties should also specify the level of effort they must expend to satisfy the conditions, with the level of commitment required denoting the materiality of the condition. Under English law, a 'best endeavours' obligation is more stringent than 'reasonable endeavours',[10] and 'all reasonable endeavours' typically falls somewhere in between the two. While 'reasonable endeavours' does not require the obligor to sacrifice its own commercial interests as is the case with 'best endeavours',[11] 'all reasonable endeavours' often requires more context to decipher and in certain situations could rise to the level of 'best endeavours'. In US deals on the other hand, parties may use 'reasonable best efforts', 'commercially reasonable efforts', 'reasonable efforts' or 'best efforts'. Unlike English law, however, the hierarchy between each of these is not as clearly delineated, which can be further complicated by parties using more than one type of 'efforts' obligation in the same agreement. In any jurisdiction, to avoid confusion or dispute, the parties may wish to define what they mean by any level of effort provided in the agreement, including any actions which they are not required to take in order to satisfy the condition.

5. Conclusion

In summary, this chapter gives a high-level overview of some of the more common conditions that might be requested by either a buyer or seller in a carve-out transaction, and how those conditions might be interpreted. Conditionality in a carve-out is likely to be more complex and bespoke than on a standard M&A deal, so careful thought should be given to the construction and drafting of this part of the sale agreement at an early stage.

---

10 *Rhodia International Holdings Ltd v Huntsman International LLC* [2007] EWHC 292.

11 *P&O Property Holdings Ltd v Norwich Union Life Insurance Society* [1993] EGCS 69; Rhodia.

Carve-out protections

Beatrice Lo
Robbie McLaren
Latham & Watkins

---

1. Introduction

This chapter focuses on some of the key contractual protections that a buyer or a seller would look to obtain in a carve-out transaction. While some of the contractual protections would be similar to any other mergers and acquisitions (M&A) transaction, it is common to see additional provisions in a carve-out transaction to deal with issues relating to the separation of the target from the seller's retained group.[1] The specific terms of warranty, indemnity and other protections will also vary depending on the particular business, the structure and the circumstances of the transaction.

A carve-out transaction could take the form of an asset sale, a share sale or a combination of both. Even if the transaction between the seller and the third-party buyer is structured as a share sale, a carve-out transaction will often involve a pre-sale reorganisation within the seller's group and this may involve intra-group asset sales to the target group. This chapter is not intended to comprehensively address all the complexities and nuances that could arise in any carve-out transaction, but seeks to highlight some of the main contractual protections to address some of the risks commonly involved in a carve-out transaction.

2. Apportionment of assets

2.1 Wrong pockets

One of the key issues in a carve-out transaction is identifying the assets and liabilities which are to form part of the transaction and accordingly providing in the sale and purchase agreement protections for:

---

1 See also the "Separations – the in-house perspective" chapter.

- the seller, to ensure it has sold or transferred all the assets and liabilities it is expecting to dispose of and not any other assets that it had wanted to retain; and
- the buyer, to ensure it receives all the assets it is expecting to acquire and related liabilities it is expecting to assume and not any other assets or liabilities.

To address the risk that certain assets have been transferred to the buyer or retained by the seller when it was not intended by either party, a 'wrong pockets' clause is often included in the sale and purchase agreement for a carve-out transaction to reallocate those assets after completion.

A wrong pockets clause will typically provide that if, following completion:

- an asset which should properly be part of the seller's group ends up with the target's or buyer's group then the relevant member of the target's or buyer's group will transfer that asset to the seller's group; or
- an asset which should properly be part of the target's or buyer's group has been left in the seller's group, then the relevant member of the seller's group will transfer that asset to the target's or buyer's group.

One of the key points to be negotiated between the parties will be what assets count as having ended up in the 'wrong' place – should only the assets that were exclusively used in the business of the other group before completion be transferred back or just the assets that were predominantly or primarily used? If, for example, an asset was not used exclusively in the seller's group but is also used in the target group but the wrong pockets clause requires that asset to be transferred back to the seller group, then consideration will also need to be given to whether the seller should also be required to grant a transitional service back to the target group for the use of that asset or whether the risk should be borne entirely by the buyer. The other key consideration is at what price any asset transfers should take place under the wrong pockets clause. To avoid further payments between the parties, it is typical to see that a transfer of assets under the wrong pockets clause is at book value or market value with the amount payable being treated as included in or as an adjustment to the purchase price.

2.2 Sufficiency of assets

Where the target business is being carved out from the seller's group, the buyer will want to ensure that the target business will be able to continue to operate once it has left the seller's group.

In an M&A transaction involving a target that is standalone, a seller will normally resist giving any warranty that the target (in the case of a share sale) or the assets included in the transaction (in the case of an asset sale), together with any transitional services, as applicable, comprise all the assets necessary for the continuation of the target business. However, in a carve-out transaction, the buyer may have a stronger argument for some form of warranty protection relating to the sufficiency of assets in the target group as the seller's group is best placed to take on the risk as to whether it has packaged all the relevant assets for sale that comprise the business.

2.3 Stranded assets

If the carve-out transaction is being structured as an asset sale or certain assets need to be transferred to the target company pre-sale, consents may need to be required before such asset can be transferred. For example, landlord consent will most likely be required to transfer any leasehold property or there may be restrictions on assignments under a contract. Further, if any contracts need to be novated, the counterparty to the contract will also need to approve and be party to the novation agreement.

For critical assets or contracts, the parties may agree in the sale and purchase agreement that obtaining any required consents for the transfer of such assets or contracts needs to be a condition to completion of the entire transaction.[2] However, if there are any assets or contracts that are critical to the target business, it would be preferable for all parties to try to deal with those before signing, if possible (otherwise the deal could be held hostage by a key supplier or customer). Alternatively, the parties could consider structuring the transaction in a different way to avoid triggering the relevant consent requirement.

For non-critical assets or contracts, some of the contractual mechanisms that are commonly used to address the risk of required consents not being obtained for the transfer of such assets or contracts to the buyer include:

---

2 See further the "Conditionality" chapter.

- an obligation on the seller to use all reasonable endeavours to obtain the consent;
- if consent is still not obtained by a long stop date, for the seller to hold the asset or contract on trust (provided that there is no restriction on this in the relevant contract);
- a back-to-back arrangement with the seller involving the seller sub-contracting its obligations under the relevant contract to the buyer or the buyer acting as the seller's agent, in either case in consideration for the seller passing through any benefits received under the underlying contract (provided that there is no restriction on sub-contracting or agency in the relevant underlying contract);
- a price adjustment mechanism; or
- termination of the contract with an indemnity from the seller for any losses incurred by the buyer relating to such termination.

2.4 Group insurance

It is common for business insurance (eg, director's and officer's liability insurance, business interruption insurance, property insurance, etc) to be obtained on a group wide basis. In a carve-out transaction, the seller's group would not typically arrange for the target to obtain separate insurance prior to completion. Instead, it would be left to the buyer to arrange its own insurance cover for the target after completion.

Where the target has an outstanding insurance claim under the seller's group policy, the buyer may wish for such claim to continue after completion. The buyer might require that the seller procure that the relevant policy is maintained and either for the seller to continue to pursue such claims and pass on any insurance proceeds, or if possible, for the target to be able to continue to pursue the claim directly with the insurer.

The buyer may also want protection for the risk of an insured event occurring, which affects the target before completion and is covered under the seller's group policy, but where no claim had yet been made under such policy. There could be a number of reasons that a claim had not yet been made, such as that the relevant claim documents are still being prepared or it is not yet known that a claim could be made. This could be addressed by the buyer or the target obtaining its own insurance relating to past events. This is the common approach for some types of insurance, such as director's and officer's liability insurance where run-off cover is generally widely available in the market.

Alternatively, the buyer could seek a provision in the sale and purchase agreement for the seller to maintain its insurance policies and for the target to be able to claim (or for the seller to claim on its behalf) in relation to an insured event that occurred before completion. Even if the seller's group insurance policies permit this, such a provision may be resisted by the seller as it could be administratively burdensome to deal with any target claims, the seller may wish to control the relationship with its insurers or the seller is concerned that the target claim may affect the level of the seller's group insurance premiums in the future. These concerns of the seller can also be dealt with in the sale and purchase agreement, for example, by providing that the seller retains conduct of any claim that the target wishes to make, for the buyer to pay the seller's costs relating to making the claim and for the buyer to reimburse or share the costs of any increase in premiums that result from the target making a claim.

3. Apportionment of liabilities

In an asset sale, only those assets and liabilities that are specified to be transferred in the sale and purchase agreement will be transferred to the buyer. Subject to certain limited exceptions,[3] the buyer will have the flexibility to exclude unwanted liabilities from the transaction and leave those behind with the seller. This is one of the major advantages of an asset sale for a buyer (and a disadvantage for the seller). If the buyer can negotiate that certain liabilities are simply not acquired, then it will not need to seek warranty protection relating to the nature or amount of those excluded liabilities. However, typically a buyer will seek an indemnity from the seller with respect to all such excluded liabilities. For any liabilities that are assumed by the buyer, the seller will seek an indemnity from the buyer in respect of any costs or liabilities incurred by the seller after completion relating to the liabilities that the buyer agreed to assume.

In contrast, in a share sale, the buyer will acquire the target company with all its liabilities and obligations. The buyer could seek an indemnity from the seller for liabilities that it did not want as part of the transaction (which could cover both a specific list of

---

3 See, eg, the "Employment and pensions aspects of carve-out transactions" chapter.

liabilities as well as a more general indemnification for liabilities that relate to the retained business of the seller). However, this is a somewhat weaker protection than simply not acquiring the liabilities in the first place and will be of limited value if the seller does not have the financial resources to pay any claim. This risk could be mitigated by negotiating a purchase price reduction, an escrow or retention amount or by obtaining insurance (see section 4 below).

4. Warranty and indemnity insurance

Insurance products to cover the risk of a breach of a warranty under the sale and purchase agreement or indemnity under the tax covenant are increasingly available in the market. The most common is warranty and indemnity (W&I) insurance which covers losses arising out of a warranty breach or an indemnity claim under the tax covenant. Insurance could be taken out by the buyer or by the seller and typically would cover only unknown or unforeseen matters. Other common exclusions from coverage include matters like fraud, criminal fines and underfunded pension schemes.

W&I insurance is a useful tool to bridge the gap between the buyer's wish to receive proper deal protection and a seller's aim to achieve a clean exit. It may also make a bid more attractive in an auction scenario if the buyer is willing to use insurance to cover risks rather than obtain recourse from the seller. In some circumstances, the seller's agreed liability cap in a sale and purchase agreement could be as low as £1 so the warranties and indemnities are given by the seller simply for the purposes of facilitating insurance coverage for any breach. A W&I policy is also useful for a buyer if the buyer is concerned about the seller's financial position or the ability to recover damages from the seller in respect of any breaches.

It is becoming more common to employ W&I insurance in transactions, although as at the date of writing, it is still only used in a minority of deals. According to the 2018 Latham & Watkins European Private M&A Market Study (the L&W Study), which surveyed over 210 deals over a two-year period, 32% of the transactions employed some form of W&I insurance, up from 13% and 22% in the 2016 and 2017 editions of the L&W Study.

Other types of insurance products that could be employed to help parties manage their risk include:

- tax or contingent liability insurance to cover known issues in a deal (eg, a known tax issue) where the quantum of the loss is potentially high but the likelihood of the loss arising is low;

Figure 1. Use of warranty and indemnity insurance[4]

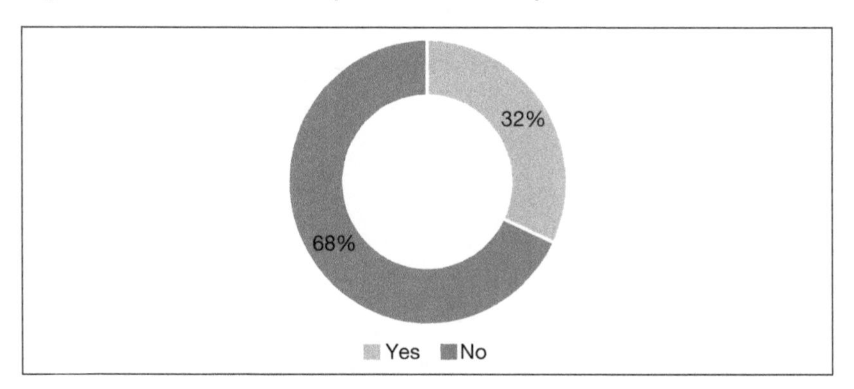

- specific insurance to cover existing litigation of the target – eg, if the loss is higher than an estimated amount; and
- specialist environmental risk cover (this could form part of a W&I policy or be a separate stand-alone policy, eg, to back up an environmental indemnity).

5. Conclusion

Compared to a typical M&A transaction for a stand-alone target group, a carve-out transaction will involve a number of additional considerations for both the buyer and the seller, which may be addressed through contractual protections in the transaction documents. In particular, there are a number of additional risks that a buyer will not expect to be burdened with, such as those related to the separation of the carve-out business or the moderation of the retained business by the seller. The apportionment of these risks will largely depend on the negotiating strengths of the parties, but given that these risks will not be covered by W&I insurance, the type of seller should also be factored in. While the types of protections and negotiation positions of the parties will clearly be deal-specific, both a buyer and the seller can be better prepared by considering in advance its approach to the common contractual positions taken in a carve-out transaction, as described in this chapter.

4 2018 Latham & Watkins European Private M&A Market Study.

Conducting due diligence

Deborah Kirk
Latham & Watkins

1. Introduction

In this chapter, I explore the diligence process that would customarily be conducted in the context of preparation for a carve-out transaction. Carve-out transactions give rise to some fairly singular diligence issues which go both to the value of the target business being purchased but equally, and perhaps more fundamentally, they go to the threats to business continuity post-completion and what is required in terms of cost and access to on-going support from the retained business in ensuring that continuity.

A buyer of a carve-out business will be seeking to understand how the operation will function on 'Day 1' (completion). If it is not a business which is entirely independent of the retained business, they will want to ask: what are the remaining dependencies on the retained business (and third-party providers) and how will these be served in an interim period and eventually severed?

The way in which diligence is conducted on these deals tends to differ somewhat from the ordinary course. There is a fair amount of reliance on the seller to develop a picture of the way in which the target business operates, including the attachments and dependencies it has on the retained business (or indeed, vice versa). A good carve-out process will begin with a seller having already conducted a fair amount of preparation, prior to engagement with the buyer, either through having actually completed all of, or aspects of, the carve-out prior to commencing a transaction process, or having a well-considered and well-documented plan to share with the buyer as to how it hopes to achieve this by or after completion, together with some orientation around the associated costs.

The end game of diligence on a carve-out transaction is to ascertain how to achieve long-term arrangements for business continuity. One consideration that should be in the mind of the buyer when conducting this diligence and planning the deal structure is the future plans for the target business. If, for example, an initial public offering (IPO) is anticipated, or a future sale is being considered in the short term, the reliance on the retained business in order for the target business to function should be a key consideration as material dependencies on the seller, or insufficient arrangements as to brand or access to data/systems, may prejudice these future plans.

A plan of how to commence the separation planning and identification is set out in the appendices.

2. The purpose of diligence

While the diligence process in a carve-out transaction will serve its usual purpose of identifying issues and risks that could impact on the buyer's willingness to do the deal, or which will need to be considered and/or addressed as part of the transaction (either by way of a purchase price reduction or protections that are crafted into the deal documentation such as indemnities or warranties in the sale documents), there is an additional type of issue characterised by the elements of overlap of asset and service use between the retained and target businesses. The buyer of a business which is being carved out will need to understand what the service lines assets are used by that business, who provides that service/access to that asset and how the target business will receive or have access to it post-completion and ultimately, long term.

The diligence process should therefore aim to flush out the dependencies between the businesses so that gaps and risks can be identified and legislated for in the documentation. This allows the buyer to strategise as to how the remaining links will eventually be severed between the business or indeed whether the level of dependency on the retained business, or the terms proposed for business continuity, makes the sale uneconomic. Ultimately, the more visibility on service lines and costs a seller can provide to a buyer prior to finalising any documentation setting out interim or transitional arrangements, the less likely a seller is to be exposed to uncertainties within the documents as to the scope of services and duration of service provision that it will be expected to provide under post-completion arrangements. On the buyer side, the more comfort that can be provided to the buyer that there is full visibility over the needs of the target business (and that the documentation provided ensures business continuity for the target by either transferring the assets or providing them under post-completion arrangements), the less exposure it is likely to suffer in terms of unforeseen costs and gaps in business operations.

3. The diligence process

A standard diligence process will require the investment of the seller in making available to the buyer (or bidders) the documentation associated with the business it is selling for a potential buyer's review (and perhaps provide some guidance in helping the buyer to understand how these underpin the universe of its business). While it is therefore incumbent on the seller to 'open its books' in this regard, diligence in context of non-carve-out transactions is primarily buyer-driven. It is for the buyer to take the lead in reviewing the documentation, raise queries and drive the diligence process. In a carve-out transaction, a fair deal more work will be expected to have been conducted by the seller prior to this point. This is because the seller is in the best place to educate a buyer as to which of its assets are used by the target business and what dependencies there are between the two business lines. In this sense, separation diligence is often primarily seller-driven and a buyer will look to the seller to guide it through the areas of business overlap and how it envisages these will be disentangled.

That said, when the shared assets and services have been identified, there will need to be an on-going dialogue between buyer and seller to assess which of these shared items a buyer wishes to acquire as part of the transaction (and how this can be achieved) and what should be done with any unwanted arrangements (and who should bear any associated stranded costs). It is more common, for example, for a trade buyer (who is making the acquisition as a bolt-on to its business) to seek to integrate service lines and supply chains into its own business, so the ability to exit certain arrangements and the cost of doing so may likely be of more interest to that buyer than the ability to continue those arrangements. Private equity or standalone buyers, on the other hand, are more likely to want to purchase a business that is fully operational with assurances that it will remain so post-completion (and the ability to split shared contracts with a limited increase in one-off costs will therefore be critical).

As with diligence in all transactions, different advisers play varying roles in this process. The process is usually commenced with operational diligence (often with the assistance of external advisers) whose purpose is to identify the service lines/assets currently used by the target business and categorising these into services/assets which are used exclusively by the target business and those which are shared with the retained business. It should then be identified, ordinarily by way of legal diligence, who provides these services or owns the assets and whether the ability to continue to benefit from that asset or service will transfer with the business. It may be that reorganisation of assets, transfer of contracts, or other changes need to be implemented prior to completion of the transaction in order to ensure that what is transferred is a fully operational business with minimal dependencies. To the extent this cannot be achieved, the answer might be to split the relevant service or asset between the two businesses by way of either short- or long-term licensing or services arrangements.

Transitional services agreements (TSAs) are often entered into for a limited period following completion of a carve-out transaction to allow time for the target business to completely transition off its retained business dependencies while ensuring business continuity. TSA services may be provided directly by the retained business or may be provided by a third party to the retained business who provide these services on a so-called 'pass-through' basis.

While the diligence process in a carve-out transaction is usually very focused on how the target business will operate post-completion and making sure there are no gaps, both the seller and the buyer should not omit to consider that there may be reverse dependencies of the retained business on the target business. This will likely impact a seller's approach on drafting any transitional documents, as the buyer is likely to request reciprocal commercial terms without good reason otherwise. It is therefore critical that the buyer does not omit to probe the seller on the reverse dependencies and how these will be addressed at Day 1.

4. Diligence request lists

If advising the target/seller, the legal advisers may wish to assist the operational diligence by providing a request list and a list of actions and goals for the target business. A request list would likely cover:

- details of the corporate entities that fall within the transaction perimeter and whether any of those entities holds assets which are used by the retained business and therefore need to be pulled out of the target business prior to completion;
- details of all contracts used in the target business (regardless of the contracting party);
- details of all regulatory approvals or licences required by the target business to operate and to the extent held by the retained business on a group wide basis;
- details of the roles of personnel which are either exclusively dedicated to the target business or which provide some of

their time working for the target business (and what percentage of their time is target focused);
- details of where the data used by the target business (including employee data, customer lists, financial information and any know how) is stored and whether this is a facility shared with the retained business; and
- details of other assets (intellectual property (IP), real property, information technology (IT) systems and hardware, etc) used by the target business and which entity owns these assets.

As with all transactions, these lists will guide the diligence process and inform the buyer as to the degree of reliance between the businesses and the extent to which assets need either to be moved into the transaction perimeter prior to completion or covered by a TSA.

5. Corporate structure

The corporate diligence from a carve-out perspective should focus on identifying the entities which own the assets identified as being used in the target business and mapping that ownership against the entities that are proposed to be within or without the scope of the transaction perimeter. Assets sitting outside the transaction perimeter will need to, ideally, be moved into a target entity prior to (or transferred as an asset directly to the purchase at) completion.

There may be additional jurisdiction or industry-specific considerations when assessing which entities should hold which assets. For example, if the assets are contracts for the delivery of regulated services, the provider of those services may need to be registered with a regulator (eg, with the UK Financial Conduct Authority (FCA)). Equally, certain jurisdictions may require assets in that territory to be owned by locally incorporated entities (ie, marketing authorisations for pharmaceutical products). Advice should be taken in the relevant jurisdiction to determine any such requirements or restrictions.

Tax advice should also be sought to examine whether there are advantages or disadvantages from a tax perspective of the proposed ownership of assets at completion and whether the carve-out of the business can be done in a more tax-efficient manner.

6. Real estate

To the extent that actual property needs to be transferred into the transaction perimeter or split between the businesses, lease and title documentation should be examined to ascertain whether there are any restrictions on, or consents required for, the proposed treatment of any real estate assets. Landlord consent is very often required for the transfer or split of a lease document, and may be required in the event that the target business is permitted access to premises post-completion on a transitional basis.

To the extent that such transitional access to premises is required following completion, the basis of the access permission needs to be determined (ie, whether a lease or a licence is most appropriate) and the underlying lease and title documentation reviewed to ascertain what is permissible on an arm's length basis and how the relevant consent should be worded.

The diligence process should not omit to cover on-premises services (eg, reception services, cleaning and other operational services, shared areas (toilets/kitchens) and any communications and internet services) and whether any of those also need to be transferred or shared on a short- or long-term basis post-completion.

7. Personnel

An analysis will need to be conducted to ascertain which of the employees used in the target business are likely to transfer automatically by operation of law under applicable legislation and whether any processes need to be undertaken involving works councils (or equivalent) in any jurisdiction. The process and planning of that needs to be conducted in a careful and compliant manner and the outcome of diligence should inform how large an exercise this is likely to be.[1] Personnel transfer issues may also become relevant under TSAs if retained business personnel commit more of their time providing transitional services, such that they transfer by operation of law to the target under the TSA. The diligence process should examine this risk such that appropriate indemnities can be sought by the buyer to address this risk if necessary.

It is worth mentioning that data protection concerns are significant in determining when is the correct time to share names of personnel with the buyer. The seller will need to determine its grounds for processing this personal data and the general advice ought to be that while numbers of personnel can be discussed, and possibly salaries (if the salary is not attributable just to one person

---

1 This is discussed in the "Employment and pensions aspects of carve-out transactions" chapter.

who can be identified by their singular role), ideally any identifying information ought not to be shared until completion.

8. Contractual diligence

When conducting contractual diligence in carve-out transactions, there are several categories of contracts that will need to be considered. The approach of the review, and the issues which are relevant, will differ depending on the status and intended treatment of the contract. The purpose of conducting such contractual diligence is to identify not just the usual risks associated with a business or share sale but also to ascertain what contracts are shared between the target and retained businesses and what (if any) options does the contract contain in relation to the parties' treatment of that contract without requiring engagement with the counterparty which could give rise to price increases, one-off costs and potential early termination fees. It is important to capture all of the relevant diligence points in the contract review in order to:

- inform the seller and the buyer of the options in relation to each contract, particularly under shared contracts; and
- ensure that when counterparty consent is obtained, it captures all waivers required for the proposed transaction (for example, if a contract is 'split' with counterparty consent prior to completion but it also contains a change of control, the counterparty could still enforce the change of control provision on completion if the consent does not also include a waiver of that provision).

There are, broadly speaking, three categories of contractual arrangements:

- *Contracts used exclusively by the retained or target business which currently sit within the 'correct' corporate entity.* These are contracts whose benefit is enjoyed exclusively by either the retained business or the target business and the group contracting party is an entity within whichever of the retained or target business benefits from the contract. In other words, these contracts are in the right place and they either stay behind to continue to service the retained business or they transfer with the target business as part of a share sale. For these contracts, aside from conducting diligence to identify onerous provisions of interest from a business operations/risk perspective (ie, exclusivity provisions), the key concerns (from a transaction mechanics perspective) will likely be change of control restrictions or triggers permitting termination for convenience. Assignment restrictions will not be relevant as the contracts are not moving, they will simply transfer with the contracting entity/entities being sold.

- *Contracts used exclusively by the retained or target business but which need to be moved in or out of the transaction perimeter, or which need to be transferred directly to the buyer or special purpose vehicle (SPV) as part of an asset sale.* These are contracts whose benefit, as in the above bullet point, is enjoyed exclusively by either the retained or target business. Either the contracting party to the contract is not a member of the group which receives the benefit of the contract. In other words, they are sitting in the wrong place. Or the transaction is an asset sale and the contracts need to be transferred to the buyer or an SPV as part of the transaction. If these contracts are to be transferred within the transaction perimeter prior to completion (so that they transfer with the target entities upon completion) then assignment provisions will be relevant, when being transferred to the right vehicle, as will change of control provisions from completion (as of course will termination for convenience provisions).
- *Contracts used by both the target and the retained business but the contracting entity is either a retained or target entity.* The treatment of these contracts will need to be determined on a contract-by-contract basis, with the input of both the buyer and the seller. The process ordinarily begins with a review of the terms of the contract to determine whether a solution can be reached without requiring the input/consent of the service provider. This is preferable as service providers will often look to renegotiate terms (including price) where a contract is 'split' between two businesses which going forward will be at arm's length. They may also seek to charge a one-off cost of splitting/terminating the contract. Finally, the 'splitting' out of the contract, legally speaking effectively results in two contracts: one between the retained business and the provider and the other between the target business and the provider. These may be on the same terms, or the target or retained business may seek to renegotiate terms. Alternatively, the contract may not be required by the target business (or indeed the retained business) and termination/partial termination options might also be explored. There is much to consider with shared contracts and, while it is important to gain an

understanding of what the agreements do and don't permit, if both parties want to continue to receive the goods or services under comparable arrangements, it is likely the third-party provider will need to be involved. This is the case even if the contract allows for assignment or partial assignment. It is a common misunderstanding that if a contract allows assignment/partial assignment, the contract can be transferred/partially transferred. While assignment does mean that the benefit of the contract can be transferred, under English law, the obligations under the contract cannot move without the consent of the provider (ordinarily taking the form of a tri-partite novation agreement). That is even the case where the contract states that the obligations may transfer without such consent. It is only in very limited circumstances, where the transferee is clearly identified, that this will be a reliable way of transferring a contract under English law and the safest approach is to obtain a novation. Permitted assignment does mean that the benefit can be transferred for an interim period without needing to involve the service provider, but without a transfer of the obligations, this is ordinarily an unsatisfactory longer-term solution. The only caveat to this may where a contract is novated 'by performance'. In simple terms, this operates by way of providing a notice to the counterparty and by performing the contract or portion of the contract in line with the notified new arrangements. If performed in accordance with those new arrangements it may be proven that the contract has novated by virtue of performance of that contract with the new party. For example, if a service provider is notified that its contract has partially transferred to the target business, that it should consider its performance of the services for the target business as being under direct contractual arrangements with that target and that going forward, it will receive monies from the target business rather than the retained business, there may be an argument that the contract novates over time. However, the difficulty with this approach regarding third-party contracts is that the behaviour of the provider often doesn't change (it may continue to provide services in the way it did previously and may not be aware that the payments are coming from a different source), meaning it arguably hasn't consented to the new structure and it could raise objection to the transfer. This is a more common approach with customer contracts in industries where customers are unlikely to identify a difference in their experience of the services/goods, but where they are required to make payments to a different receiver/ account in accordance with their notice. This is helpful as it signifies a change in behaviour which arguably signals acceptance of the transfer of the contract to the new recipient of the monies. In brief, novation by performance is a strategy that should be adopted only for those contracts where risk of objection is seen to be very low and where there will be some change in behaviour required of the counterparty that could be pointed at as evidence of acceptance. Even then, a buyer may want to insist that the most material customer contracts, for example, are transferred by way of formal novation signed by the incoming, outgoing and counterparty to the contract.

The diligence around contracts and the exercise of identifying shared contracts, deciding which contracts will be split with the buyer and which will be replaced and establishing which contracts ideally would be finalised by completion, is not always achievable and the work may need to continue post-completion. During this time, the relevant services may need to be provided under a TSA or through 'back to back' arrangements until the longer-term solution has been finalised. The process of engaging service providers and negotiating the contract split and associated costs is usually seller-driven with input where required from the buyer. Not until negotiations have finished with the counterparty will the deal parties really know the cost exposure associated with this exercise. It should be monitored closely and costs tracked diligently so that both seller and buyer can keep track of their exposure under the sale documentation (which may provide for all manner of cost-sharing or cost-allocating structures, depending on deal dynamics and negotiating power). Where signing and completion is split (with a sizeable gap in between), this exercise is almost always conducted between those two dates with the sale document providing a process for the parties working together to find appropriate solutions. Where signing and completion are simultaneous, the exercise will likely continue after completion, with either the main sale document providing for the process and the TSA providing the framework for seeking consent to allow services on a pass-through basis. Where consents to pass-through services under a TSA have not been obtained from vendors prior to completion, this represents a compliance risk for both parties due to the continued provisions and use of services/licences from the seller to what is now a third party (the target business).

9. Intellectual property and information technology systems

Intellectual property (IP) diligence on a carve-out transaction should seek to, like with diligence on other assets, identify the owner of:

- the IP which is used exclusively by the target business and ensure that IP will transfer with the business; and
- the IP that is shared between the target and retained businesses, so that parties can agree how these will be treated following completion of the deal.

The position regarding shared IP can be difficult to manage, particularly when it comes to 'splitting' a brand on a long-term basis.

Where the shared IP constitutes 'non-brand' IP, eg, patents or know-how, and involves one party making use of the assets owned by another, if the use of the IP is primarily by one of the two businesses, a standard approach would be that the business making the greatest use of the asset will retain it and license use of it to the other. The diligence should focus on examining the use of the IP by the target business and to ensure that:

- any proposed structure of ownership/licensing arrangement is appropriate; and
- the scope of any licence to the target business is broad enough in terms of duration and scope to meet the needs of the business operations.

What can often be more difficult is where the shared IP is used by each business in a different manner, either in terms of the field of use or the territory. While this seems like a cleaner delineation of the uses of the IP, the negotiations as to whether a licence should be provided or ownership of the relevant part of the portfolio should be transferred can often be less straightforward. Where diligence reveals shared brands or patent families, a structural decision needs to be made as to how the portfolio will be shared between the parties post-completion: whether one entity will retain the whole portfolio and grant a licence to the other on a long-term basis or whether the portfolio will be split, with each party taking ownership of the rights in its field/territory.

This can be particularly problematic where a brand is involved, as poor use of a brand can have a negative effect on goodwill of the brand as a whole, not necessarily that attached to the brand in a particular territory or for a particular product category post-sale. This is the reason why, in a carve-out transaction, either the seller or buyer often agrees to rebrand those parts of the business the subject of a shared brand (sometimes with transitional licence arrangements to allow a run-off of all uses post-completion). However, where co-use of the brand is agreed post-completion, any licences should provide for robust restrictions on negative uses of the brand. Equally, where ownership of the portfolio is split, co-ownership or co-existence arrangements should be put in place to ensure each business is not negatively impacted by the operations of the other. Diligence should focus on not only ensuring that the seller has ownership of the rights in the field/territory of the transaction perimeter but also where the portfolio gaps are, with a view to future expansion. In the light of those gaps, a strategy will need to be worked out as to how the parties will approach any unchartered territory going forward to avoid future disputes between them and how they will work together in respect of third-party infringements or applications.

Due diligence regarding ownership, status and expiry of patents and trademarks (and any other registered IP) can be conducted using publicly available databases operated by the relevant registries. Using these, however, raises challenges, primarily due to the number of them that are often in foreign languages. There are several commercially available databases that connect with the national and supra-national registries and amalgamate registered IP information. These are extremely useful if conducting diligence of a trademark or patent portfolio and offer a one-stop shop for multi-jurisdictional searches.

As stated above, if an IP portfolio is not split and instead, the target (or retained business) agrees to transition off a brand post-completion, the diligence efforts should be focused around understanding the current uses of the brand and determining how long the business will need to cease its use. Where the shared IP is know-how, the diligence should focus on where this is held (is it documented/in the minds of personnel), how it will be transferred (if transfer is necessary) and whether it has adequately been protected to date, by way of non-disclosure agreements (NDAs), confidentiality restrictions on employees and adequate internal processes around documentation of and restricted access to confidential materials.

Other IP may also be shared between the parties, such as bespoke software and systems. Again, the diligence in this area will be focused on how replaceable is that software and how long will be required to establish independent replacement systems for the target. This could include cloning the software such that the target has its own instance of the code which can then be adapted to the specific needs of the business, but this requires permission from the retained business so may require a longer-term licence. The diligence process should be focused on identifying these needs and understanding the plan for the target to operate independently. Where the businesses determine that a long-term (possibly perpetual) licence of bespoke software is required between the parties, the licensee will need to ensure it has adequate maintenance and support services, either from the licensor or elsewhere.

10. Data sharing

In addition to data protection concerns regarding the sharing of personnel data, additional diligence will need to be undertaken to understand where the data collected and used by the target business is stored, who hosts and manages this database and who has access to it.

The buyer will need to understand how segregated (or otherwise) the target business and seller data is systematically and to the extent an exercise needs to be conducted to separate that data, how will this technically be achieved and will this be possible before completion. To the extent it will not be achieved by completion, TSAs may be required to allow post-completion access to data relevant to one party's business that is held by another. If diligence identifies that technically each party can access the data relating to the other party's business post-completion, steps will need to be taken to prevent this, both technically and legally. The parties should also be mindful about the extent to which their diligence efforts, either prior to signing or before singing and completion, involve the sharing of commercial information, so as to ensure this does not constitute gun-jumping or other anti-competitive behaviour.

To the extent that any transfer of personal data needs to occur, as mentioned above in relation to personnel, it is preferable that this takes place post-completion and, even then, in a manner that ensures compliance with applicable data protection laws. The diligence process needs to identify where the data sits, how it was collected and on what terms, who is the current data controller and what uses of the data are permitted going forward. Notices may need to be sent to the individuals informing them of the transaction and the documentation will usually legislate a process for this and even contain agreed language.

11. Minimising Day 1 exposure

Ultimately, the diligence process in a carve-out transaction aims to minimise operational and financial exposure of the parties such that on Day 1 each party has access to the goods and services required to run its business, whether by way of a transfer, TSA or replacement arrangements. Equally, the parties will want to ensure their exposure to increased or stranded costs is minimised.

A successful diligence process in a carve-out transaction will begin early and relies on good planning, engagement between the parties to identify needs going forward and adequate time to negotiate with third parties and mitigate stranded costs exposure.

Transitional services

Gail Crawford
Frances Stocks Allen
Latham & Watkins

---

1. Introduction

This chapter examines transitional services in the context of carve-out transactions, that is, the provision of agreed services on a transitional basis by a seller group to a buyer, in order to facilitate the successful and minimally disruptive carve-out of divested assets and businesses.[1]

It is common particularly, for example, in the context of a large and complex divestment of assets, that a range of services may need to be provided by the seller group on a transitional basis, and that this may represent a significant driver of value to the buyer and a significant commitment of resources by the seller group. Given that different buyers will require different transitional services, for different periods of time, and different sellers may be willing or able to agree to different scopes and durations of service provision, a transitional services agreement will typically document a bespoke combination of services and durations of service provision.

The primary reason for the provision of transitional services is buyer driven, in order to facilitate the ongoing performance of the divested business without material diminution in value on closing. A seller may agree to provide transitional services to a buyer for a number of reasons, key amongst these being the requirements to maximise the purchase price achieved for the divested assets, speed up the transaction and/or to ensure that any applicable contractual, legal or regulatory obligations are met during any post-closing period during which the seller will remain responsible.

In preparation for the divestment or acquisition of divested assets, both the seller and the prospective buyer, plus their respective advisers, should plan for the operational spin out of the divested

---

1 The authors would like to acknowledge the significant contribution of Terese Saplys as well as the assistance of colleagues Daniel Smith, Shaun Thompson and Catherine Drinnan (all at Latham & Watkins) in the preparation of this chapter.

assets from the seller's group and their integration into the buyer's business, in order to minimise disruption to the business. Typically, this planning requires significant stakeholder engagement at both organisations, and may be best orchestrated, depending on the complexity of the transaction, by external consultants.

If you are selling assets, or advising a seller, in connection with a carve-out transaction, you should undertake as part of the internal due diligence phase of your transaction planning for the divestment an in-depth assessment of the operational support your likely buyer(s) will require to support the transition of the divested assets from your operational structure. It is important to consider that different buyers may have different requirements – for example, a trade buyer currently operating in the same industry as the seller who is acquiring the assets as a bolt-on transaction is likely to require a very different scope and duration of support from a seller than a new build shell company financed by private equity investment would.

In order to maximise the purchase price received for the divested assets, a seller may need to be flexible as to the scope and duration of transitional services it is willing to provide. However, this incentive needs to be accompanied by an assessment of the restrictions that the provision of these transitional services agreement will place upon the seller's ability to make changes to their remaining organisation and assets after the carve-out sale is completed, including terminating and/or re-allocating employees, terminating and/or replacing service providers and restructuring your operations.

In addition, a seller should consider that, particularly where the divestment involves the transfer of employees or is made in connection with a broader reorganisation, the assets and employees the seller's organisation retain after the conclusion of the carve-out transaction may not be sufficient to enable the seller to perform the contracted transitional services in the way the seller would have been able to prior to the carve-out transaction. Thus, when drafting the transitional services agreement, the seller must ensure that all contractual provisions (for example service level commitments and any employee turnover restrictions) are achievable given the seller's plans for the retained business during the term of the proposed transitional service provision.

If you are considering buying divested assets, or are advising a party considering acquiring divested assets, in connection with a carve-out transaction you should assess at an early stage what transitional services you will require to separate the divested assets from the seller's business and transfer them to your organisation, without disrupting the day-to-day operation of the business associated with the divested assets and thereby reducing their value. Ideally this analysis will be undertaken at the time you and your advisers are valuing the assets, to ensure that the costs and complexity of separation and transfer (whether provided by the seller or otherwise) are factored into your calculation of the purchase price and the stand-alone operating cost model for the divested business.

2. Scope of services

Typically, medium to large organisations will provide financial, reporting, human resources, facilities, information technology, regulatory and legal services on a centralised basis and the proposed divested assets may therefore benefit, prior to divestment, from some form of intra-group service provision. In a carve-out transaction, these core services are the services which, at a minimum, are likely to be required by the divested business, at least on a short-term basis, to avoid material disruption and a potential diminution of value following the closing of the transaction. In addition to these core services, other services may have been performed at the corporate level and these may by required for a transitional period to facilitate the separation of the divested assets from the seller's business and integration into the buyer's business. For example, the provision of sales or promotion services or the supply of goods may have been provided intra-group prior to the transaction and these may be required to be provided by the seller following the closing of the transaction, in particular where such service provision requires the provider to hold governmental or regulatory licences or approvals, or where the transfer of the supply of goods to the buyer or a third party would involve a detailed transfer of technology. The replacement of these services will need to be factored into the stand-alone operating cost model for the divested business.

Occasionally, a key driver of value on a carve-out transaction will be the longer-term supply of goods or services at a preferential rate from the seller to the buyer, in which case these services may either be included in the transitional services agreement or in a more detailed, longer-term services or supply agreement, which is still part of the separation activities for the transaction, but subject to different terms.

A seller will usually require that the transitional services which are to be provided in connection with a carve-out transaction are specifically agreed between the parties on a service-by-service basis, and set out in a detailed services schedule to the agreed transitional services agreement, so that they have certainty as to what exactly they are meant to be providing, for how long and any specific requirements for the provision and wind down of such services. A buyer must therefore be careful to document a sufficiently broad suite of transitional services (including in terms of the types and categories of services to be provided, their duration and any separation or exit support required) to facilitate the separation of the divested assets from the seller's business whilst preserving their value and minimising disruption. The process of documenting this services schedule can be completed either prior to signing or prior to the closing of the divestment transaction, but a buyer should be aware that they may find it harder to obtain the breadth and duration of services they require if they are not negotiated until after signing, due to the reduction in leverage that may occur once a purchase agreement has been signed.

3. Reverse transitional services

Depending on the scope of the assets to be divested and, particularly, where transferring employees are included in the bundle of divested assets, reverse or reciprocal services may need to be provided by the buyer back to the seller. Such services are typically performed by the transferred employees or using the divested assets, in the manner conducted prior to closing, for a limited period. Most often, such reverse transitional service provision is required because the transferring employees spent some of their time performing services for the retained business as well as in relation to the business of the divested assets.

Typically, though specific terms will depend upon the negotiations between the parties, reverse transitional services will be provided by the buyer on the same or similar terms as the transitional services that are to be provided from the seller to the buyer. However specific circumstantial reasons may result in the parties negotiating, for example, a different service standard, duration, or employee turnover obligation in the reverse transitional services agreement. This drive for mutuality of terms can be helpful in the negotiating process, to prevent either party adopting a zero-sum game approach to their terms and keeping discussions reasonable, if both parties will experience the same term as a recipient and as a provider. We note that, whilst in this chapter we generally refer to the provision of transitional services with the relevant seller acting as service provider and the prospective buyer acting as service recipient, most of our analysis could be applied in the reverse with respect to a reverse transitional services agreement.

4. Additional services

Where it is not possible to ascertain prior to closing of the transaction the complete scope and all details of the transitional services that are likely to be required, it may be useful to include a mechanism in the transitional services agreement which provides that the buyer will receive (either automatically or on mutual agreement) certain services that are identified as being required following the closing of the transaction.

The parties will need to discuss and agree as part of contractual negotiations whether the scope of potential additional services that can be added via such mechanism should encompass new services (eg, adding in human resources (HR) services where none were previously agreed), or whether the additional services mechanism should be restricted to new or unexpected tasks within the agreed service areas (eg, a new monthly report within a finance reporting service area). Typically, a seller will prefer to limit any additional services mechanism to permit only the addition of new tasks, particularly where the seller plans to restructure operations following closing of the transaction, to give certainty as to which resources might be required to be retained in order for the seller to service its commitments to the buyer under the transitional services agreement.

In addition, the parties should discuss and agree how the seller will be compensated for any additional services added via this mechanism. Will they be included within the agreed service charges or will they be separately chargeable? If they will be separately chargeable, will the same charging principles apply as already apply to the agreed services (eg, at cost, where the seller's actual costs of agreed kinds are reimbursed by the buyer, or at cost plus an agreed percentage margin, to reward the seller for the service provision)? These decisions will typically be driven by the agreed scope of what additional services might be added, whether this right will apply only at the outset of the transitional service provision for a limited period, the nature of the services to be provided (including, eg, whether the services require the payment of fees or service charges to a third party, including for the provision of any third-party consents or licences), and the parties' respective negotiating power.

5. Service level

A well-documented services agreement should set out the agreed standard, or service level, at which the relevant services will be provided to the service recipient. Where the services are provided on a transitional basis in connection with a carve-out transaction, they will commonly refer to the standard at which the relevant services were provided by the seller on an intra-group basis prior to the completion of the carve-out transaction, over a defined period that begins sufficiently in advance of the announcement of the transaction as to protect against a possible diminution of the standard of service provision once the transaction was announced. This look-back period is referred to as a 'reference period'. Depending on the context of the particular transaction, the reference period may relate to a certain number of months (typically six to 12 months) either before the purchase documentation was signed or the completion of the transaction.

Where it is expected that the period between signing and closing will be longer than a few months (eg, due to potential antitrust issues or in connection with a pre-closing reorganisation), a potential buyer should be aware that there is a significant risk of loss of value in the divested business in the post-signing, pre-closing period when, despite the seller complying with ordinary course conduct covenants in the purchase agreement, individual employees may take less care in the conduct of their duties in the context of the uncertainty the transaction creates in relation to their individual employment. In these circumstances, it is advisable for the buyer to seek that the reference period relates to the pre-signing period as well as taking steps, once the deal has been announced, as agreed with the seller, to win over local management on the merits of the transaction and the attractiveness of the buyer.

In practical terms it may be difficult, particularly where the seller did not document internal service provision standards, to ascertain to what standard exactly a particular service was provided in the pre-closing or pre-signing period, and this becomes more pronounced the further away from the present the reference period is set. This can introduce uncertainty and produce an increased risk of disputes under the transitional services agreement but is commonly accepted commercially, given that few sellers will accept a higher standard (eg, best industry practice, good industry practice) on the basis that they are not in the business of providing these types of services. As a seller commits to the provision of transitional services to facilitate the carve-out transaction, they are likely to be reluctant to commit to the type of service level a commercial service provider might provide. Indeed, a seller may require the inclusion of language to the extent that the seller is not in the business of providing services, to reduce the inference of additional duties or service standards into the transitional services agreement.

Other common standards for service levels include best industry practice or commercially reasonable efforts. However, to the extent that the seller is in the business of providing the same types of services to the market, and the seller is charging market rates for provision of such services on a transitional basis to the buyer (even if at a small discount), then the buyer should negotiate for the seller to provide the transitional services to the same standard as provided to the market. This is because, in the above circumstances, there is no reason why the delivery of the services to the divested business should be any more difficult to perform than when the same services are provided to a third party (particularly given that the seller was previously accustomed to providing these services to the divested business internally).

Typically, transitional services will be provided by a seller's employees, either directly or indirectly (eg, where certain services are provided by a third-party supplier to the seller or its affiliates, and are then provided to the buyer on a pass-through basis by the seller's employees). As a seller's ability to meet its service level commitments will depend to a large extent on the quality of service provided by individual employees, a buyer may wish to include in the transitional services agreement a measure of control over the seller's service providing employees, for example, by creating a mechanism under which the buyer has a right to request or require that underperforming employees are reassigned so that they no longer perform the services. By way of further example, a buyer may wish to negotiate to include in the transitional services agreement an obligation on the seller to maintain key employees or a minimum number of employees who, prior to closing of the transaction, were engaged in the provision of the transitional services on an intra-group basis in the course of their ordinary employment duties. This is particularly relevant where the seller intends to make redundancies following closing of the transaction or to otherwise reduce the size of the retained business.

6. Governance

Due to the complexity of a transitional services agreement, it is common and typically helpful to include a governance mechanism in order to attempt to deal with any disputes arising in relation to the provision of the transitional services outside of court or arbitration proceedings. Typically, such a mechanism will include a steering committee responsible for the overall service provision, monitoring and day-to-day dispute resolution, as well as escalations to senior executives of unresolved disputes. Depending on the volume and nature of the transitional services, it may even be beneficial to include service leads, with responsibility for day-to-day communications and decision making.

7. Transferring employees

An important issue to address in any transitional services agreement will be which and how many employees of the seller will provide the relevant transitional services, particularly the jurisdictions in which they are based, as specific local law issues may need to be addressed in the transitional services agreement. For example, where the service providing employees are based in the United Kingdom, the Transfer of Undertakings (Protection of Employment) Regulations 2006 (TUPE) may apply. TUPE is derived from EU legislation, and therefore different national implementing legislation in other European jurisdictions may also apply to service providing employees based in other EU member states, and this will need to be addressed specifically in the transitional services agreement.

Under TUPE, in circumstances where a transitional service is taken in-house by the buyer or is taken over by a new third-party service provider engaged by the buyer, there is a risk that, on termination of the provision of the relevant service by the seller under the transitional services agreement, the seller's employees who were providing that service to the buyer immediately before such termination will automatically transfer under TUPE to the new party providing the services (ie, the buyer or the new third-party service provider). The default legal position in such circumstances is that the transferee entity will automatically inherit the impacted employees on their existing terms and conditions of employment as well as any outstanding and ongoing liabilities relating to their employment and its termination (such as any ongoing employee litigation, go-forward salary and employee benefit costs and severance costs).

The likelihood of a TUPE transfer occurring is highly fact based and therefore an assessment will need to be made on a case-by-case basis as to the likelihood of the transfer occurring and the volume of impacted employees. For example, if the relevant seller employees are to be redeployed by the seller into its retained business on termination of relevant transitional services and will retain their jobs as a result of such redeployment, the risk of those individuals claiming to have or being deemed to have transferred under TUPE is low. However if, following the termination of the relevant transitional services, the seller will no longer require the services of the relevant employees (eg, if the seller has continued to employ them purely to provide services under the transitional services agreement), then there is a material risk that they will be transferred under TUPE and if there are a large number of such employees, the costs associated with such TUPE transfers could be materially significant to the transaction as a whole.

As a result of the risk of a TUPE transfer occurring, it is common for the parties to include a clause in a transitional services agreement stating that neither the seller nor the buyer intend that TUPE will apply on the commencement, operation or termination of any of the services under the transitional services agreement, that the relevant employees will remain employees of the seller and that the seller will continue to be responsible for paying their salaries and providing them with access to any relevant employee benefit arrangements (subject to any agreed cost reimbursement under the transitional services agreement). It has become market practice to support this clause with an indemnity for any liabilities incurred in relation to the service providing employees' employment and its termination, as well as also, at times, an obligation to carry out an information and consultation process with or on behalf of any transferring employees prior to the transfer, if any seller employees do in fact transfer on the commencement, operation or termination of the services under the transitional services agreement. Each side will need to assess the size and probability of the potential TUPE risk and consider whether any restrictions would be appropriate as to the scope of such indemnity prior to signing the transitional services agreement.

8. Term

The term of a transitional services agreement will be primarily a matter for commercial discussion between the buyer and seller, but may also be informed by any delay to the transfer of assets which is required due to regulatory or other reasons. The buyer should, as part of their diligence activities, determine how long they think they need to separate the acquired assets from the seller's retained organisation, including finding alternate sources for the relevant transitional services. This may involve considerable time and resources to hire and train employees, obtain licences from or contracts with third parties and finding new facilities, for example, and must be conducted simultaneously with the buyer's efforts to communicate changes to the market and its employees and to start exploiting the acquired assets and justify the price paid for them to shareholders, creditors and investors. As is well documented, the first 100 days following the closing of a transaction are the most important and turbulent time for the buyer's new business, so it is common for a buyer to seek at least six months of transitional service provision from the seller, to allow for some continuity and security during those important first months.

9. Extension

A buyer is likely to want to include in the transitional services agreement the right to extend the duration of transitional service provision, at least once on a service-by-service basis, in case the planned transition does not progress in accordance with the planned separation time line to avoid a damaging 'cliff edge' end to service provision. A seller is likely to resist such a right, again on the basis that the seller will need certainty of when and how their retained resources are committed to the provision of transitional services. A common compromise is to limit the number of automatic extension terms, both in terms of number and duration, and to potentially include a ratchet pricing mechanism that applies during an extension term (ie, which would increase the cost to the buyer of the relevant service(s) for the duration of such extension term) to incentivise the buyer to continue to seek to transition from service provision by the seller to in-house or third-party service provision in a timely fashion.

10. Separation planning

An important practical factor to consider is the need to plan separation – planning for when both acquired assets and service provision will transfer will go a long way towards reducing the possibility for unforeseen delays and disruptions to the acquired business. A key factor of this separation planning exercise is to determine how the buyer requires the provision of the various transitional services to end – eg, will the service provision cease to be provided on the same day across all functional areas or does it make more sense for the acquired business for the services to end on a service-by-service basis, as and when the buyer is ready to transfer service provision in house or to a third party. A seller may prefer a 'big bang' type approach, to increase certainty, but for practical reasons a phased service-by-service approach is likely to be most aligned to the buyer's needs.

11. Termination rights

A transitional services agreement may provide the buyer with the right to terminate individual services, the entire agreement, or both, for convenience. The parties should ensure that any such termination rights do not conflict with the service exit timelines set out in any agreed separation plan. To the extent that the parties agree to include the right to terminate by service, it is customary that the charges payable to the seller for provision of the services are reduced to the extent the seller can avoid incurring or mitigate costs following the date notice of termination is given.

In addition to a termination for convenience right in favour of the buyer, a transitional services agreement will typically include a mutual right to terminate upon the insolvency of or the uncured material breach of the other party. In addition, the seller may wish to include a right to terminate upon change of control of the buyer, on the basis that the seller is typically not in the business of providing services of the kind they have agreed to provide to the buyer, and they may not be willing to provide them to another party, particularly but not limited to where such party may be a competitor of the seller.

12. Third-party contracts

The provision of transitional services (depending on their nature) may require the seller to grant access to, or to use in its service provision, certain third-party software, systems or information by or for the benefit of the buyer and the divested assets. However, the contract between the relevant third-party provider and the seller group may restrict such access or use, requiring the third party's consent to be sought. As part of the pre-transaction due diligence process, the seller should therefore invest time identifying which of its third-party contracts will be impacted by the provision of the transitional services and which, if any, of them require the consent of the relevant third party (or, for example, the provision of notice). Typically, the seller and buyer will then include detailed mechanics in the transitional services agreement to cover the scenario where the consent of the relevant third party is not obtained prior to closing of the divestment transaction, with the seller using an agreed endeavours standard to obtain the third party's consent within a specified time period following such closing. In addition, it is common that the seller will want to include an obligation on the buyer to comply with the terms of any relevant third-party agreement, to the extent that such terms are known to the buyer and relevant to the receipt of the transitional services.

13. Intellectual property matters

An important consideration when drafting a transitional services arrangement and the separation of divested assets generally, is to what extent the business of the divested assets will need to continue to make use of retained trademarks or other intellectual property (IP) of the retained business for a transitional period. For example, where product rights are divested, if inventory is currently branded with the corporate trademarks of the seller, the buyer will need a transitional licence to use such corporate trademarks until such time as the buyer has been (or should have been) able to replace such branding with its own.

Additionally, as with any other form of services agreement, the transitional services agreement should clearly state the ownership and rights to any related IP. It is fairly typical that a transitional services arrangement should not amend the ownership rights of a party to its background IP (where such background IP of the buyer is deemed to include any IP rights included within the divested assets), and that newly developed IP, to the extent not constituting an improvement to such background IP, will be owned by the buyer. Depending on the circumstances, it may be appropriate for such newly developed IP to be licensed to the seller (with a license to the buyer) or in some cases owned by the seller (with a license to the buyer) for example to the extent such newly developed IP is of general applicability to the seller's business or has been developed without reference to the buyer's confidential information (including that comprised within the divested assets).

14. Dependencies

Typically, a seller will require the buyer to provide certain information or materials in order to perform certain of the transitional services, for example, the approval of budgets and targets, within a specific time period. These types of buyer activities are commonly referred to as dependencies, where they would, if not performed or incorrectly performed, prevent the performance of the services by the seller. A seller will typically want to include in a transitional services agreement carve-outs from certain seller obligations to the extent the buyer does not perform its dependencies, for example, the seller's obligation to provide a service at the required service level, or the seller's liability for delay in the provision of a particular service.

From the buyer's perspective, it is important that these dependencies are specifically identified and set out in detail, along with a specified process which the seller is mandated to follow in order to allow the seller to rely upon the buyer's failure to perform a dependency as a carve-out of its obligations under the transitional services agreement. Without specified dependencies and a detailed mechanism for how they are to be notified to the buyer and resolved, buyer dependencies can create significant risk to the buyer, as a result of the uncertainty of service provision they create.

15. Liability

The liability provisions of a transitional services agreement are typically heavily negotiated and will largely depend on the negotiating power of the respective parties as well as the scope and nature of the transitional services. Where the parties' liability is not determined by the underlying purchase documentation, it is common to include a cap on each party's liability at a multiple of the service charges paid or payable under the transitional services agreement, as well as to exclude indirect and consequential damages from each party's liability and, occasionally, direct loss of profits. However, particularly, where the seller will be effectively running the divested business for the buyer during the transitional period, the buyer must very carefully assess the proposed basket of exclusions and limitations, to ensure that they have a meaningful basket from which to make claims if the seller fails to perform the transitional services in accordance with the agreed transitional services agreement.

16. Indemnification

The indemnity provisions of a transitional services agreement are also subject to the negotiating power of the respective parties, and similarly may be driven by the underlying purchase documentation, as well as the geography of the agreement. US transitional services agreements often include a broader suite of indemnities, including occasionally indemnification claims as between the parties as well as by third parties for breach of the agreement itself. In the United Kingdom, typically, indemnities are limited to third-party claims such as claims alleging infringement of such party's IP rights, claims for breach by the seller of third-party contracts that are relevant to, or necessary for, the provision of the transitional services, claims for breach of confidentiality provisions and non-compliance with applicable laws (including data protection laws) and claims relating to the fraud or wilful misconduct of each party in relation to the provision or receipt of the transitional services.

17. Data processing

Following the entry into effect of the European Union Regulation 2016/679 (commonly known as the General Data Protection Regulation or the GDPR), it is important that as part of the due diligence stage of the transaction, the seller and buyer assess whether the divested assets include any personal data, as defined by the GDPR, and whether any such personal data will need to be processed by the seller on behalf of the buyer in the performance of the transitional services. To the extent that personal data, as defined by the GDPR, will be processed by the seller on behalf of the buyer in the course of providing the transitional services, the transitional services agreement should include data processing provisions that are appropriately robust in the context of the particular transaction and which meet the requirements of Article 28 GDPR.

18. Anti-corruption

Where the seller will continue to run the divested business for a period of time on behalf of the buyer, or where for example, sales, promotion or other customer-facing services will be provided as part of the transitional services, the buyer may be criminally liable for any bribery or other corrupt practice committed by or on behalf of the seller in the provision of the transitional services.

As part of the buyer's overall due diligence of the transaction, the buyer should assess the risk of bribery or other corrupt actions being conducted, including by reviewing the geographical location of the required transitional service provision, any interaction by the seller with government officials on behalf of buyer, and the nature of the services themselves. The buyer should also assess the strength of the seller's anti-corruption compliance policies, procedures and training, and the extent to which these will continue to apply to the transitional services following the completion of the transaction. These measures will not only reduce the risk of corrupt activity taking place for which the buyer may be found responsible, but also increase the likelihood that the buyer may rely on a defence of 'adequate procedures' if they subsequently are found to have failed to prevent bribery by the seller in the performance of the transitional services.

The buyer should also ensure to include in the transitional services agreement itself appropriate contractual anti-corruption provisions so that the buyer is protected from the consequences of any corruption which may occur as part of the performance of the services, for example representations and undertakings in relation to past corrupt activity, covenants regarding future activities, periodic compliance certifications, and the rights and obligations of the parties in the event of suspected or alleged corruption activity.

Antitrust

Gregory Bonné
Jonathan Parker
Latham & Watkins

---

1. Introduction

This chapter considers the application of EU merger control rules to transactions that involve the acquisition of business units or collections of assets that have been carved out of a larger group structure. The acquisition of a business from a seller group may give rise to mandatory merger control obligations in one or more jurisdictions. In relation to the EU, which is the focus of this chapter, a mandatory merger filing is required where two conditions are satisfied. First, there must be a notifiable 'concentration' where there is a change of control over the target business on a lasting basis which results, in respect of carve-outs, from the acquisition by one or more 'undertakings' over the whole or parts of another undertaking. Secondly, this 'concentration' must have an 'EU dimension', where the turnover of the relevant undertakings concerned must exceed specified thresholds. Under the EU Merger Regulation,[1] in the event that a mandatory merger filing is triggered, no additional merger filings are required in any EU member state. Therefore, the EU provides a 'one-stop shop' mechanism for transactions that fall within the EU Merger Regulation's jurisdiction. Additional merger filings may be required outside the EU but a consideration of such filings is beyond the scope of this chapter.

This chapter briefly outlines the circumstances in which a carve-out transaction will qualify for an EU merger filing. The second section considers the concept of a notifiable 'concentration' and the acquisition of control of one or more 'undertakings' as they are applicable to carve-outs, including identification of each of the acquiring and target businesses. The third section sets out when such a concentration will be deemed to have an 'EU dimension' and the entities that should be taken into consideration for turnover calculation purposes. The fourth section considers the stand-still

---

1 Council Regulation (EC) No 139/2004 on the control of concentrations between undertakings (EU Merger Regulation).

obligation that applies to all notifiable mergers under the EU Merger Regulation, including carve-outs, and recent developments from the European Court of Justice.

2. Concentration

A concentration is deemed to arise where a change of control on a lasting basis results from:

- the merger of two or more previously independent undertakings or parts of undertakings; or
- the acquisition by one or more undertakings of direct or indirect control of the whole or parts of one of more other undertakings.[2]

Carve-out transactions fall into the second category of transaction, which specifically includes the acquisition of "parts of one or more other undertakings". In determining whether there is a reporting obligation under the EU Merger Regulation, it is necessary to identify both the acquirer and the target business as the relevant parties to the transaction.

2.1 Acquisitions of control

The EU Merger Regulation only applies to acquisitions of control over undertakings. Acquisitions of non-controlling interests are not notifiable. Control can be acquired on an individual basis (sole control) or can be acquired jointly with other undertakings (joint control). There is no minimum level of shareholding that must be acquired for an acquisition to be notifiable. The concept of control is relevant to all transactions for EU merger control purposes, including carve-out acquisitions. The basic principle is that the acquirer must acquire control over the target and, as explained below, the key concept under the EU Merger Regulation is whether an acquisition confers 'decisive influence', irrespective of the level of shareholding that has been acquired.

2.2 Acquirer of control

Control may be acquired by one or more 'undertakings' acting alone or by several undertakings acting jointly.[3] The concept of an 'undertaking' is broadly defined and extends to almost any entity engaged in an economic activity and generating turnover, irrespective of the

---

2 EU Merger Regulation, Article 3(1).

3 Consolidated Jurisdictional Notice, para 11.

exact legal form. Control may also be acquired by one or more 'persons', which includes public bodies, private entities as well as natural persons.[4] Acquisitions by natural persons are only considered to bring about a lasting change in the structure of the undertakings concerned where those natural persons carry out further economic activities on their own account or if they control at least one other undertaking.[5]

(a) Acquisitions of direct and indirect control

Control is normally acquired by persons or undertakings which are the holders of the rights or are entitled to rights that confer control under the relevant contracts.[6] However, there may also be situations where the formal holder of a controlling interest differs from the person or undertaking having the power to exercise the rights conferring control. In these situations, control is acquired by the person or undertaking that in reality enjoys the power to exercise control.[7] As a result, a controlling shareholding that is held by different entities in a group is normally attributed to the undertaking exercising control over the various shareholders.[8] This is applicable to all acquisitions of control irrespective of whether it concerns only part of a business.

(b) Means of control

Control is defined by the EU Merger Regulation as the possibility of exercising decisive influence over an undertaking. It is not necessary that decisive influence is or will be actually exercised. The possibility of exercising control can exist on the basis of rights, contracts or other means, either separately or in combination. The most common means for the acquisition of control is the acquisition of shares or assets, often combined with a shareholders' agreement in cases of joint control.[9] Control can also be acquired on a contractual basis where the contract leads to a similar control of the management and the resources of the target undertaking as in the case of an acquisition of shares or assets.[10]

---

4 *Ibid*, para 12.
5 *Ibid*, para 12.
6 *Ibid*, para 13.
7 EU Merger Regulation, Article 3(3)(a); Consolidated Jurisdictional Notice, para 13.
8 Consolidated Jurisdictional Notice, para 13.
9 Consolidated Jurisdictional Notice, para 17.
10 *Ibid*, para 17.

(c) *Change of control on a lasting basis*

Transactions are only notifiable under the EU Merger Regulation where there is a change in control over an undertaking on a lasting basis and, as a result, a lasting change on the structure of the market. Accordingly, the EU Merger Regulation does not apply to temporary changes of control and such transactions are not notifiable. This may be relevant to transactions involving the contribution of assets to a joint venture for a specified period of time or to agreements where undertakings have come together for the purpose of acquiring another company with the intention of dividing up the acquired assets according to a pre-existing plan. However, this does not exclude from the EU Merger Regulation's jurisdiction transactions where the underlying agreements are entered into for a specified period of time, as long as the agreements are renewable. In addition, the EU Merger Regulation will also apply to transactions where the agreements have a definitive end date, without the ability to renew, where the agreements will last a sufficiently long period of time for a lasting change in the control of the undertakings concerned to have occurred.[11] In this regard, there is no minimum period of time that a change of control must last but the Commission has considered a period of three years to be insufficient.[12]

2.3 Acquisition of a business or part of a business

The object of control, or the target of a transaction, can be one or more undertakings that constitute legal entities; it may also be part of one or more undertakings, or the assets (or some of the assets) of such entities.[13] With respect to carve-outs, where the proposed transaction involves the acquisition of a legal entity, often in the form of a stand-alone business unit from a seller group, identifying the object of control is straightforward. However, where the transaction involves the carve-out of less than a stand-alone business unit, additional factors must be considered.

The acquisition of control over assets will only be notifiable under the EU Merger Regulation if those assets comprise a business with a market presence to which revenues can be attributed.[14] The

---

11 *Ibid*, para 28.

12 Case COMP/M.3858, *Lehman Brothers/Starwood/Le Meridien*, Commission decision of 20 July 2005.

13 EU Merger Regulation, Article 3(1)(b); Consolidated Jurisdictional Notice, para 24.

14 Consolidated Jurisdictional Notice, para 24.

acquisition of assets can typically be considered to be an undertaking if it concerns the following.

- *Transfer of customers*. The transfer of a business' client base can fulfil these criteria if this is sufficient to transfer a business with a market turnover.[15]
- *Revenue generating intangible assets*. A transaction confined to intangible assets such as brands, patents or copyrights may also be considered to be a concentration if those assets constitute a business with a market turnover. The transfer of licences for brands, patents or copyrights, without additional assets, can also fulfil these criteria if the licences are exclusive at least in a certain territory and the transfer of such licences will transfer the turnover-generating activity.[16]

There are no bright-line rules applied when determining whether the acquisition of certain assets or parts of a business constitutes an undertaking; it is a qualitative exercise based on the available facts. The key principle is that the target assets must be revenue generating or be capable of revenue generation within a short period.

The package of assets can be deemed to be an acquisition of an undertaking under the EU Merger Regulation even if those assets were not previously revenue generating (or only generated intra-group turnover) provided that the acquirer can generate revenue within a short period. If third parties are not yet supplied, in order for the assets to be considered an undertaking, the following features should typically be present depending on whether it is goods sold or services provided.

- *Manufacturing for the provision of goods*. In the case of manufacturing the package of assets should contain production facilities, product know-how (it is sufficient if the assets transferred allow the build-up of such capabilities in the near future) and, if there is no existing market access, the means for the purchaser to develop a market access within a short period of time (eg, including existing contracts or brands).
- *Provision of services*. As regards the provision of services, the assets transferred should include the required know-how (eg, the relevant personnel and intellectual property) and those facilities which allow market access (such as, eg, marketing facilities).

---

15 *Ibid*, para 30.
16 *Ibid*, para 24.

There are multiple examples of the Commission reviewing carve-out asset acquisitions across different industries and set out below are a few non-exhaustive examples.

- In the pharmaceutical industry, Novartis purchased the auto-immune indications of the pharmaceutical substance ofatumumab from GlaxoSmithKline (GSK).[17] Ofatumumab was an anti-CD20 monoclonal antibody and Novartis had recently purchased its oncology indications from GSK. The target business contained the rights to develop, manufacture, promote and market the drug, as well as tangible assets such as biological materials and cells, clinical trial data and supply contracts. The Commission held that this was a concentration because the necessary intangible and core tangible assets for bringing the drug to market were being transferred and the business acquired by Novartis could be reasonably expected to enter the market within a reasonable period of time.
- In the airline industry, easyJet's acquisition of certain assets held by Air Berlin for operation in Berlin Tegel airport,[18] which included:
  - slots at Berlin Tegel airport and at some destination airports (eg, Palma de Mallorca);
  - overnight parking stands associated with the acquired slots;
  - Air Berlin's customer bookings in respect of the relevant operations (if any);
  - historic data relating to the target; and
  - certain aircraft furnishings and related equipment.
- Relying on the Consolidated Jurisdictional Notice, the Commission considered that: "In relation to outsourcing, the Consolidated Jurisdictional Notice (CJN) clarifies that the assets transferred should include at least core elements that would allow the acquirer to build up a market presence in a time-frame similar to the start-up period for joint ventures (ie, three years). Similarly, the acquisition of control over assets will constitute a concentration if the acquisition includes the core elements allowing the acquirer to build up a market presence within a relatively short time period."[19] The Commission considered that slots were a particularly

17 Case M.7872 – *Novartis/GSK (Ofatumumab autoimmune indications)*, dated 18 December 2015.

18 Case M.8672 – *easyJet/Certain Air Berlin Assets*, dated 12 December 2017.

19 Case M.8672 – *easyJet/Certain Air Berlin Assets*, 12 December 2017, para 15.

important right which gives access to congested airports. As a result of acquiring these slots and other ancillary assets, it was deemed that easyJet would be able to develop airline operations at the airports at which Air Berlin used to operate.

- In the retail sector, Otto acquired control of certain assets of Primondo and Quelle in the home-shopping sector (eg, enabling home-shopping via catalogues and the Internet) including trademarks, trademark applications, a patent, domain names, copyrights and rights of use of client data.[20] The Commission found that the transaction concerned the acquisition of an undertaking under the Merger Regulation since in the home-shopping sector companies do not typically have their own production facilities or shops, and the assets purchased including trademarks and domain names are significant assets which are vital for the acquisition of customers and turnover.
- In the chemicals industry, Nufarm acquired a portfolio of crop protection products from Adama and Syngenta.[21] These included herbicides, fungicides, insecticides, seed treatment products and plant growth regulators. It included the rights to a number of crop protection product registrations, pipeline registrations and intellectual property (IP) rights related to these product registrations and necessary to maintain such registrations. Nufarm was also granted an irrevocable, exclusive, transferrable, royalty-free licence to obtain access and use the product registration data related to the products and lead artificial intelligence (AI) data.

2.4 Successive transactions

In order to ensure that the EU Merger Regulation's jurisdiction is not circumvented by breaking down a transaction into a series of sales of assets over a period of time, if two or more transactions (each of them bringing about an acquisition of control) take place within a two-year period between the same persons or undertakings, they may be treated as a single concentration arising on the date of the last transaction, irrespective of whether or not those transactions relate to parts of the same business or concern the same sector.[22] This allows the Commission to take into consideration the turnover

---

20 Case M.5721 – *Otto/Primondo Assets*, 16 February 2010.
21 Case M.8725 – *Nufarm/Century*, 6 March 2019.
22 EU Merger Regulation, Article 5(2); Consolidated Jurisdictional Notice, para 50.

applicable to the target for each successive transaction over a two-year period for the purposes of calculating whether the single concentration has an EU dimension. That is, the turnover of the target businesses over the relevant period will be aggregated. The rules concerning successive transactions are particularly pertinent for carve-out transactions since several smaller packages of assets may be transferred over time which on a combined basis constitute the transfer of a larger business. These rules prevent the acquirer from avoiding the Commission's competence to review the transaction in such circumstances.

3. EU dimension

The EU Merger Regulation applies to concentrations that are deemed to have an 'EU dimension' on the basis that they meet certain turnover thresholds. This is often straightforward in relation to the acquisition of an entire company but can present additional challenges in relation to carve-outs where a business unit or a collection of assets from a seller group are being acquired. The first step is to identify the relevant entities whose turnover will be taken into account for the purpose of assessing whether a transaction has an EU dimension. The second step is to calculate the relevant turnover of those entities in accordance with the requirements of the EU Merger Regulation.

3.1 Identification of relevant entities

To determine whether the EU Merger Regulation's turnover thresholds are met, it is necessary to identify the entities whose turnover must be taken into consideration for the purposes of these thresholds. In relation to acquisitions of control, which will be most relevant for carve-out transactions, the relevant undertakings are, on the acquirer side, the undertakings acquiring sole or joint control. Therefore, the turnover of any non-controlling acquirers will not be included for the purposes of determining whether the turnover thresholds are met.

On the target side, the relevant entities are those over which control is being acquired. In this regard, the EU Merger Regulation provides that, where a concentration concerns the acquisition of part of one or more undertakings, only those parts that are the subject of the transaction should be taken into account for the purposes of calculating turnover (ie, the turnover of the entire seller group is not included).[23] The seller's turnover should not be taken into consideration for these purposes. Therefore, in situations involving the

23 EU Merger Regulation, Article 5(2).

acquisition of parts of a company, the undertakings concerned will be the acquirer and the acquired part(s) of the seller.

3.2 Calculation of turnover

Once the relevant entities have been identified, their annual turnover should be calculated for the purposes of applying the EU turnover thresholds. This can be challenging for carve-out transactions where the target may not be a legal entity with annual accounts and could be an asset package with no clearly defined turnover. In all circumstances, turnover should be calculated in accordance with the principles set out below.[24] Additional guidance has been provided on what steps might be appropriate for a carve-out transaction where there is no readily identifiable target turnover.

- *Ordinary activities.* Amounts to be included in the calculation of turnover should correspond to the 'ordinary activities' of the undertakings concerned. For these purposes, 'ordinary activities' means the turnover achieved from the sale of products and/or the provision of services in the normal course of business and will usually exclude sales of fixed assets and extraordinary income. The Commission's preference is to rely on the turnover included by the undertakings concerned in their audited accounts. Where audited accounts are not available, as may often be the case in carve-out transactions, the parties should endeavour to calculate turnover based on the revenue of the business transferring and the market reality. That is, for example, the amount of sales made to customers transferring with the asset package or any intragroup revenues which will become third-party revenues post-acquisition or revenues which can be directly attributed to assets being divested on a *pro rata* basis as part of the wider business being retained by the seller.
- *Net turnover.* The turnover to be taken into account is based on 'net sales' after the deduction of sales rebates, value added tax and other taxes directly related to turnover.
- *Reference period.* Turnover should be based on the audited accounts relating to the closest complete financial year to the date of the transaction. An adjustment of these figures should only be made in the event of disposals and/or acquisitions that have been made by the undertaking concerned since the

24 Note that different rules apply to calculating the turnover of credit and other financial institutions as well as insurance undertakings.

end of the last complete financial year (see below). Where the business unit or the assets being acquired have no reference period of their own, parties should normally use the annual financial reporting period applicable to the selling entity.

- *Exclusion of intra-company sales*. Turnover should not include the sale of products or the provision of services between any parent or subsidiary companies where the entire target group of companies is transferring. This is to avoid double-counting. However, in relation to carve-out transactions, it may be relevant to use intra-group sales for the calculation of turnover where this aspect of the business will become outsourced post-transaction, ie, the acquirer will be providing the goods or services to the seller under a third-party supplier/customer relationship.
- *Disposals/acquisitions*. Adjustments must be made to the last audited accounts if there have been any disposal or acquisitions (of businesses or assets) or closure of part of a business by any group undertaking since the end of its last financial year, which are not reflected in the accounts. Where an acquisition has been made, the turnover of the acquired entity for the entire previous fiscal year should be added to that of the undertaking concerned (ie, not just the turnover since the date of the acquisition). If an agreement for the sale of a business has been signed, but has not completed, turnover from the previous financial year should not be adjusted unless the sale is a precondition of the current transaction (ie, there is certainty that the sale will occur).
- *Joint ventures*. The turnover of joint venture companies in which an undertaking concerned has an interest is to be allocated equally according to the number of jointly-controlling companies (ie, if an undertaking has a joint venture with two other companies, only 33.3% of the joint venture's turnover should be included in the undertaking's total group turnover). Turnover should not be allocated on the basis of the level of shareholding.
- *Turnover of subsidiaries*. Where the Purchaser has subsidiary companies that form part of its group structure because, for example, it owns more than half the share capital or business assets, the whole turnover of the subsidiary in question must be taken into account regardless of the actual shareholding that the undertaking concerned holds in the subsidiary.

- *Geographical allocation.* As a general rule, turnover should be allocated by reference to the location of the customer at the time of purchase (as this is taken to be the place where competition generally takes place). For the sale of goods, if the place where the customer was located at the time of purchase was different from either the billing address or the place of delivery, turnover should usually be allocated to the place of delivery. For the provision of services, turnover should usually be attributed to the location of the provision of the service to the customer.

There are additional rules which apply to the calculation of turnover for investment funds but these are beyond the scope of this chapter.

3.3 EU Merger Regulation thresholds

The EU Merger Regulation contains two, alternative, sets of turnover thresholds to determine whether a concentration has an EU dimension.

The first set of turnover thresholds are as follows:

- the combined aggregate worldwide turnover of all the undertakings concerned exceeds €5 billion;
- the EU-wide turnover of at least two of the undertakings concerned exceeds €250 million; and
- the undertakings concerned do not achieve more than two-thirds of their individual aggregate EU-wide turnovers within one and the same member state.

The 'two-thirds' provision in the turnover thresholds was originally intended to exclude from the EU Merger Regulation's jurisdiction transactions that principally affected a single member state. However, as the primary set of thresholds failed to capture significant transactions occurring within a member state that could have effects across the EU, the Commission introduced a second set of turnover thresholds aimed at those transactions falling short of having an EU dimension but which nevertheless have a substantial impact in at least three member states. This prevents multiple filings being made within the EU in relation to the same concentration.

The secondary set of turnover thresholds are as follows:

- the combined aggregate worldwide turnover of all the undertakings concerned exceeds €2.5 billion;
- the EU-wide turnover of at least two of the undertakings concerned exceeds €100 million;

- the combined aggregate turnover of all the undertakings concerned exceeds €100 million in at least three member states;
- in each of those three member states, the turnover of at least two undertakings concerned exceeds €25 million; and
- the undertakings concerned do not achieve more than two-thirds of their individual aggregate EU-wide turnovers within one and the same member state.

4. Stand-still obligation

Many merger control regimes, including the EU, impose a stand-still obligation as a necessary safeguard of *ex ante* merger control. Under the standstill obligation, reportable transactions can be closed and implemented only after formal authorisation by the relevant antitrust authority. This rule also applies to reportable carve-out transactions. For carve-out transactions this can cause particular problems where it is necessary to carry out a number of implementation steps to prepare for the transfer of the asset package and any customers, or where services are to be carried out under a transitional services arrangement during any such integration planning period.

Neither the European Commission nor the EU Courts have set clear standards for permissible integration planning or preparatory steps toward integration pre-merger clearance. The recent European Court of Justice (ECJ) judgment in *Ernst & Young P/S v Konkurrencerådet* of 31 May 2018, is the first time that the European courts have opined on the extent of the standstill obligation and its observations are directly applicable to carve-out transactions.[25]

In 2013, KPMG Denmark concluded a merger agreement with Ernst & Young for the acquisition of its auditing and accounting business in Denmark. KPMG Denmark was part of KPMG International, an international network of independent auditing firms, linked by cooperation agreement and, as such, the business was to be carved out of the wider KPMG network. In accordance with the merger agreement, on the same day after signing the merger agreement, but before merger clearance from the Danish national competition authority had been received, KPMG Denmark gave notice (with effect 10 months later) to terminate its cooperation

25 *Ernst & Young P/S v Konkurrencerådet*, Case C-633/16, Judgment of the Court (Fifth Chamber) of 31 May 2018 (*EY/KPMG* Judgment).

agreement with KPMG's international network. Three days later, KPMG International established a new auditing business in Denmark and several clients switched auditors. The Danish national competition authority was notified of the transaction and cleared it subject to conditions. However, in December 2014, the Danish authority determined that KPMG Denmark had breached the Danish standstill obligation (which replicates the EU standstill obligation) by giving notice to terminate the cooperation agreement *before* clearance of the notified transaction. The Danish authority reasoned that the termination was merger-specific. In other words, KPMG would not have served the notice, absent the merger. KPMG challenged the decision before the Danish courts and as the Danish rules on merger control are based on the EU Merger Regulation, and the Danish competition authority referred in large part to the Commission's decision-making practice and to the case-law of the EU judicature in the contested decision, the referring court considered that the interpretation of Article 7(1) of the EU Merger Regulation raised questions which should be dealt with by the ECJ.

The ECJ found the following.

- Integration planning and preparatory steps that do not contribute to the change of control of the Seller do not infringe the standstill obligation.
- Standstill obligations do not apply to activities which "despite having been carried out in the context of a concentration, are not necessary to achieve a change of control of an undertaking concerned by that concentration..." because "those transactions, although they might be ancillary or preparatory to the concentration, do not present a direct functional link with its implementation."[26]

The *EY/KPMG* Judgment provides welcome clarification that integration planning or preparatory steps towards integration that do not contribute to the change of control of the target do not infringe the standstill obligation. Operations that do not fall under Article 7(1) of the EU Merger Regulation because they are only coincidental to the operation leading to a change in control remain subject to control under Article 101 Treaty on the Functioning of the European Union (TFEU). As such, merging parties must still ensure that integration planning and preparatory steps towards integration do not

26 *EY/KPMG* Judgment, para 49.

infringe the prohibition under Article 101 TFEU on competitors engaging in illegal cooperation or improperly exchanging competitively sensitive information.

In the context of a carve-out acquisition, a seller must maintain operational control over its business pending antitrust clearance and continue to act on its own behalf during the interim period. However, in preparing for clearance, an acquirer and seller can take actions as a result of the transaction, as long as those actions do not cede control of the target business to the buyer, such permissible actions could include seeking customer consents for a change in control, deferring new information technology (IT) investments, or imposing hiring freezes.

Carve-outs involving listed companies

Claire Keast-Butler
Cooley
Anna Ngo
Latham & Watkins

1. Introduction

This chapter outlines the specific considerations for carve-out mergers and acquisitions (M&A) transactions involving listed companies, either as vendor or purchaser, with a focus on companies whose shares are traded on the main market of the London Stock Exchange (the LSE) with a premium listing on the Official List of the UK Financial Conduct Authority (the FCA) (referred to in this chapter as 'premium listed companies').[1]

As an alternative to an M&A transaction, a listed company may instead consider carving-out the relevant business unit and undertaking an initial public offering (IPO) of the relevant subsidiary (which we refer to in this chapter as a 'carve-out IPO'). Alternatively, the listed company may consider a demerger transaction whereby the relevant business unit is segregated and its ownership is spun-off to the listed company's shareholders, typically resulting in those shareholders holding shares in two separate listed companies (which we refer to in this chapter as a 'demerger' but can also be referred to as a 'spin-off'). A carve-out IPO may be combined with a demerger, or followed by a spin-off by the listed company of its retained stake. While a detailed analysis of carve-out IPOs and demergers is beyond the scope of this book, we also outline in this chapter certain high-level capital markets considerations in respect of carve-out IPOs and demergers.

The choice among the different types of business separation transactions depends on myriad issues, including the listed

1 Note that the FCA introduced new a new regime in July 2018 which enables 'sovereign-controlled companies' to have a premium listing with certain modifications to the continuing obligations regime, in particular in respect of related party transactions.

company's rationale for pursuing a business separation transaction, the likely tax consequences for the company and its shareholders, as well as legal and accounting considerations. If a listed company needs to raise cash, it is likely to pursue an M&A transaction and/or a carve-out IPO (or potentially both options in parallel as a 'dual track' transaction), which will result in it receiving cash proceeds. Execution of an IPO is dependent on favourable market conditions and is unlikely to result in a 100% exit for the listed company, which may result in an M&A transaction being the favoured outcome. By contrast, a demerger does not raise cash, but may be pursued if the listed company's main aim is to separate business units to enhance shareholder value. Recent examples of high-profile carve-out IPO and demerger transactions include the IPO of the wealth management business (Quilter) following its demerger from Old Mutual plc in 2018, the listing of Gocompare.com Group plc following its demerger from esure Group plc in 2016, and the listing of CYBG, the holding company of Clydesdale Bank, Yorkshire Bank and Virgin Money UK following its demerger from National Australia Bank in 2016.

2. Carve-out M&A transactions

2.1 Approval requirements

(a) Board approval

The listed company's board of directors will need to approve the transaction in accordance with their statutory and fiduciary duties to the company. For a listed company incorporated in the United Kingdom, the directors will need to act in a way that they consider, in good faith, would be most likely to promote the success of the company for the benefit of its members as a whole. In doing so, the directors must have regard (among other matters) to: the likely consequences of any decision in the long term; the interests of the listed company's employees; the need to foster the company's business relationships with suppliers, customers and others; the impact of the company's operations on the community and the environment; the desirability of the company maintaining a reputation for high standards of business conduct; and the need to act fairly as between members of the company.

(b) ***Shareholder approval***

In certain circumstances, approval of the transaction by the listed company's shareholders may be required. For a premium listed company, shareholder approval will be required under the Listing Rules published by the FCA if an acquisition or disposal of a carved-out entity or business amounts to a class 1 transaction, reverse takeover or related party transaction.

Class 1 transactions: An acquisition or disposal by a premium listed company will be a class 1 transaction if any one of four 'class tests' results in a percentage ratio of 25% or more. These tests compare the gross assets the subject of the transaction to the gross assets of the premium listed company, the profits attributable to the assets the subject of the transaction to the profits of the premium listed company, the consideration for the transaction to the aggregate market value of all of the ordinary shares (excluding treasury shares) of the premium listed company and in the case of an acquisition only, the gross capital of the company or business being acquired to the gross capital of the premium listed company. The FCA has a discretion, where a calculation under any of the class tests produces an anomalous result, or the calculations are inappropriate to the activities of the premium listed company, to modify the relevant rule to substitute other relevant indicators of size, including industry-specific tests.

A class 1 transaction requires:

- announcement via a regulatory information service containing prescribed details of the transaction (the notification should be made as soon as possible once the terms of the transaction have been agreed);
- an explanatory circular to be sent to the premium listed company's shareholders; and
- prior shareholder approval and the transaction to be conditional on that approval being obtained (see section 2.3 below for details of the content requirements for a class 1 circular).

A premium listed company cannot agree to pay a sum in excess of 1% of its current market capitalisation pursuant to a break fee or 'reverse break fee' arrangement in connection with a carve-out M&A transaction without specific shareholder approval (as that will amount to a separate class 1 transaction). This includes 'no shop' and 'go shop' type provisions requiring payment of a sum to a party if the seller finds an alternative buyer, a requirement to pay another party's wasted costs if a transaction fails and non-refundable deposits. Payments in the nature of damages (liquidated or unliquidated) for breach of an obligation with an independent substantive commercial rationale for example, the typical business protection covenants that apply between exchange and completion of a share or asset purchase agreement or cooperation and information access obligations relating to obtaining merger or other clearances, are not break fee arrangements.

Reverse takeovers: Additional requirements may apply in the case of a listed company purchaser where the carved-out entity or business is larger than the listed company purchaser according to one of a number of metrics (referred to as a 'reverse takeover').

For premium listed companies, as well as companies with a standard listing of shares or depositary receipts, a reverse takeover is an acquisition where any of the percentage ratios set out above is 100% or more or which in substance results in a fundamental change in the business or a change in board or voting control of the company. The FCA will generally seek to cancel the listing of the listed company purchaser's shares on completion of a reverse takeover and the listed company will be required to reapply for listing for the enlarged group (including publishing a prospectus on the enlarged group).

Similar reverse takeover provisions apply in respect of purchasers with shares admitted to trading on the AIM market operated by the LSE, pursuant to its AIM Rules for Companies.

Related party transactions: Shareholder approval may be required for a smaller transaction (ie, where one or more of the percentage ratios under the class tests is 5% or greater) if it is entered into by a listed company purchaser or vendor with a person who is a 'related party', for example a sale of a business unit to an entity controlled by a director or major shareholder. A related party for these purposes includes a 10% plus shareholder in the premium listed company or any of its subsidiaries, a director of the premium listed company or any of its subsidiaries, a person exercising significant influence over the premium listed company or an associate of any such person. A related party transaction is any transaction between a premium listed company and a related party, an arrangement pursuant to which a premium listed company and a related party both invest in, or provide finance to, another undertaking or asset or any other similar transaction or arrangement between a premium listed company and any other person the purpose and effect of which is to benefit a related party (in each case other than a transaction or arrangement in the ordinary course of business).

2.2 Disclosure obligations

Information on a carve-out transaction may constitute inside information for the listed vendor or purchaser for the purposes of the EU Market Abuse Regulation (Regulation 596/2014) (MAR). MAR requires inside information to be disclosed to the public as soon as possible. However, a listed company may (on its own responsibility) delay disclosure provided that each of the following three conditions is met.

- Immediate disclosure is likely to prejudice the listed company's legitimate interests. It may be legitimate for the listed company to delay disclosure where there are ongoing negotiations, or related elements, where the outcome or normal pattern of those negotiations would be likely to be affected by immediate public disclosure – this includes negotiations related to mergers, acquisitions, splits and spin-offs, purchases or disposals of major assets or branches of corporate activity, restructurings and reorganisations.
- Delay of disclosure is not likely to mislead the public.
- The listed company is able to ensure the confidentiality of the information. In the event of a leak, the listed company must disclose the inside information to the public as soon as possible.

Care should be taken to establish insider lists and internal records should be maintained in accordance with the requirements of MAR. The listed company should review and consider on an ongoing basis whether the grounds to delay the disclosure of inside information still remain. On announcement of the carve-out transaction, the listed company will be required to notify the FCA that disclosure of the information was delayed and, if the FCA requests, provide a written explanation as to how the conditions set out above were met.

2.3 Class 1 disclosures and financial statement requirements

If a premium listed company is entering into a carve-out M&A transaction, as vendor or purchaser, and that transaction amounts to a class 1 transaction (see section 2.1 above), then it will need to prepare a class 1 circular for the acquisition or disposal which will need to comply with the content requirements in the Listing Rules and requires the approval of the FCA prior to publication and circulation to shareholders. The premium listed company will be required to appoint a sponsor to advise it and to liaise with the FCA on its behalf. The sponsor also needs to give certain confirmations to the FCA as required under the Listing Rules.

(a) *Class 1 circular content requirements*

As well as complying with the general content requirements for all circulars, and giving all the information about the transaction which has been given in the announcement, a class 1 circular must include certain financial and general information about the premium listed company and the assets which are subject of the transaction, covering both pre- and post-acquisition details. The purpose is to provide a full explanation of the proposed transaction and its effects on the premium listed company, so that shareholders are then able to make an informed decision about whether or not to vote in favour of the transaction. The circular is required to include an express responsibility statement from the premium listed company and its directors. The directors may be exposed to personal liability if they make the declaration negligently.

Other specific content requirements include:

- disclosure of risk factors which are material risk factors to the proposed carve-out transaction, will be material new risk factors to the premium listed company's group as a result of the proposed carve-out transaction or are existing material risk factors to the group which will be impacted by the proposed carve-out transaction;
- inclusion of trend information in respect of the premium listed company and the carved-out entity or business;
- summary of material litigation in respect of the premium listed company and the carved-out entity or business;
- description of any significant change in the financial or trading position of the premium listed company or the carved-out entity or business since the date of the last financial statements (or a statement that there have been no such significant changes);
- summary of material contracts entered into other than in the ordinary course of business by the premium listed company and the carved-out entity or business;

- statement that the premium listed company has sufficient working capital for its present requirements, that is for at least the next 12 months (this is a single statement for the premium listed company and its subsidiary undertakings on the basis that the disposal or acquisition, as applicable, has taken place); and
- details of where certain documents (including the sale and purchase agreement, or equivalent, for the carve-out M&A transaction) are on display and available for inspection.

(b) Financial information requirements

The class 1 circular will be required to include certain historical financial information (HFI) in respect of the carved-out entity or business.

Class 1 acquisitions: For a class 1 acquisition by a premium listed company purchaser, the key requirements are as follows.

- The class 1 circular will need to contain HFI covering three full financial years (or, if the carved-out entity or business has been in existence for less than three years, such shorter period) covering all relevant entities. This should include for each period a balance sheet and explanatory notes, an income statement and its explanatory notes, a cash-flow statement and its explanatory notes, a statement showing either all changes in equity or changes in equity other than those arising from capital transactions with owners and distributions to owners, the accounting policies and any additional explanatory notes. Unless a carved-out entity has been run as a stand-alone entity with its own financial statements, this is likely to require the preparation of carve-out financial statements.
- If the carved-out entity has itself made acquisitions in this three-year track record period, additional HFI in respect of the acquired entities may be required.
- Generally, the HFI must be presented in a form that is consistent with the purchaser's accounting policies. This may require a restatement from local GAAP to IFRS.
- In most cases, an accountants' opinion is required to be included in the class 1 circular which sets out whether, for the purposes of the class 1 circular, the HFI gives a true and fair view of the financial matters set out in it. This opinion must be given by an independent accountant who is qualified to act as an auditor (typically referred to as the 'reporting accountants').

Class 1 disposals: For a class 1 disposal by a premium listed company vendor, the key requirements are as follows.

- The HFI on the carved-out entity or business is limited to the last annual consolidated balance sheet, the consolidated income statements for the last three financial years (drawn up to at least the level of profit or loss) and the consolidated balance sheet and consolidated income statement (drawn up to at least the level of profit or loss) for any interim period for which the premium listed company has published financial statements.
- The HFI should be extracted, without material adjustment, from the consolidation schedules that underlie the premium listed company's audited consolidated accounts or interim financial information and must be accompanied by a statement to this effect.
- If the HFI is not extracted from the consolidation schedules, it must be extracted from the premium listed company's accounting records and where an allocation is made, the HFI must be accompanied by:
  - an explanation of the basis for any financial information presented; and
  - a statement by the premium listed company's directors that such allocations provide a reasonable basis for the presentation of the financial information for the target to enable shareholders to make a fully informed voting decision.
- If the premium listed company has not owned the carved-out entity or business for the entirety of the HFI period, the information may be extracted from the carved-out entity or business' accounting records.
- There is no requirement for an accountants' opinion or report on the HFI.

***Pro forma* financial information:** There is no requirement for a premium listed company to include *pro forma* financial information in a class 1 circular. However, it is common to include *pro forma* financial information in order to illustrate the expected impact of the transaction on the premium listed company. If included, the *pro forma* financial information should be prepared in accordance with the requirements of the Prospectus Regulation (Regulation (EU) No 2017/1129), including that the *pro forma* financial information must be accompanied by a report prepared by the reporting accountants.

Profit forecasts and profit estimates: If a premium listed company has made any estimate or forecast about its profits (or the profits of a significant part of its group) or the profits of the carved-out entity or business (or a significant part of the carved-out entity or business) for any period for which financial information has not yet been published, it will be required to include that profit forecast or estimate in the class 1 circular. The premium listed company will need to reconfirm the profit forecast or estimate and state that it has been properly compiled on the basis of assumptions stated and that the basis of accounting is consistent with the accounting policies of the listed company or, if appropriate, include an explanation of why the profit forecast or profit estimate is no longer valid. There is no requirement to include an accountants' report on the profit forecast or profit estimate in the class 1 circular.

Synergy benefits: It is common for a class 1 circular prepared by a premium listed company purchaser to include details of estimated synergies or other quantified estimated financial benefits (synergy benefits) expected to arise from a transaction. In that case, the class 1 circular also has to include:

- the basis for the belief that those synergy benefits will arise;
- an analysis and explanation of the constituent elements of the synergy benefits (including any costs) sufficient to enable the relative importance of those elements to be understood, including an indication of when they will be realised and whether they are expected to be recurring;
- a base figure for any comparison drawn;
- a statement that the synergy benefits are contingent on the class 1 transaction and could not be achieved independently; and
- a statement that the estimated synergy benefits reflect both the beneficial elements and related costs.

Supporting documents from accountants: The reporting accountants will also need to prepare various private reports to support the class 1 circular which will be addressed to the premium listed company and the sponsor. These include:

- a working capital report that considers the basis for the working capital statement in the circular;
- a private report on any profit estimate or forecast which is repeated in the circular; in the case of an acquisition by a premium listed company, a report on the financial reporting

procedures of the carved-out entity or business being acquired; and

- comfort letters in respect of the significant change statements in the circular and any other financial information that is extracted from the premium listed company's accounts and included in the class 1 circular.

There may also be a report from the reporting accountants to support the verification of the synergy benefits statements in the circular.

(c) ***Equity offering documentation***

If a premium listed company purchaser is financing the acquisition with an equity offering that has a pre-emptive element (such as a rights issue or placing and open offer), a prospectus will be required in connection with that offering. The class 1 circular and prospectus are often prepared and sent to the premium listed company's shareholders as one single combined document.

2.4 Timing considerations

If a carve-out M&A transaction amounts to a class 1 transaction for a premium listed vendor or purchaser, the principal drivers of timing for that process will be the timing required to prepare the financial statements for inclusion in the circular (and the various accountants reports and comfort letters), as well as the time needed for the review process with the FCA. In broad terms, we would expect the drafting and approval process for a class 1 circular for an acquisition to take approximately six to eight weeks and for a disposal to take approximately four to six weeks.

3. Carve-out IPOs

3.1 Choice of market and eligibility requirements

In the United Kingdom, the carved-out entity will have a number of routes to market. In the event it is seeking admission of its shares to trading on the Main Market of the LSE, it can seek a premium listing or standard listing of its shares on the FCA's Official List, or it may elect to seek a listing through the LSE's High Growth Segment. As an alternative, the demerged entity could also consider applying to quote its shares on AIM, the LSE's junior market. In the case of a carve-out IPO, the key drivers for the choice of market, in particular, whether the carved-out entity could qualify for a premium listing, would include the following.

(a) ***Financial track record***

In order to be eligible for a premium listing as a commercial company under Chapter 6 of the Listing Rules, the carved-out entity will be required to have a financial track record, including the requirement to have a revenue earning track record, and demonstrate that it operates an independent business (both of these points are covered in more detail below).

(b) ***Continuing obligations***

In the event the carved-out entity was eligible for a premium listing, it would be required to comply with extensive continuing obligations. In particular, the relationship between the carved-out entity and its former parent company would need to be considered. If the former parent company retains a stake of 10% or more in the carved-out entity (and for the 12 months after its holding falls below 10%), thereby qualifying as a 'substantial shareholder' under Chapter 11 of the Listing Rules, then the carved-out entity would be subject to the related parties regime under the Listing Rules. Any transactions entered into between the carved-out entity and its substantial shareholder may require shareholder approval, even if the transaction was undertaken on an arms-length basis.

(c) ***Independent business requirements***

Under the Listing Rules, a company must demonstrate to the satisfaction of the FCA that it carries on an independent business as its main activity in order to be eligible for, and to maintain, a premium listing. The independent business requirement is intended to ensure that a premium listed company is operating a meaningful business in its own right, and does not, for example, simply exist as part of a wider enterprise. Factors that are relevant to the determination of independence include situations where a majority of the revenue or the company's financing is attributable to one person or group, and/or where the company has no strategic control over revenue or the commercialisation of its products or no freedom to implement its business strategy. These requirements may present challenges in the context of a carve-out IPO. In particular, the FCA will review closely the following situations.

- Where a company has been carved out of a wider group, and which has retained close ties with its former parent. The FCA notes that such ties may take the form of extensive services being provided by the former parent, beyond normal outsourcing arrangements or transitional services agreements.

Particular regard should be had to circumstances where the carved-out entity is required to source those services from its former parent, or may not have control over information that is essential to decision making at the carved-out entity's level.

- Where key contracts are contingent on the relationship with the former parent, or where the carved-out entity's business is predominantly generated through the former parent group.
- Where a company cannot access financing other than through the parent group (other than where this is a choice exercised by the carved-out entity for commercial reasons).

(d) ***Controlling shareholder rules***

Typically, the parent company will retain a significant stake following completion of a carve-out IPO. A company with a 'controlling shareholder' under the Listing Rules, being a shareholder with 30% or more of the shareholding in the company will need to be able to demonstrate that, despite having a controlling shareholder, it is able to carry on an independent business as its main activity in order to be eligible for, and maintain, a premium listing. Factors that may indicate a company does not satisfy controlling shareholder requirements include where a company has granted or may be required to grant security over its business in connection with the funding of a controlling shareholder (or member of the controlling shareholder's group), where a controlling shareholder appears to be able to influence the operations of the carved-out entity's operations outside of its normal governance structures or via material shareholdings in one or more significant subsidiary undertakings, where a controlling shareholder appears to be able to exercise improper influence over the carved-out entity and/or where the carved-out entity cannot demonstrate that it has access to financing other than from the controlling shareholder.

The FCA has noted that circumstances where a controlling shareholder is able to influence a company in a way which subverts its normal governance process includes:

- using financing or other business arrangements to unduly influence the strategy of the carved-out entity; and/or
- using significant stakes in subsidiaries of the carved-out entity to exert indirect control over the group as a whole.

The Listing Rules also require companies seeking a premium listing as a commercial company to have a relationship agreement in place at all times with a controlling shareholder, including certain mandatory provisions designed to ensure that the carved-out entity can operate independently from the controlling shareholder. This can also give rights to the controlling shareholder, for example director appointment rights.

(e) *Other 'readiness' considerations*

In addition to listing location and segment considerations, thought should also be given by the parent company and the carved-out entity as to listing 'readiness'. As ancillary considerations to any tax, accounting and other separation workstreams (which are beyond the scope of this chapter), some thought should be given as to the listing structure, and whether a new holding company should be inserted above the carved-out entity. For example, a new UK holding company could be inserted above the carved-out entity, which would make it easier for the carved-out entity to gain entry to the FTSE indices – premium listed companies that are UK incorporated are eligible for FTSE indexation with a 25% free float, whereas non-UK incorporated companies are required to have a free float of 50%.

(f) *Corporate governance considerations*

If the carved-out entity is to seek a premium listing, it would be expected to comply with the UK Corporate Governance Code, which requires it to have a board of directors that has an appropriate combination of executive and non-executive, in particular independent non-executive, directors, such that no one individual or small group of individuals dominates the board's decision making. The UK Corporate Governance Code, which operates on a 'comply or explain' basis, states that at least half the board, excluding the chair, should be non-executive directors whom the board considers to be independent. On this basis, the parent and carved-out entity should consider what additional board and senior hires are required for the carved-out entity.

The process of on-boarding any new directors to the board should be carefully choreographed, particularly with those members who may be unfamiliar with the demerged business. This is particularly relevant against the requirement for directors to take responsibility for the content of the prospectus under the UK Prospectus Rules. The legal and financial advisers to the carved-out entity should focus on the requirements of any board education to enable the directors to comfortably take responsibility for the prospectus.

Additionally, as part of the 'readiness' conversations, thought should be given to unwinding any pre-existing incentive arrangements of the existing members of management of the carved-out entity, and the introduction of incentive arrangements that are compliant and consistent with the UK Corporate Governance Code and UK corporate governance best practice.

3.2 Approval requirements

(a) Board approval

A carve-out IPO would need to be approved by the listed company's board of directors in accordance with their statutory and fiduciary duties to the company, as well as by the new board of directors of the carved-out entity. Please see section 2.1(a) above for additional considerations for a company incorporated in the United Kingdom.

(b) Shareholder approval

In the case of a premium listed company, a carve-out IPO could require shareholder approval as a class 1 transaction if any of the class tests set out in section 2.1(b) above produces a percentage ratio in excess of 25%. The class tests are run on the basis of the interest being disposed of by the premium listed company through the IPO process. If the carve-out IPO will result in the carved-out entity no longer being consolidated in the premium listed company's accounts, it would be treated as having disposed of 100% of the carved-out entity for the purposes of the gross assets test and the profits test even if it retained a substantial minority stake.

3.3 Disclosure obligations

Information on the carve-out IPO or demerger transaction may constitute inside information for the parent company under MAR. Additional considerations are set out in section 2.2 above.

3.4 Public documentation requirements

(a) Class 1 circular

As noted above, a carve-out IPO could constitute a class 1 disposal requiring publication of a shareholder circular. Additional detail on the content requirements for a class 1 circular are set out in section 2.3 above.

(b) *Prospectus*

A prospectus providing information on the carved-out entity will be required to admit the shares of the carved-out entity to listing on the Official List of the FCA and, in the event of a carve-out IPO that is not limited only to institutional investors, in connection with the offering of the shares. The process of preparing a prospectus will need to be factored in to the overall transaction timeline, particularly if there is little pre-existing disclosure on the carved-out entity. Assuming that research will be published on the carved-out entity by investment banks forming part of the underwriting syndicate (as would be usual), under new FCA rules that came into effect in July 2018 a base registration document will need to be published earlier in the IPO process; typically this would be seven days prior to the publication of such research reports. Both the prospectus and the registration document would need to be reviewed and approved by the FCA.

In order to be eligible for a listing on a stock exchange in the EEA, the carved-out entity will require HFI to cover the previous three financial years. Carve-out financials will be required to be prepared for the carved-out or demerged group. The latest audited accounts must be no more than six months old prior to the date of the prospectus; interim accounts can be included in the prospectus to satisfy this requirement. In addition, for US accounting comfort purposes, the latest audited or reviewed accounts cannot be older than 135 days from the date of listing. The HFI must be prepared in accordance with IFRS as adopted by the European Union or an equivalent accounting standard. The timetable for any carve-out IPO should factor in any accounting conversion process from local GAAP to IFRS.

In particular, to be eligible for a premium listing, the Listing Rules also require that the HFI represent at least 75% of the carved-out entity's business for the track record period, and which demonstrate that it has a revenue earning track record.

(c) *AIM admission document*

In the event of a carve-out IPO on AIM, the carved-out entity would be required to publish an AIM admission document rather than a prospectus (provided that the IPO was limited to institutional investors only). The content requirements for an AIM admission document are based on the content requirements for a prospectus, with certain modifications and items excluded. An AIM admission document does not require a review and approval process with the FCA or any other regulatory body.

3.5 Timing considerations

The timing for a carve-out IPO will generally be the same as for other IPOs. For an IPO on the premium segment of the Official List, we would expect the transaction to take five to six months, but may well be longer if the carve-out is complex and/or the preparation of HFI for the carved-out entity takes a lengthy period. It is usually possible to complete an IPO on AIM in a slightly shorter period.

4. Demergers

4.1 Choice of market and eligibility requirements

Most demergers by listed companies will involve the listing of the demerged entity. Many of the same considerations set out in section 3.1 above will also apply in the case of a demerger. However, as the listed company will not retain a stake in the demerged entity, the controlling shareholder rules set out section 3.1(d) will not be relevant.

4.2 Approval requirements

(a) Board approval

A demerger transaction would need to be approved by the listed company's board of directors in accordance with their statutory and fiduciary duties to the company. Please see section 2.1(a) above for additional considerations for a company incorporated in England and Wales. In making its decision to effect a demerger, the board of the listed company does not owe fiduciary duties to the newly demerged company or to any prospective shareholders of the demerged company in that capacity.

(b) Shareholder approval

In the case of a premium listed company, a demerger transaction could require shareholder approval as a class 1 transaction if any of the class tests set out in section 2.1(b) produces a percentage ratio for the disposal of the demerged entity by way of the demerger in excess of 25%.

In addition, shareholder approval is likely to be required as a matter of corporate law to implement the demerger, for example to declare a dividend *in specie* or approve a reduction of capital (as applicable). If the demerger involves a scheme of arrangement under Part 26 of the Companies Act 2006, the scheme will need to be approved at a court-convened shareholder meeting.

4.3 Securities law considerations

(a) *Disclosure obligations*

Information on the demerger transaction may constitute inside information for the parent company under MAR. Additional considerations are set out in section 2.2 above.

(b) *Public offer considerations*

A demerger is not considered to be an 'offer to the public' by the demerged entity since the shareholders receiving shares in the demerged entity have not made an investment decision to receive such shares pursuant to the Financial Services and Markets Act 2000. The shareholders receive the shares in the demerged entity as a function of the transaction without having the right to elect to receive the shares.

4.4 Public documentation requirements

(a) *Class 1 circular*

As noted above, a demerger transaction could constitute a class 1 disposal requiring publication of a shareholder circular. Additional detail on the content requirements for a class 1 circular are set out in section 2.3 above.

(b) *Prospectus*

A prospectus providing information on the demerged entity will be required to admit the shares of the carved-out or demerged entity to listing on the Official List of the FCA. This will be the same as for a carve-out IPO as set out at section 3.4(b) above, save that unless the demerger is being undertaken in conjunction with an IPO where research is being published by investment banks in the underwriting syndicate, there will be no requirement to publish a separate base registration document.

4.5 Timing

The overall timing of a demerger will be driven by the overall complexity of the transaction and the potential demerger structure, including whether it requires court sanction to become effective. The capital markets considerations, including the preparation of a listing prospectus for the demerged entity in order for it to be listed upon the effectiveness of the demerger, should be run in tandem with the overall corporate timetable. As described, ample time should also be given to IPO 'readiness' factors for the demerged entity, particular if it is seeking a premium listing on the Official List, which will necessitate compliance with the UK Corporate Governance Code. We would expect a demerger transaction to take nine months or longer to complete.

Tax issues

James Leslie
Karl Mah
Latham & Watkins

---

1. Introduction

The aim of this chapter is to provide a broad overview of certain tax issues which can arise on carve-out transactions including: pre-sale issues to be considered, the key, and potentially contentious, structuring decisions which will need to be agreed between buyer and seller, and an overview of the main contractual issues which may arise when negotiating a carve-out transaction. It should be emphasised at the outset that this chapter is only intended to provide a broad overview of the tax issues which may arise on carve-out transactions. A comprehensive commentary on this topic is worthy of a book in itself. In addition, the tax treatment of the seller, target entity or entities, and the buyer will depend on the precise facts and circumstances of the transaction and the tax position and residence of each of the parties.

Cross-border transactions will require the input of local counsel in each relevant jurisdiction. This chapter will assume the seller and the buyer are unconnected UK corporate entities resident for tax purposes in the United Kingdom and all assets to be sold are situated in the United Kingdom, however many issues discussed (such as purchase price allocation and tax risk allocation) will also be relevant in non-UK jurisdictions.

A fundamental consideration at the outset will be whether to structure the transaction as an asset sale or a share sale. The two can produce significantly different outcomes from a tax perspective and each can have their benefits and pitfalls depending on the circumstances of the parties and the transaction in question. Share sales are perhaps more common in the market for various reasons (often including, but by no means limited to, tax). As such, this chapter will focus on tax issues arising on share sales. However, as a starting point it is useful to understand some of the key tax issues which can arise on asset sales for a comparison to be drawn between the two.

2. Asset sale

In general, where assets are transferred, any tax liabilities relating to such assets remain with the selling entity rather than transferring across to the buyer. Equally, any tax losses attributable to such assets will generally remain with the selling entity. As a result, fewer contractual tax protections tend to be required in an asset purchase agreement than in a share purchase agreement (where historical tax liabilities will generally transfer with the target entity).

However, while an asset sale may, at first, appear simpler from a tax perspective than a share sale, the tax consequences can in fact be more complex. Depending on the type of assets transferred, significant transfer taxes may be incurred and, while these will generally be payable by the buyer, they may affect the global price a buyer is willing to pay for the assets (so that economically such transfer taxes may also be a seller cost).

2.1 Purchase price allocation

From a tax perspective, an asset sale is essentially a transfer of a bundle of individual assets. Therefore, while a global purchase price for such assets may have been agreed between the buyer and the seller, this global price will need to be allocated between each asset (or at least between the various classes of assets transferred). The buyer and the seller may have conflicting interests with respect to the allocation of the purchase price.

For instance, the seller may (subject to any tax relief or exemption) realise a chargeable gain on the disposal of an asset calculated on the difference between its base cost (broadly, the cost of acquiring the asset) and the sale price allocated to that asset. It is therefore likely that the seller will wish to allocate a greater amount of the purchase price to those assets with a higher base cost and a lower amount of the purchase price to those assets with a lower base cost in order to minimise any chargeable gain/maximise any loss. By contrast, the buyer will be keen to allocate a greater proportion of the purchase price to those assets which are most likely to be re-sold (so creating a higher base cost in such assets and reducing any future potential chargeable gain/maximising any chargeable loss).

The allocation of the global purchase price between assets is a matter for negotiation. However, it should be noted that there are various provisions in the UK chargeable gains and capital allowances legislation (as to which, see below) which allow HM Revenue & Customs (HMRC) to reallocate consideration if it is not 'just and reasonable'. Any allocation should therefore fall within the 'just and reasonable' boundaries. Many jurisdictions impose similar legislation, so the buyer and seller should try to agree a purchase price allocation in the purchase agreement if possible.

One potential advantage for the buyer in an asset sale is that, depending on purchase price allocation, it will receive a step up in base cost for the assets purchased. In a share sale there will generally be no disposal of the assets by the target company, so the buyer will indirectly inherit the base cost of any assets held by the target companies, which may be an issue for the buyer if any of the assets are 'pregnant with gain'.

2.2 Value added tax

Whether value added tax (VAT) is chargeable on an asset sale or not will depend on the assets being sold; however, the seller will usually expect to be made whole for any VAT element for which it is required to account on the supply of assets. The buyer may be able to recover at least some of the VAT element paid to the seller (by making onward taxable supplies), and an analysis of the buyer's expected VAT recovery position should be carried out early in the transaction.

Where the bundle of assets being sold constitutes a business in its own right, the asset sale may be treated as a transfer of going concern (TOGC) for VAT purposes. Where this is the case, the transfer of the assets is treated as neither a supply of goods nor a supply of services, and so falls outside the scope of VAT. If only part of a business is being sold, that part must be capable of being carried on as a separate operation. Various conditions will need to be met in order for TOGC treatment to apply (for instance, the buyer will need to use the assets to carry on the same kind of business as that carried on by the seller prior to completion), and the parties will want contractual protection for additional comfort that the conditions will be met. The VAT risk should be allocated in the purchase agreement in the event that HMRC assert that TOGC treatment is not available.

It is worth noting that while the supply of land and buildings is generally exempt from VAT, an 'option to tax' can be exercised. If an option to tax is exercised over land and buildings the supply of such land and buildings will be subject to VAT at the standard rate (and VAT incurred in making such supply may therefore be recoverable). TOGC treatment can still apply to a transfer of land and buildings over which the option to tax has been exercised; however, additional conditions will need to be met. For instance, the buyer will also need to opt to tax the land and buildings in question from completion. It should be noted that stamp duty land tax (SDLT) is chargeable on the VAT inclusive price of the property in question. Therefore, if the transfer of land and buildings is subject to VAT, this may result in an increase in the SDLT due.

2.3 Capital allowances

Some assets being sold, such as fixed plant and machinery, may benefit from capital allowances. Capital allowances are essentially depreciation for tax purposes, allowing the owner of the asset to offset a fixed percentage annually of the cost of such asset against taxable profits. The buyer will likely want to allocate to those assets which qualify for capital allowances as much of the global purchase price as possible in order to maximise any future capital allowances. However, if the purchase price allocated to the assets benefiting from capital allowances exceeds the tax written down value brought forward in the seller's books, a balancing charge will be triggered for the seller (ie, the seller is treated as having received taxable income equal to the amount of the excess), while to the extent the purchase price is lower than the tax written down value brought forward, a balancing allowance will be triggered for the seller (ie, the seller is entitled to a tax deduction equal to the difference between the tax written down value of the asset and the purchase price for such asset).

In relation to land that includes fixtures, provided certain conditions have been met, a joint election may be entered into by the buyer and the seller in order to set an agreed allocation of the purchase price for the purpose of capital allowances (such election should not impact the chargeable gains position of the buyer or the seller, but will need to be 'just and reasonable').

2.4 SDLT

Transactions in land situated in the United Kingdom will, subject to any available exemptions or reliefs, be subject to transfer taxes. The applicable transfer tax will vary according to the location of the land in question. In England and Northern Ireland, SDLT will be the applicable tax; in Scotland, land and buildings transaction tax will be applicable and in Wales, land transaction tax. This may represent a significant cost to the buyer and so the buyer may be eager to allocate as little as possible to any land or buildings being sold as part of the transaction. Any such allocation must be done on a just and reasonable basis.

3. Share sale

A clean sale of the entity or entities owning the business to be sold will often be preferable for a seller who may wish to walk away completely from the business being sold, and this is achievable more easily with a share sale. However, any tax liabilities of the target are likely to transfer with it on sale, so greater contractual protection will generally be required by a potential buyer.

3.1 VAT and stamp taxes

The sale of shares in a UK company is exempt from VAT and, assuming only commercial (as opposed to residential) property is owned by the target company, SDLT will generally not be applicable on a share sale. The buyer will however generally be liable to stamp duty at the rate of 0.5% of the consideration paid for the shares of the target company. Assuming there is a written instrument of transfer (most commonly a stock transfer form), that instrument will need to be presented to HMRC for stamping and stamp duty paid within 30 days of completion of the transaction.

3.2 Capital gains and substantial shareholding exemption

While the sale of shares could *prima facie* result in a chargeable gain for the sellers, any gain on the shares may be exempt under the substantial shareholding exemption (SSE). SSE is not however available on an asset sale so capital gains tax may be payable on the sale of such assets, thus reducing the net proceeds received by the seller and therefore reducing the amount of cash available to be distributed to shareholders. Various conditions need to be met in order for SSE to apply and the seller should undertake a detailed analysis as to whether the conditions will be satisfied well in advance of any potential sale. In particular, the seller will need to have held at least 10% of the target's ordinary share capital for a period of one year beginning no more than six years before the date of the disposal, and the target company must be a trading company (or a holding company of a trading group). It should be noted, however, that SSE is not optional. SSE will apply automatically where the conditions are met and it not only exempts any chargeable gain, but will also render as unallowable any loss which may otherwise have been realised. The SSE may therefore be unwelcome to the seller if the sale of the business would otherwise produce a significant loss for chargeable gains purposes.

Where a pre-sale reorganisation is necessary in order to ensure all the assets of the carved-out business sit within the target entity, various de-grouping charges can apply on sale of the target to a third party. As discussed below, buyers will generally expect robust protection against any such charges in the transaction documentation.

4. Pre-sale reorganisation

Whereas under an asset sale the buyer can essentially cherry pick which assets are to be transferred as part of the carve-out transaction, in a share sale the target business and all its assets will need to be packaged within a company or group of companies to be sold. As a result, a pre-sale reorganisation will often be necessary to ensure all the relevant assets sit within the target entity or entities. It will be essential for all parties that such reorganisation is achieved in a tax efficient manner. Depending on the nature of the seller group and the business to be transferred, pre-sale reorganisations can be extremely complex and time consuming and so careful planning should take place as far in advance as possible of any potential sale (even if implementation occurs shortly before sale).

Where assets are to be transferred within a group of companies, various reliefs/exemptions may be available in order to effect the reorganisation in a tax neutral manner. However, many of the reliefs can be complex and prescriptive in nature. Effecting the reorganisation in a tax neutral manner is often only half the battle as various anti-avoidance provisions exist which may operate to clawback any reliefs claimed during the reorganisation on a subsequent sale of the target. It is therefore essential in any pre-sale reorganisation that not only is the reorganisation itself tax efficient, but any subsequent sale will also be as tax efficient as possible. This chapter highlights a few of the issues which can arise for sellers and buyers with respect to pre-sale reorganisations.

Where assets are transferred within a chargeable gains group (broadly, under common 75% ownership) such a transfer will often be on a 'no gain/no loss' basis. This generally means the transferee will inherit the transferor's base cost in the asset. However, if the transferee of the assets leaves the capital gains group within a six year period of the transfer (a so called 'de-grouping'), the transferee will, unless it remains in a capital gains group with the transferor, be deemed to have disposed and immediately reacquired the asset for its market value which may crystallise a chargeable gain or allowable loss (and potentially create a step up in basis for the transferee). Any chargeable gain or allowable loss will be treated as increasing or decreasing (as the case may be) the disposal proceeds of the shares sold by the seller, thereby increasing or decreasing any gain or loss realised by the seller on a disposal of the shares. It should be noted that any gain can be reallocated to another member of the seller's chargeable gains group. For instance, the seller may wish to reallocate any gain to another member of the group which has capital losses which can be used to offset such gain. Such a de-grouping charge may be mitigated if SSE is available.

The treatment of intangible assets (such as goodwill and intellectual property) will depend on whether the assets were acquired or created on or after 1 April 2002. Intangible assets acquired or created prior to 1 April 2002 will be subject to the chargeable gains regime outlined above while those acquired/created after this date will be subject to the 'intangibles regime'. Under the intangibles regime, assets may also be transferred between members of a group on a tax neutral basis. Nevertheless, as with assets subject to the chargeable gains regime, a de-grouping charge can arise where an intra-group transfer of intangible assets has taken place and the transferee subsequently leaves the group (and the transferor company does not leave with it) within a six year period of such transfer. Unlike under the chargeable gains regime where the de-grouping charge will arise in the seller group, under the intangibles regime the charge will arise in the target, potentially being a cause of concern for the buyer. It is, therefore, especially important to distinguish between intangible assets which are pre-April 2002 and those which are post-April 2002. A buyer should take particular care during the due diligence process to make this distinction and seek appropriate contractual protections. It is possible for the parties to make a joint election to reallocate the de-grouping charge to the seller.

If shares are to be transferred as part of the pre-sale reorganisation, relief from stamp duty may be available to mitigate the 0.5% stamp duty charge that is *prima facie* payable on the transfer of UK shares. The relief is not automatic and any documents subject to stamp duty will need to be submitted to HMRC and stamped (as not chargeable to stamp duty). The application for the relief is prescriptive and care should be taken to ensure all conditions for the relief are met. HMRC can take several weeks to 'adjudicate' that no stamp duty is payable, so this should be built into the timing of any pre-sale reorganisation. Moreover, relief can be denied where the intra-group transfer is connected with any arrangement under which the transferee and transferor would cease to be connected for stamp duty purposes. It is therefore important that any such transfers take place well in advance of any sale where the transferee is to leave the stamp duty group.

Relief from SDLT should also be available where land or buildings are to be transferred intra-group. However, as with stamp duty, care will need to be taken to ensure there are no arrangements in place which will disqualify any such relief. SDLT relief can also be 'clawed-back' in certain circumstances, such as where the transferee leaves the SDLT group within a three-year period of the relevant transfer.

A buyer of the carve-out business may attach significant value to any trading losses available to the target which may be used to offset future taxable profits. A seller may be able to monetise any such losses by ensuring they transfer with the target entity to the buyer and by negotiating an increase in the purchase price reflecting this value. *Prima facie* any losses will remain within the entity in which they were generated but, if certain conditions are met, where a trade is transferred as part of a pre-sale reorganisation, carried forward losses arising from that trade can transfer with the trade to the successor company. It is worth noting that any arrangements for the sale of the target company which indicate that beneficial ownership of the target has transferred to a person outside the corporation tax group of the seller may jeopardise the availability of the carried forward losses.

5. Contractual protections on a share sale

Nearly all share purchase agreements will contain at least some degree of tax warranty protection. As well as any specific warranties a buyer may require as a result of its due diligence, the tax warranties can as a minimum be expected to cover the following general areas:

- payment of taxes (within any applicable time limits);
- filing of all tax returns (within applicable time limits);
- all tax returns correct and complete (in all material respects);
- no tax avoidance schemes have been entered into;
- no disputes with any tax authority;
- applicable transfer pricing rules have been complied with;
- VAT registration and compliance with VAT legislation;
- all documents required to be stamped have been duly stamped;
- the Target will not be liable for any de-grouping charges on completion of the transaction; and
- tax residence and any taxable presence in a jurisdiction outside the target's jurisdiction of tax residence.

While the general scope of the tax warranties on a carve-out transaction will be similar to any other share purchase, any pre-sale reorganisation steps undertaken by the seller should be carefully analysed to ensure such reorganisation does not create any additional future tax exposure for the target. To the extent such a risk is identified, warranty protection should be sought by the buyer. Of particular importance on a carve-out transaction will be the possibility of de-grouping charges and, as a minimum, buyers will usually expect warranty protection for any such charges which arise on completion.

The statute of limitations for tax authorities to make claims against tax payers can run for a number of years, and as such the limitation period for claims under tax warranties (and the tax covenant) is often longer than for non-tax claims (typically four to seven years) for UK targets.

If any specific tax issues come to light during due diligence or the disclosure process (including in relation to any pre-sale reorganisation steps), the buyer should consider whether a specific indemnity or price reduction is appropriate. Often, however, the buyer will also insist on a general tax indemnity (often known as a tax covenant) to cover any unexpected pre-completion taxes. Whether a tax covenant is given by the seller will be a matter of commercial negotiation.

While the principle of a tax covenant (which may be a schedule to the share purchase agreement or a separate document) is relatively straightforward, it is often a heavily negotiated and intricate document. Below is an outline of the provisions which will typically be found in a UK tax covenant.

6. The tax covenant

6.1 The covenant

The tax covenant will effectively allocate any taxes arising in the target on or prior to completion to the seller by containing a covenant to pay the buyer an amount equal to any tax on income, profits or gains arising prior to completion or triggered by any 'event' (which is usually drafted extremely widely and will include any omissions) occurring on or prior to completion. The covenant should also cover any interest and penalties arising from such taxes. The tax covenant will usually be structured so any payments will flow between the buyer and the seller as an adjustment to the purchase price so as to mitigate the risk that such payments are subject to tax in the hands of the recipient.

The tax covenant for a carve-out transaction will usually be similar to a tax covenant on a standard mergers and acquisitions transaction. As the tax covenant generally protects the buyer from taxes of the target arising on or before completion, any de-grouping charges should already be covered by the general tax covenant. However, it is common for a specific covenant covering the pre-sale reorganisation (and any related de-grouping charges) to also be included. As the seller is generally in complete control of the pre-sale reorganisation, buyers will often argue than some of the limitations applicable to the general covenant should not apply to the specific pre-sale reorganisation covenant.

It will also be important to understand at the outset the commercial deal on the value being attributed to any tax reliefs in the target company. To the extent value has been attributed to tax reliefs (eg, those shown in the completion accounts/locked-box accounts) the buyer will also expect to be protected should such reliefs turn out not to be available (often known as a 'buyer's relief') or if such reliefs are used to shelter any taxes the seller would otherwise be liable to pay under the covenant. On the other hand, to the extent reliefs are available in the target which have not been paid for (often known as a 'seller's relief'), the seller will likely view those as a 'freebie' which it will expect the buyer to use in order to shelter a liability of the seller under the tax covenant. The drafting on buyer and seller reliefs will need to be carefully constructed in order to accord with the commercial deal and these are often heavily negotiated parts of the tax covenant. This can be particularly important in a carve-out transaction where a pre-sale reorganisation may affect the reliefs available to the target company.

6.2 Limitations

Given the blanket protection for all pre-completion taxes, the seller will usually require certain carve-outs to the tax covenant which, again, are often heavily negotiated. At a minimum, the seller will generally not expect to be liable to the extent the tax liability in question:

- has already been taken into account in the purchase price (eg, through completion accounts or locked-box accounts);
- has already been discharged (at no cost to the target or the buyer);
- is due to a change of law after completion; or
- is due to any action of the buyer after completion.

As above, if specific covenants are included in relation to a pre-sale reorganisation, buyers may argue that at least some of the limitations (such as tax arising as a result of any action of the buyer after completion) should not apply to such specific covenants.

In a locked-box deal, any tax on any income, profits or gains arising in the ordinary course of business between the locked-box date and completion will also generally be carved out (on the basis that such profits will be for the buyer's benefit, so the buyer should bear the economic burden of tax on such profits).

6.3 Certain procedural matters

Given that the seller will generally be liable for any pre-completion taxes, it is likely to want some input on tax returns prepared by the target post-completion which relate to pre-completion periods. The seller will usually want control over tax returns for accounting periods ending before completion (although the buyer is likely to require comment rights). While the buyer will usually be responsible for any tax returns for periods ending after completion, the seller is likely to require some input for the accounting period in which completion takes place. This position is usually acceptable to buyers provided it is clear that it will not be required to submit any tax returns which it considers to be incorrect or will materially increase its future liability to tax. Control of pre-completion tax returns is likely to be particularly important to a seller on a carve-out transaction if the expected tax treatment of the pre-sale reorganisation depends on making an election post-completion which relates to a pre-completion period.

The seller is also likely to require some right to contest, in the name of the company, any tax claim against the company by a tax authority for which it is liable under the covenant. However, the buyer will want to ensure these provisions contain certain protections (eg, indemnification of costs and not having to take any action it considers materially prejudicial to its business). These provisions are often the most heavily negotiated aspect of a tax covenant.

6.4 Other provisions

Various other provisions may also be included for the seller's benefit. These may include ensuring the buyer uses reasonable endeavours to recover tax for which the seller is liable under the covenant from any third party (to the extent it is able), giving the seller the benefit of any overstatement of tax liabilities in the accounts, and giving the seller the benefit of any reliefs arising as a result of the matter giving rise to the claim under the covenant. A detailed discussion of these provisions is beyond the scope of this chapter; however, the above serves to illustrate some of the complexities involved in drafting and negotiating a tax covenant.

6.5 Warranty and indemnity insurance

The use of warranty and indemnity (W&I) insurance is becoming increasingly popular among buyers, particularly where the seller is not willing to take any risk by giving a tax covenant. While insurance policies vary, it is worth pointing out that an insured tax covenant may offer less protection than a standard covenant. In general, W&I insurance will not cover known risks (such as issues identified as part of due diligence), loss of tax reliefs, secondary tax liabilities or transfer pricing adjustments. In particular, on a carve-out transaction, W&I insurance is unlikely to cover any de-grouping charges arising as a result of a pre-sale reorganisation, so it will be all the more important for the buyer to conduct thorough due diligence of any such reorganisation and seek protections directly from the seller if necessary. W&I insurance may well still prove worthwhile for buyers, but clients should be aware of some of the potential limitations and the specific policy should be closely reviewed.

Employment and pensions aspects of carve-out transactions

Catherine Drinnan
Latham & Watkins

1. Introduction

The exact nature of the employment and pensions issues that arise in relation to a carve-out transaction will of course depend on the structuring of the transaction itself and the organisation of the group prior to the transaction. This chapter considers some of the key issues that will arise on various different types of carve-outs.

It will be critical for the seller to assess in advance whether any pre-sale reorganisation is required, as potential purchasers will expect a detailed proposal for this so that any related liabilities can be factored into the price they are prepared to pay for the business.

2. Transferring employees between relevant entities

Even if the carve-out is being effected as a sale of companies, rather than assets, to the purchaser, it is very often the case that there will need to be some movement of employees between group companies prior to completion of the transaction. This may be because there are employees technically employed by the company that is being sold (perhaps for historic reasons) but who do not actually work in the business of the company that the purchaser is acquiring (and vice versa), or because a new company is being set up for the purchaser to acquire, with all relevant employees and assets being transferred to that company prior to completion of the transaction. The below principles therefore apply to a carve-out effected by an asset sale, or where such an intra-group transfer is required.

The Acquired Rights Directive[1] (as implemented by applicable local legislation, being Transfer of Undertakings (Protection of Employment) (TUPE)[2] in the United Kingdom) provides employees with protection if the business they are assigned to is transferred to another entity. In such a scenario, they are entitled to follow their work, with their length of service and terms and conditions intact. It will therefore very often be the case in a European carve-out that these provisions will apply to any movement of employees between entities. An information and consultation process will need to be carried out prior to the transfer. Requirements for this vary per jurisdiction but it will typically be with the works councils or unions, or the employees themselves if there are no employee representative bodies. The length and complexity of the consultation will generally depend on the effect the transfer will have on the employees – if redundancies or changes to terms and conditions are proposed (collectively, 'measures'), it will take longer. The transferor employer carries out the pre-transfer consultation process, and the transferee will need to provide input on any measures it proposes.

In respect to individual employees, a detailed analysis will need to be carried out to determine whether the employee is in fact assigned to the relevant business – in some cases this may be very obvious eg, it is clear from the employee's job title and duties that they spend all their working time on the business to be carved out, but it can be less clear cut, most obviously in the case of shared services employees or often senior management who oversee a number of businesses.

A purchaser may therefore wish to include protections in the transaction documentation regarding employee transfer, such as it being a condition to completion that either a percentage of the employees or particular key employees have agreed to transfer their employment to the target company.

As a matter of law, the Acquired Rights Directive provides that the new employer steps into the shoes of the former employee and all rights and liabilities under the relevant employment contracts

---

1 Council Directive 2001/23/EC of 12 March 2001 on the approximation of the laws of the member states relating to the safeguarding of employees' rights in the event of transfers of undertakings, businesses or parts of undertakings or businesses.

2 Transfer of Undertakings (Protection of Employment) Regulations 2006 (SI2006/246).

transfer to the new employer. So, for example, if the employee had brought a harassment claim against his or her former employer, liability for that claim would transfer to the new employer. It has therefore become market practice in asset transactions for employment liabilities to be split at completion, with the seller remaining liable for pre-completion liabilities, and the purchaser taking responsibility for completion onwards. The parties also usually indemnify each other for their own failure to comply with their information and consultation obligations. It is also common for provisions to be included whereby the seller provides the purchaser with indemnity protection if employees whom the parties did not expect to transfer do in fact transfer, and the purchaser commits to making offers of employment to employees whom the parties did expect to transfer but who claim they should not.

In a pre-completion reorganisation, technically the Acquired Rights Directive transfer will be intra-group and the seller may be resistant to the purchaser becoming involved. However a purchaser should always ask to have input into the reorganisation documentation and it will be a point for commercial negotiation as to whether the target company into which employees are transferring is granted indemnity protection in the same way as a third-party purchaser typically would be. In addition, the purchaser should seek protection for the target entity in relation to redundancy costs or other liabilities for any employees who were due to transfer out to a retained seller group company but who do not in fact transfer.

If the Acquired Rights Directive does not apply to an employee, or if the transaction includes entities outside Europe which do not have equivalent legislation, then the employee's consent will likely be needed to effect the transfer. Jurisdiction-specific advice will need to be taken in every case as to the optimal method of achieving this – for example, should the employee be asked to resign, be terminated, or enter into a tripartite agreement with the former and the new employer? The position regarding severance benefits under each approach will differ and should be considered carefully in the commercial context of the transaction – the current employer will generally be liable for these. If the employee is offered the ability to transfer with his or her length of service preserved and on the same terms and benefits, it may be a fairly simple decision but sellers need to be aware that if the current employer offers generous redundancy terms the employee may try to argue that the new employment is not suitable alternative employment and he or she should be entitled to redundancy pay. In Germany, for example, this concern also applies to an Acquired Rights Directive transfer as if the employee refuses to transfer and the current employer no longer has a role for him or her (which would be expected to be the case as the business he or she was working for has been sold out of the group) he or she is entitled to be made redundant. This can be contrasted with the position under, for example, English law, where an employee who objects to a TUPE transfer is treated as having resigned and is not entitled to any payment (unless his or her resignation is as a result of a detrimental change to his or her terms and conditions proposed by the new employer).

2.1 Consultation in respect of a share sale

As noted above, if the carve-out involves an Acquired Rights Directive transfer, an information and consultation exercise will almost always be required. In many jurisdictions, if it is simply a transfer of shares, ie, the purchaser is acquiring target companies from the wider seller group and all the employees and assets are already in the correct company, then often there does not need to be such a process. As a matter of good practice, it would be common to communicate with employees and their representative bodies, typically after signing and before completion if there is a gap. In English law, there is no statutory requirement to inform or consult on a share sale, but any formal agreement with employee representative bodies should be checked to ensure the company has not committed to any particular obligations in excess of the statutory position. Obviously, if redundancies are proposed as part of the transaction, where 20 or more redundancies are proposed in a 90-day period, the consultation requirements under the Trade Union and Labour Relations (Consolidation) Act 1992 will apply.

There are a number of European jurisdictions where consultation may be mandatory even if it is a share transaction, and we summarise the most common as follows.

Where a sale of shares leads to a direct change of control in a French company, the employee representative bodies (ERB)[3] of the target company must be informed and consulted with. Information and consultation obligations might also apply to the seller entity and to the purchaser entity, if these do have an ERB. An 'information

---

3 The ERB may include the works council and in some cases the Health and Safety Committee. The Social and Economic Council will replace all current ERB at the latest by 1 January 2020.

note' must be provided to the ERB, setting out the consequences of the sale on employees' employment and there must be successive meetings with the ERB to discuss the sale. The ERB must then provide their opinion on the sale. They do not have any veto rights and the sale or acquisition can proceed even where the ERB provides a negative opinion.

The length of this process can be negotiated with the ERB. In the absence of agreement, timing ranges generally from one to two months, but exceptionally also up to four months, depending on a number of factors including whether the ERB decides to engage an external expert to assist them with the process. The consultation must take place at such a time when the ERB can genuinely influence the decision as to whether or not to proceed with the sale, meaning that consultation has to occur pre-signing. It will not be possible to consult after signing, even if completion is made conditional on the consultation finishing. As parties are generally reticent to commence consultation before signing as there is no certainty that the transaction will go ahead, it has become a common practice that the purchaser makes a binding offer for the business (the so-called 'put-option'), with an agreed form purchase agreement attached to the offer, and then the agreement is signed after consultation is complete. The put-option approach will only be available if the purchaser does not have an ERB consultation obligation at its end, ie, the purchaser can enter into a binding agreement without any prior ERB procedures.

Where the sale is not direct (ie, the French company being sold is a subsidiary of the target company), there are arguments that consultation is not required, in particular if there are other operating companies between the direct target company of the share sale and the French company.

Further, French *Loi Hamon* might apply if the sale concerns more than 50% of the shares of a French target company and if such French target company has less than 250 employees (*Loi Hamon* obliges the seller to notify employees of the French target entity individually of the proposed sale as to allow them to make a non-binding purchase offer themselves). Like the ERB process, the outcome of such procedure, if ever employees make an offer which is very rarely the case in practice, is not binding for the seller, ie, *Loi Hamon* does not provide for a right of pre-emption.

In Germany, on a direct sale, the economic committee and the works council of the target must be informed and consulted with before the sale takes place, however they do not have the power to delay or block the sale. In order to give the economic committee and the works council enough time to discuss the planned sale with the target, as for France, the strict legal position is that they must be informed of the sale before the target makes a final decision on the sale (ie, before signing the purchase agreement). However, in practice, these bodies are usually only informed immediately before or after signing (particularly where confidentiality is a pressing concern). Failure to provide the required information in a truthful, complete and timely manner may constitute an administrative offence which carries a fine of up to €10,000. On an indirect share transaction, the prevailing view is that such bodies only need to be informed if the change in ownership has a significant impact on the employees of the German company.

Under Dutch law, a target must consult its works council, if any,[4] in respect of a share sale. The target company must give the works council the opportunity to offer advice on the impact of the sale and while such advice should have a meaningful influence on the sale, the works council does not have to approve the proposed sale. While different Dutch law firms take different approaches, in practice it is often the case, particularly where the sale of the Dutch company is indirect and the transaction does not significantly affect the Dutch employees, that this process takes place between signing and completion of the proposed transaction, with completion being conditional on positive advice from the works council being received. The works council must issue its advice within a reasonable period of time.

If a company employs over 50 people and is involved in the acquisition of direct or indirect control over all or part of the activities of another company, the provisions of the Social Economic Council's Resolution concerning the Merger Code 2015 (SER-besluit Fusiegedragsregels 2015) (Merger Code) will apply. The Merger Code is not formal law, but a quasi-legislative code of conduct, the application of which is however regarded as obligatory.

The essence of the Merger Code is the obligation of companies involved in a merger to (unless one of the exemptions mentioned in the Merger Code applies) notify and consult with the trade unions prior to the sale. This must be done at a stage where the trade unions can still substantially influence the realisation and the conditions of the sale, and as noted above in relation to works

4 Companies with at least 50 employees must establish a works council.

council consultation, is often included as condition to completion. Parties sometimes take a view that where the sale is indirect and/or the Dutch business is not material to the target business as a whole, there is no need to comply with this requirement.

3. Pensions considerations

The complexity of managing the legal aspects of ensuring continuity of benefit arrangements for employees affected by the carve-out will be dependent on the structure of the transaction, the complexity of the benefit arrangements, and whether the benefits are currently provided at an employer or wider group level. The Acquired Rights Directive imposes restrictions on changes that can be made to benefits, and in addition employee contracts may contain contractual promises to a particular level or type of benefit.

In this chapter we next focus on the issues that may arise in relation to defined benefit pension plans in the United Kingdom (UK DB Plans) as these can be critical and require careful legal assessment in advance of the transaction.

4. UK defined benefit pension plans

The existence of a UK defined benefit (DB) Plan in a company group will be a very important consideration to address in the context of the carve-out. UK DB Plans are:

- almost always in deficit on at least one measure of valuation;
- subject to onerous regulatory and funding requirements; and
- operated by trustees who are required to act independently of the sponsoring employer(s) in the best interests of members of the plan.

Each UK DB Plan has a principal employer, which is the sponsoring employer which, broadly, has the most responsibility towards the pension plan (including having certain powers and obligations under the plan's governing rules). In addition to the principal employer, the plan may have other sponsoring employers who are participating employers in the plan. These entities have an obligation to pay contributions to the pension plan on an ongoing basis but, typically, have fewer powers and duties than the principal employer. The cessation of participation by a participating employer in a UK DB Plan (including as a consequence of a carve-out transaction) will need to be properly addressed, as discussed further below.

There are several ways of calculating the deficit of a UK DB Plan and a plan must undergo a new actuarial valuation at least once every three years. It is important to emphasise that a UK DB Plan's accounting deficit is irrelevant in terms of calculating the liabilities which a sponsoring employer owes to the plan.

The key UK DB Plan deficit calculation measures are:

- the technical provisions deficit, which drives the level of ongoing employer contributions which are payable to the plan; and
- the buy-out deficit, which is the cost of securing the plan's liabilities in full with an insurance company (which will in practice always be higher than then the accounting and technical provisions deficits, often significantly).

A buy-out deficit is triggered only in limited prescribed circumstances, including sponsoring employer insolvency and if the plan in question is wound up. However, as discussed further below, it will be important to address any buy-out deficit trigger issues in the context of a carve-out transaction.

The trustees of a UK DB Plan have certain powers which they can use to protect their pension plan. These powers include a statutory power to call for a new actuarial valuation at any time (which may lead to an increase in the plan's deficit and employer contributions to the pension plan) and to change the plan's investment strategy (firstly having consulted with the sponsoring employer(s)). In addition, the trustees may have additional powers under the governing rules of their pension plan, including the power to require additional employer contributions to the plan and/or to wind up the plan (triggering the buy-out deficit as due and payable). These powers can give the trustees a strong negotiation position in relation to a transaction. In a carve-out transaction, the trustees will be concerned if the transaction will have a detrimental impact on their pension plan and the ability of the retained group to fund and support the plan after completion of the transaction. They may seek to use any powers available to them in this context, or involve the UK Pensions Regulator (the Regulator).

5. The Regulator

The Regulator is a UK statutory body which has a duty to protect the security of the benefits of members of UK DB Plans. In order to do so, the Regulator has 'moral hazard' powers which it can use to require additional funding or other financial support to be put in place for a UK DB Plan (up to the level of the relevant plan's buy-out deficit). This obligation can be imposed on a sponsoring employer of a UK

DB Plan and any entity who is connected with or an associate of that employer within the meaning of the relevant legislation. This legislation is broadly drafted and means that entities such as companies in the same group as a sponsoring employer, shareholders who control one-third or more of the voting power of the employer or its parent and company directors are all connected to a UK DB Plan sponsoring employer for the purposes of the Regulator's moral hazard powers. Connection for these purposes lasts for up to six years following any disposal, which means that a shareholder who sells a UK DB Plan sponsoring employer will remain a potential target of the Regulator's powers in relation to the UK DB Plan sponsored by the relevant company for this six-year period.

The Regulator is (in theory at least) able to exercise its moral hazard powers on a global basis, which means that any entity (wherever located in the world) which is connected to a UK DB Plan sponsoring employer could be the subject of the Regulator's moral hazard powers. In order to exercise its moral hazard powers, the Regulator must satisfy a number of statutory tests, including that it must show it is acting reasonably.

In a carve-out transaction, the Regulator will be concerned if the transaction has a detrimental impact on the ability of a UK DB Plan's sponsoring employer(s) and its wider group to support the UK DB Plan following the carve-out. For example, if a retained group in which a UK DB Plan sits has been considerably weakened by the sale of a profitable part of its business without some of the consideration from this sale being paid into the plan, this is likely to cause the Regulator concern, which may lead to it seeking to exercise its moral hazard powers as a result of the carve-out. It is possible to apply for clearance (ie, a statement from the Regulator that it will not use its powers in relation to a particular transaction) on a voluntary basis to the Regulator. However, clearance is a rarely used process, primarily because it can take several weeks (or longer) for a clearance application to be determined, there is no guarantee that clearance will be granted and the Regulator will often demand some additional funding or support be provided to the relevant UK DB Plan as a condition to granting clearance. In practice, if the UK DB Plan is material, the parties will seek to reach agreement with the trustees prior to signing the purchase agreement.

6. Carve-out – acquisition of a UK DB Plan's principal employer

In a carve-out transaction where the purchaser acquires the principal employer of a UK DB Plan, the default position is that the purchaser will inherit the pension plan as a result of acquiring the principal employer. In addition, the purchaser will become connected to the UK DB Plan for the purposes of the Regulator's moral hazard powers for its period of ownership and the up to six year post-disposal time period discussed above. It is important that the purchaser bears this in mind, as having a UK DB Plan in a group can heavily restrict corporate activity, should that activity be detrimental to the pension plan. This may be the case, for example, where the purchaser intends to wind-up, sell or remove assets from the group; pay significant dividends (or otherwise remove value from the group); or grant security. In all of the aforementioned situations, the trustees may demand increased contributions, or seek to involve the Regulator, and consideration should be given as to whether to apply for clearance at the relevant time.

In relation to the carve-out, if there are any companies participating in the relevant UK DB Plan who are not acquired by the purchaser, they should cease participating in the plan prior to/ on completion of the transaction. There are various mechanisms which can be used to implement a cessation of participation by a participating employer in a UK DB Plan (a 'Cessation Employer'). The most common mechanism is a 'flexible apportionment arrangement' (FAA).

Under an FAA, subject to trustee consent and several statutory tests being satisfied (including that the trustees must be satisfied that the continuing sponsoring employer(s) will be able to support the plan going forward), the liabilities which the Cessation Employer owes to the plan will be apportioned on a contingent basis to one or more companies who will continue to sponsor the plan. However, the Cessation Employer will remain connected to the relevant UK DB Plan for the purposes of the Regulator's moral hazard powers for up to six years following the carve-out transaction.

7. Carve-out – acquisition of a UK DB Plan's participating employer

If the purchaser acquires the shares of a UK DB Plan participating employer (a 'target employer') but the plan's principal employer is retained by the seller group, the default position is that the relevant pension plan will remain behind with the seller group. However, the participation by any target employer in the relevant UK DB Plan will need to cease prior to completion of the carve-out transaction. The most common mechanism to do this would be via an FAA, under the same process discussed above. This would result in the purchaser acquiring the relevant target employer without that company owing any further obligations or liabilities to the relevant UK DB Plan. However, the target employer (and any other company which the purchaser acquires from the seller group) will remain connected to the UK DB Plan for the purposes of the Regulator's moral hazard powers for up to six years following the carve-out transaction.

8. Carve-out – asset purchase

In general terms, TUPE does not protect ongoing benefit accrual in a UK DB Plan, which means that if any transferring employees were accruing benefits in the seller group's UK DB Plan immediately prior to the transfer of their employment to the purchaser, the purchaser would not be obligated to provide the relevant individuals with defined benefit pension accrual following completion of the carve-out. However, there is a risk that the purchaser could inherit an obligation under TUPE in the future to meet the cost of certain benefits which may be payable to the transferring employees following the asset purchase which are derived from their membership of the seller's UK DB Plan. This applies to benefits payable on the early retirement or redundancy of an eligible transferring employee. The risk of inheriting such TUPE liabilities would be an important diligence issue for the purchaser in any asset purchase transaction.

The UK DB Plan will stay behind with the seller group and will continue to be the responsibility of the seller. As no target employer is being purchased, there may not be any need for cessation of participation issues to be considered, although there may still be an issue for the seller if one of the employers ceases to employ active members of the pension plan (ie, because they have all transferred out to a purchaser company) at a time when other seller group companies continue to employ active members. These circumstances will also trigger a cessation of participation debt, albeit this will purely be a seller concern rather than an issue for the purchaser. In addition, the purchaser would not, as a result of an arm's length asset purchase, become connected to the UK DB Plan for the purposes of the Regulator's moral hazard powers (although it should be noted that connection may be found if the purchaser has acted as a shadow director of the pension plan employers).

Separations – the in-house perspective

Edward Heaton
BT

1. Introduction

Separation and integration planning and activities add a particular complexity to carve-out mergers and acquisitions (M&A) transactions for corporates. For in-house teams, their involvement will last much longer than their private practice counterparts; they will become involved earlier in the process and will need to get more embedded into internal strategic decisions about how to approach the separation or integration, while they will also deal with integration matters long after the underlying transaction has completed.

On both the buy and sell side, in-house lawyers should ensure that the business, and in particular the finance function, understands the impact that the separation process can have on the viability of a transaction. This chapter will explore the different aspects of separation that can lead to a cost and suggest some approaches as to how those costs could be allocated in a transaction. As a buyer or a seller, these costs cannot be ignored and the business case for pursuing the transaction will need to factor these in.

As a key example, the buyer cannot assume that the purchase price and transaction fees will be its only expenditure in acquiring the target. To the extent that the seller does not agree to fund some or all of the separation costs, the buyer will need to reach a view on the further expenditure required during the transitional period as these can have a very significant effect on the financial profile of the deal. Similarly, sellers will need to assess whether substantial separation costs that they agree to assume mean that, actually, there is a dis-synergy in undertaking the divestment or, in other words, financially, it would be prudent to retain the target.

As well as looking at some of the particular sensitivities that in-house teams should be alive to from finance, operational and legal perspectives, this chapter will also look at bringing stakeholders along the path.

2. Why early stage planning matters

The in-house legal team should aim to get involved at the early stages of a transaction in order to help assess the viability and complexity of the target. Businesses should be given legal support throughout the financial and operational separation and integration planning as the in-house legal team is likely to be concerned with this just as much as the underlying transaction.

On the sell side, all of these separation activities will be (or should be) completed before the main M&A preparations of producing marketing materials, setting up data rooms and drafting transaction documents can commence. All of those key M&A activities will be impacted by the approach taken to separation. Different companies take different approaches to the integration of their businesses and pooling of systems, but even a target that is considered 'stand alone' can have hidden synergies and reliances that need to be unpicked and made visible to buyers. On the buy side, there will also be different approaches to the speed and depth with which the target can be integrated into the buyer group's own systems and processes.

Another reason for addressing these issues early, in addition to ensuring that the M&A materials are based on an executable separation plan, is to ensure that appropriate management attention on the sell side is given to these issues. As transactions move towards execution and completion, attention of management can drift towards other business imperatives and away from post-completion matters (often the transitional period is seen as requiring a lot of sell side effort with little reward). For buyers, this is unlikely to be the case as they will identify areas of opportunity post-completion, with each business division taking ownership and driving this integration.

3. Operational separation and the transitional services agreement

3.1 Operational planning

Operational separation planning needs to be an initial focus of the seller. Processes involved in running the target that have been built up over time need to be analysed and assessed as the relevant teams are unlikely to think of the relevant processes as consisting of individual elements. The individual elements, however, will need to be understood for comprehensive separation planning to be done and this will also assist buyers to determine what services will initially be required by the target post-closing to operate in the ordinary course until such time as they implement their own resources and functions.

One example of a process with many layers is finance; the finance team will know how they go about accessing their past invoices, but do they know which server they are stored on? Do they know which software is used to manage invoices and where it is licensed from and on what terms? Do they know the extent to which that information is comingled with other parts of the business?

Early in the preparation process, management should be encouraged to think about the end-to-end processes in the target in the broadest possible way. The best approach is often to get multi-specialist teams to sit with a blank sheet of paper and consider how the target runs by producing process maps (see Figure 1 below for an example). Each step can then be assessed to determine who is involved, what systems are utilised and whether the target is dependent on any external providers or licences etc, and whether such elements are within the scope of the divestment or need to be provided during the transitional period. This early engagement might also assist with identifying what services can be transitioned to the target ahead of completion such that they will not be required to be provided by the seller under a transitional services agreement (TSA). External consultancy providers are also available and they might provide additional resource, expertise and a fresh perspective in drilling down into each process step (given they are not subject to any prior knowledge of the target's operations).

Other approaches to identifying separation requirements that focus on the target's legal framework or finance functions risk missing important constituent parts. For example, looking at annual external spend misses one-offs that might have happened in previous years, spend that might have come from another group company, etc. Similarly, looking at internal recharges risks missing informal support arrangements and those that are simply not recharged. In the same manner, looking at legal arrangements that the target is a party to also risks missing those that are sourced by other group members, for example umbrella insurance policies or trading terms.

Buyers should also conduct a similar integration planning exercise and deal teams should reach out to their business functions

Figure 1. Example process map for billing and collections process

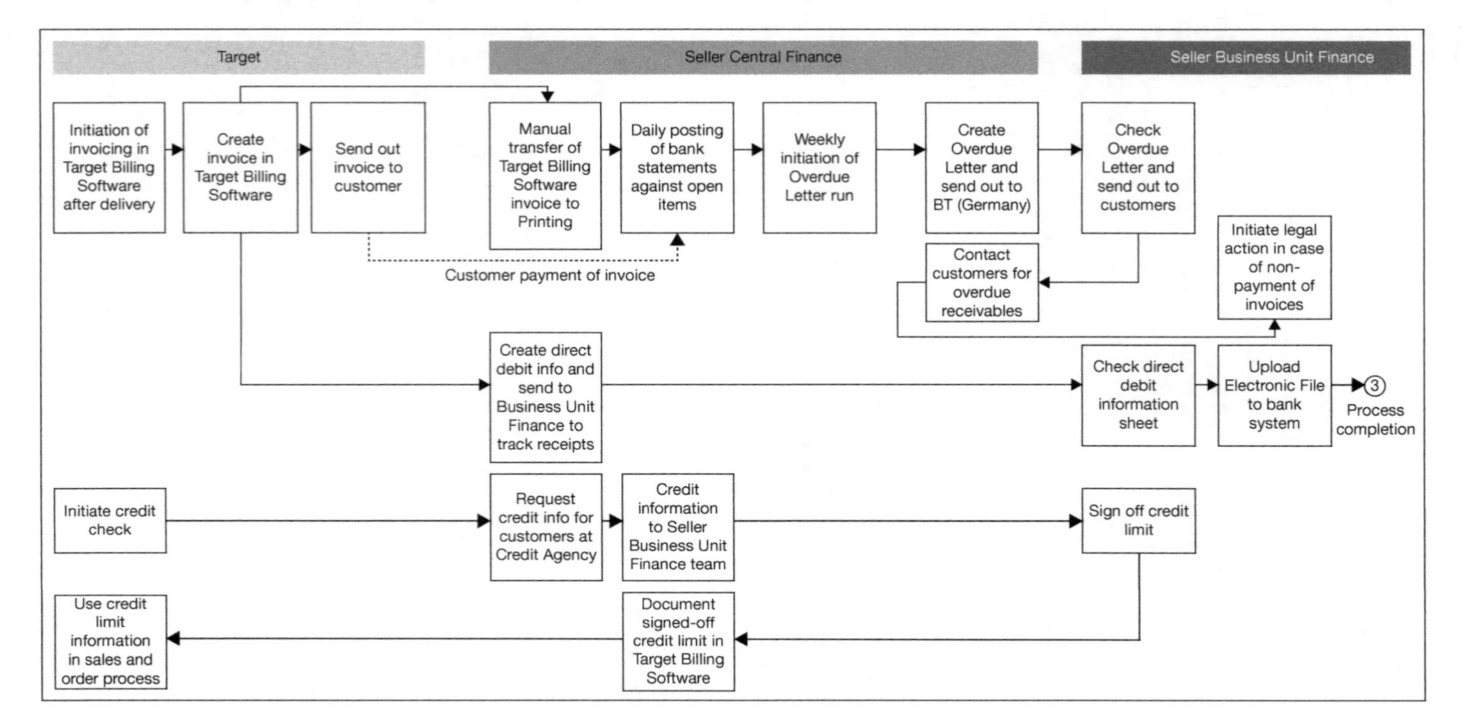

to identify processes they would, based on their own operations, expect to see in the target.

3.2 Legal planning

(a) *Initial considerations for the seller*

A seller's view on whether to undertake full vendor due diligence will depend on a number of factors relevant to the target and the type of transaction process to be run. However, separations, as opposed to divestments of more stand-alone businesses, will invariably require some legal review of the target by the seller. While sellers can still determine that it will leave buyers to carry out their own diligence, it is desirable for the seller to undertake a focused review of the target to understand the options for implementing a separation and any implications on the proposed structure. Buyers will invariably be guided by such assessment although they are likely to conduct their own in any event to verify the diligence and the synergy opportunities.

The in-depth analysis of legal risks relating to separations is covered elsewhere in this book but, at the minimum, the in-house lawyer should confirm the following:

- Customer contracts:
  - Does the contract contain any exclusivity or 'most favoured nation' provisions or other restrictive provisions on the target?
  - Does the target share contracts with other parts of the seller's organisation and, if so, can they be split easily?
  - Is engagement with the customer necessary and, if so, is that to seek consent for a split of the contract or is a more substantive engagement process with the customer required?
  - If engagement is required, who is to carry out that process, the seller and/or the buyer?
  - If no engagement is required, does the contract permit the seller to subcontract its obligations to the buyer?
- Supplier contracts:
  - (The first four considerations applicable to customer contracts also apply to supplier contracts.)
  - Are any supplier contracts personal to the seller or can they resell such services (especially where such supplies are required to be provided under the TSA)?

    - Is the seller's purchasing power materially reduced as a result of the divestment and can the retained business continue to meet any minimum purchase requirements (if any)?
- Legal entity structure:
    - Are the contracts, people and assets of the target held by an entity that is in scope for divestment and do they relate exclusively to the target? If not, should these be 'hived up' to the target or should all assets relevant to the target be 'hived out' to a newly-formed company?
    - If there is to be a pre-completion reorganisation: firstly, are there any change of control provisions or restrictions on assignment that could affect a material contract; and, secondly, does the target have all regulatory consents required to operate the business post such reorganisation?
    - How much corporate knowledge is there about the medium- to longer-term history of the target? Has the target always carried on the same business? Is there a risk that historic rights, assets or contracts have been 'parked' in the target but which should actually remain with the retained group?

Once the separation analysis has been concluded, this should produce a list of the target's dependencies. A commercial decision will then need to be made as to how the target can continue to access these post-completion, the main options being:

- the service is withdrawn at completion and the buyer sources an alternative (whether internally or through a third party);
- the seller provides the services as a transitional service; or
- the parties implement a longer-term outsourcing of the service to the seller's organisation.

In the in-house environment, it's particularly important to think about the commercial merits of these options. There is a temptation towards over-reliance on TSAs as these tend to be the simplest to implement, while keeping closest to the status quo. However, the TSA does present its own risks and the in-house lawyer should be aware that their organisation (whether on the buy or sell side) will have to live with any deficient scoping or provisioning of services for an extended period of time, potentially long after the transaction has otherwise delivered its value to the group.

(b) *TSA considerations*

Scope of services: A general rule of thumb for sellers is to keep the scope of services to be provided under a TSA as limited as possible, with buyers encouraged to move off them as quickly as possible (buyers will also be incentivised to move off the TSA services as soon as possible to avoid paying further fees for such services). Under the strictest approach, the buyer should be challenged to have implemented its own integration steps in every instance possible before completion. The only services that should be provided under the TSA are those that the seller is satisfied cannot physically or legally be implemented by the buyer for Day 1 (although buyers are also likely to seek the inclusion of a 'sweeper' to capture any services that have been later identified as necessary but not covered by the TSA).

The two primary reasons for this limited scope of services to be provided under the TSA is:

- the seller's group is unlikely to be in the business of providing these services to third parties; and
- the seller's group is unlikely to have the organisation set-up to deliver such services.

In the former instance, the services will not have gone through the same quality control processes that would generally be used for the group's end-customer products in order to underwrite the group's ability to perform them in a compliant manner (especially where the standard of services to be provided is high). To some extent, this can be reflected through limited service credits and modest caps on liability in the TSA, but it is preferable to have an agreement you can comply with. Furthermore, failures in delivering the TSA that cause issues for the buyer may well motivate them to look for recovery elsewhere, for example via breach of warranty claims or post-completion adjustment mechanisms.

In respect of the latter, a bespoke delivery unit may be required for particularly onerous or broad TSAs and the costs of setting one up will need to be factored into the financial case for the sale. There are also potential regulatory costs to factor in, for example, any transfer by the seller to the target of personal information will need to comply with applicable data privacy laws. These costs should also cover ensuring that the individuals running that organisation have proper incentives. If individuals are taken out of their day job to run these services, their regular incentives (particularly those remunerated on a sales basis) will not be sufficient to reward them.

For the buyer, ensuring that there is a continuation of the business from completion is key and, to the extent the buyer requests services to be supplied under the TSA which are burdensome for the seller to enable business continuation, the buyer should expect to pay a premium on such services.

Other considerations when scoping the TSA services are whether the services are actually provided by a third party and whether it is actually suitable to provide the required services. In respect of the former, services which are provided to third-party suppliers may be personal to the seller and which cannot be resold to the buyer. By agreeing to provide such services (whatever the quantum) in contravention of the underlying agreement, can cause issues on a group-wide basis for the seller if this results in harm to a valuable supplier relationship. In respect of the latter, for example, intra-group financing arrangements which the target will no longer be the beneficiary of, consideration needs to be given as to how any intra-group balances are settled and if any cash needs to be extracted from the target. This is also likely to have tax considerations for sellers and should be considered in the transaction as a whole.

Notwithstanding the above, there are two particular circumstances when the seller should consider whether to be more generous than the narrow approach advocated above:

- if the seller is required to give a strong sufficiency of assets warranty, giving a more substantial amount of support under the TSA can make it less likely that a failure in the target leads to a warranty claim; or
- where the customers of the seller's retained group will still be relying on the target's services, there's a strong motivation on the seller's part to assist with the business continuity of the target.

From the buyer's perspective, generally its focus should be on testing the *completeness* of the proposed separation items. A buyer is better served spending time ensuring it understands whether all items have been considered, whether they are proposed as a transitional service or something the buyer has to source itself, rather than focusing too much on negotiating the scope of proposed transitional services.

Legal considerations: Whenever considering how services are structured (either on a business as usual basis or where an organisation is implemented specifically for these services), it is important to consider how employment law impacts the parties' flexibility. Specifically, for transactions with a nexus to an EU country, this means considering how the Acquired Rights Directive (ARD)[1] will apply to the employees engaged in providing these services.

In the United Kingdom, Transfer of Undertakings (Protection of Employment) (TUPE) can lead to an automatic transfer of employees who have been providing transitional services over to the buyer or its new service provider. This risk will be more prevalent where a new operational unit is required to be established by the seller to perform the TSA. This risk should be assessed and can either be accepted or the parties should agree up-front who bears the cost of re-deployment or redundancy of those individuals.

Time periods for the provision of services: Although there is a desire on both sides for the target to cease its reliance on services supplied by the seller, buyers will be keen to ensure that the duration of the TSA provides it with enough time to fully integrate the target into its own operations. Accordingly, buyers might seek the ability to extend the TSA for an additional period (at an additional cost) in the event it has not fully transitioned the target. Buyers may even seek the early termination of services at no cost in the event they achieve integration early and a seller's view on this is likely to depend on the risk of stranded costs.

(c) ***Scoping integration requirements with a buyer***

As noted above, sellers should only seek to provide a narrow set of services under a TSA. Such services, should be limited to those being provided as at the time of completion. When approaching the process of workshopping the TSA services, it can be tempting for buyers to start to ask for bespoke variations on the services. Sellers should remain cautious about agreeing to these variations and challenge buyers as to whether those variations can be provided elsewhere.

The TSA should not be a cheap or easy alternative for the buyer, but instead a solution where separation by completion is not possible and where the seller provides existing services to the same specification. Varying the existing services or introducing new elements

1 The Acquired Rights Directive (Directive 2001/23/EC), implemented in the United Kingdom by the Transfer of Undertakings (Protection of Employment) Regulations 2006 (SI 2006/246) (TUPE).

creates additional risk for the seller as such services will be untested, thereby increasing the likelihood that a seller fails in its support for the divested business under the TSA. Instead, the emphasis for separation workshops should be to identify new ways of covering any gaps. Buyers can be resistant to changes for a transitional period as it can lead to a 'double hop' separation. This can lead to additional service failure risk for the buyer to its end-customer.

In addition to agreeing the scope of services to be provided, buyers are likely to seek additional protection that the relevant senior technical staff who currently provide the services (and which are to be provided under the TSA) are retained by the seller. This provides the buyer with the comfort that the target should receive the same level of service and support as it currently enjoys, while for the seller it should protect against potential claims from the buyer for a drop in the standard of supply.

(d) Drafting the TSA

Generally, the TSA is split between the front end (which is usually led by the legal team) and the back end (which is operational and needs to be led by the appropriate parts of the business).

In-house teams can really come into their own in assisting with the back end. The closer contact in-house teams have with the business and the greater knowledge of how the business (and the target in particular) is organised and operates can be of great value. If the TSA workstream is likely to be complex, time consuming and/or particularly risky, in-house teams should consider assigning a dedicated in-house resource, even if that needs to be an external contractor/secondee.

By conducting all of the early stage planning, this will enable a comprehensive position on the type of services and cost of such services to be provided by the seller under the TSA (although part of this is dependent on what functions the buyer has capacity to provide internally), rather than seeking to engage in such discussions with management during the pressure of transaction timelines.

(e) Timing for finalisation of the TSA and separation plans

One point frequently discussed in the context of TSAs, and separation planning more broadly, is whether they need to be in fully final form prior to signing a transaction or whether (if there is a split signing and closing), elements of the agreement can be left to be settled after signing. Generally, this means considering whether the full detailed technical and operational service specifications are completed prior to signing. This is likely to depend on the scope and complexity of the services. Generally, the buyer has most to lose by not having a fully agreed set of services prior to signing, as it is left exposed with a poor bargaining position through which to make demands of the seller after it is committed to the transaction.

However, there are a number of reasons why a buyer may wish to accept this risk. They may wish to proceed to signing swiftly (for example, in a competitive auction process) and want to secure the transaction before having had the opportunity to fully scope how they will provision the separation and integration services. This affords the buyer with flexibility and more time to consider whether services should be sourced in-house from their own group or from an alternative third-party provider rather than from the seller.

One alternative to having (or not having) a full set of documents at signing is for the parties to specify some level of cooperation between them to agree mutually acceptable terms after signing. As with any agreement to agree, at least under English law, these obligations are difficult to enforce, so a buyer should be aware of the limitations of these sorts of principles. A buyer is much better placed if it has a clear plan for at least the target's business-critical requirements prior to signing.

4. Pre- and post-completion considerations

4.1 Running the TSA services and separation/integration in general

The scope of separation is likely to require the involvement of a number of parts of the seller's organisation, each with different points of contact. Buyers are unlikely to accept that they must interface with different teams and personnel, each of whom may have different ways of working and approaches. To ensure the buyer's needs are met, a single point of contact in the seller's organisation is desirable. This individual should be someone who is sufficiently senior to take ownership of service issues with the buyer and resolve these appropriately within the seller's organisation. The buyer should also appoint their counterpart and ensure that there is regular contact between both managers to keep the separation and integration on track.

Appointing a separation/TSA manager to this sort of role will also help the seller ensure that they are complying with the requirements of the TSA in terms of service levels, response times, deliverables etc. This person can also have oversight of, and be responsible for, billing the TSA services.

This person should be brought in early on in the process and should ideally also have a role in the separation activities. This will give the manager a good view on the relationship between services that are being assumed by the buyer or its third-party suppliers and those which will be provided by the seller through the TSA.

There will be occasions where one separation/integration manager is not sufficient, particularly where the exact scope of the services has not been settled prior to signing of the transaction. Here, a transition or separation committee constituted of representatives from various business divisions from both the seller and the buyer can be useful. The committee can be given broad authority to agree an approach to dependencies, whether they are separated from closing or drafted into the TSA, who bears the costs of separation, when is the appropriate time to start irreversible separation work, etc.

If new processes are being set up from scratch, it should be considered how their effectiveness can be assessed. For business critical processes like payroll/invoicing, etc, the seller can consider with the buyer whether the new systems should be implemented as a shadow system some time before completion. This can allow the parties to perform a dry run of the system, for example a dummy invoicing run, to identify any failures in implementation and avoid such problems being discovered for the first time in a live operational environment. Where this kind of detailed separation support is provided by the seller, the parties will need to consider whether the seller should be entitled to charge for their time. This addresses a wider question of incremental costs relating to the separation. The seller's approach to this should be considered early in the process; is the transaction being set up to give assurance to a buyer that their purchase price includes a fully functioning business or will the target be marketed as requiring the seller to bear certain separation costs? For ongoing costs of the new systems, it is likely to be appropriate for these to be borne by the buyer as part of the ordinary operating costs of the business following completion. The question as to cost and who should bear these is, ultimately, a matter of commercial negotiation and will depend on the bargaining strength of the parties and the wider financials of the deal.

At all times during the pre- and post-completion period, both the seller and the buyer (and their respective separation and integration teams) should be mindful of antitrust concerns to ensure that no actual steps are taken to implement the integration until completion has occurred and, to the extent relevant, competition clearance has been obtained.

4.2 Other seller obligations

Other sales process areas that require consideration relate to the running of due diligence, disclosure and the continued success of the business. In-house teams should liaise with the human resources (HR) department to devise an incentive plan that rewards management of the target's business to secure its continued success during the period. However, in-house teams will need to be careful with the messaging and ensure that management understand that they should not be artificially boosting business, chasing low margin revenue, looking for opportunities to squeeze suppliers, etc. In addition, management should be encouraged to remain loyal to the seller until an appropriate time in the process as transactions can be called off at any time.

5. Reverse separation support

When identifying the scope of reliance between the target and the retained group, it should also be considered whether the removal of the target from the seller's group is going to leave a capability gap for the seller, for example back office support.

When considering whether the retained group will need to rely on the target, it is important to consider not just business as usual work of the retained group but also the tasks necessary to allow the seller to fulfil its obligations under the transaction documents, for example, the transaction documents are likely to allocate responsibility for creation of completion accounts. If the seller is to provide the initial draft of such accounts, will there be sufficient resources available to the seller to draft these, or, if they are to review the buyer's draft, will they have adequate access rights and information sharing rights to assess the accounts?

Where there are reverse services to be provided by the target to the seller's group, the buyer is likely to diligence these services carefully to ensure that, from completion, it can continue to provide these services (having not previously supplied them). Sellers should also be mindful that placing onerous obligations on the buyer with respect to the level of service to be supplied is likely to result in the buyer asking for reciprocal protections for the services it receives from the seller.

Long-term agreements can also help to ensure that the retained group can continue to service its customers following completion. The approach may be very different compared to the TSA. Charging and risk allocation should be considered carefully. The low liability caps and minimal margin charges normally associated with TSAs are unlikely to adequately allocate risk and reward where the services feed directly into the seller's customer experience.

Another important post-completion issue that may arise relates to warranty claims. This is not an area where the buyer's assistance can be sought. However, sellers should consider before letting business knowledge leave their group, how they would deal with contesting a warranty claim. Is information relating to the target to be retained? Will the seller continue to have access to copies of emails and documentation produced in the target while under its ownership? When the seller no longer has access to management and other employees with the most in-depth knowledge of the target, this access to information will be crucial for information gathering and such protections should be sought within the transaction documents by the seller. Otherwise, a seller could find that they struggle to resist a claim.

6. Conclusion

In a carve-out transaction, it is clear that in-house legal teams can have a large and important role to play when determining the scope of the services to be provided under the TSA. As well as undertaking their own internal legal review of the target's contracts, early engagement with the business teams will help the in-house team better assess the nature of the target and where its dependencies are. This will ensure that the seller's organisation is better aligned internally and assist external counsel with drafting the TSA and the transaction documents more generally.

Jurisdiction clauses: litigation vs arbitration

Moeiz Farhan
Jeffrey Sullivan
Gibson, Dunn & Crutcher

1. Introduction

The principal purpose of a jurisdiction clause is to set out the parties' choice as to the forum and method by which any disputes arising out of their agreement are to be resolved. These clauses are often considered as an afterthought once the commercial terms of a deal have been agreed, but there are important points to be considered when drafting a jurisdiction clause that can have far-reaching implications for the strategy and timing of any subsequent dispute.

This chapter explores the points that lawyers responsible for drafting transactional documents should consider when deciding what sort of jurisdiction clause to include in their agreement. In particular, this chapter considers the relative advantages and disadvantages of opting for either litigation or arbitration as the chosen mechanism for dispute resolution. Put simply, litigation refers to the submission of a dispute by the parties to the national courts of a particular country.[1] Arbitration, on the other hand, refers to the adjudication of disputes by an independent tribunal appointed for that purpose in accordance with the parties' agreement to arbitrate.

In the following sections we discuss some of the key points that should be considered when deciding what sort of jurisdiction clause to include in an agreement. Every transaction is unique of course and some of these considerations may be more relevant than others depending on the circumstances of the particular issues involved.

---

1 The parties may nonetheless choose to have their dispute determined in accordance with the law of a third country. For example, the parties may choose to have their disputes determined by the English courts in accordance with French law. In those circumstances (subject to English conflict of laws rules) the English court will apply French law, as pleaded and proved, to determine the case.

2. Procedural issues

2.1 Which procedural rules will apply?

The first issue to consider is what procedure will be more appropriate in light of the potential disputes that may arise under the agreement. The procedural rules governing litigation will vary from court to court. For example, if the parties agree to submit their dispute to the English courts, that dispute will be governed by the English Civil Procedure Rules. One advantage to using a well-known and established set of procedural rules in a national court (such as the English Civil Procedure Rules) is that there tends to be well established precedent for how the rules work and the mechanisms that are available under those rules. In other words, there is a degree of predictability to choosing litigation in this respect.

Arbitration, on the other hand, perhaps offers less predictability than litigation in terms of procedure. However, because arbitration is inherently a consensual mode of dispute resolution, the parties have much more flexibility with respect to the procedure. In general terms, there are three main options to parties:

- arbitration under the auspices of a particular institution (ie, in accordance with its procedural rules and subject to its supervision), such as the London Court of International Arbitration (LCIA) or the International Chamber of Commerce (ICC);
- *ad hoc* arbitration, where the parties and the tribunal independently determine the procedure to be adopted; and
- *ad hoc* arbitration but subject to institutional rules.

The difference between the first and third option is that the institution plays no supervisory role in the latter case.

This control over arbitration procedure extends to the freedom to decide the 'seat' of the arbitration, ie, the jurisdiction whose laws will govern the arbitration. Parties will often choose a neutral seat, particularly in contracts with a cross-border element or where the parties to the contract come from different jurisdictions. The choice of seat will have a number of important practical implications, including the extent to which interim or supportive remedies are available from local courts, and will also determine where an award is deemed to have been made (which can be important for the purposes of enforcement – addressed below). Factors that parties should consider include: whether the seat is in a New York Convention state; whether the seat has adopted the United Nations Commission on International Trade Law (UNCITRAL) Model Law on International

Commercial Arbitration (the Model Law) or a variation thereof, which in 2006 was amended to establish a comprehensive regime on interim measures; the bases on which the arbitration law of the seat allows a final award to be challenged or set aside.[2]

2.2 The adjudicator

The next procedural point to consider is whether it is beneficial to have a degree of control over the adjudicator of the dispute. Parties that submit their dispute to litigation in the courts of a particular country will usually have little or no say in the judge(s) that are appointed to determine their dispute.[3] The same is not true with respect to arbitration. Whilst parties are sometimes content to leave the appointment of the arbitrators that will determine their disputes to a recognised institution or arbitral body (such as the LCIA or ICC), it is increasingly common for parties to demand a say in the appointment of their tribunal.

Modern arbitration agreements tend to provide not only for party-nominated arbitrators (with a chairman to be agreed by the parties' nominees, or decided by a recognised institution or arbitral body) but also in some cases for the necessary experience or expertise an individual must possess before he or she will qualify for appointment. This can be an effective way of ensuring that any disputes are determined by arbitrators with practical experience of the relevant industry or of particular legal issues.

The parties may, for example, provide in the jurisdiction clause that any arbitral appointee must have experience in the sorts of valuation and accounting issues that frequently arise in mergers and acquisitions (M&A) disputes. Carve-out transactions, in particular, often raise difficult questions relating to the transitional relationship between the parent company and the business unit being divested. The ability of the parties to access arbitrators with M&A experience, including in the issues that typically arise in the context of carve-outs (for example, scope of services, exclusivity, standards of performance and intellectual property (IP) rights), will be highly advantageous.

That said, the jurisdiction clause must also provide a degree of flexibility regarding the qualification of the potential arbitrator. If the clause provides that arbitrators must have a certain set of

---

2 Importantly, 'seat' is not the same as 'venue'. It is possible, for example, for an arbitration to be seated in Singapore but for all the hearings to take place in London.

3 In some jurisdictions, most notably the United States, juries will also play an important role in determining issues of fact before the courts.

characteristics that is too narrow and specific, it could severely limit the pool of potential arbitrators when the dispute arises.

2.3 Case management

Parties should consider the advantages and disadvantages of the procedural flexibility that tends to be associated with arbitration. The greater degree of autonomy that the parties have over procedure in arbitration can in some cases result in a faster and more streamlined resolution of the dispute. This is because arbitral tribunals and parties can adapt procedures to fit the circumstances of the particular case (eg, a greater or lesser focus on oral evidence) and to the respective legal cultures of the parties and their representatives.

However, arbitral tribunals tend to lack (or be reluctant to utilise) the robust case management powers that a number of national courts possess. As a matter of practice, deadlines in arbitration tend to be more flexible than in the courts. Moreover, courts will possess, and be more willing to impose, stronger penalties on parties that fail to abide by procedural orders.

A court's case management powers typically also provide for the summary determination (or dismissal) of claims. For example, in the courts of England and Wales it is possible for a court to strike out a claim on the basis that it discloses no reasonable grounds for bringing or defending the claim,[4] and to give summary judgment on a claim where it is of the view that the claimant or defendant has no reasonable prospect of succeeding or successfully defending the claim or a particular issue in the claim.[5] Some arbitral rules provide tribunals with similar case management powers, but generally speaking, arbitral tribunals are much less willing to determine disputes on a summary basis.

Applying for summary judgment can be a useful (and cheaper) way of disposing of cases where there are no complex issues of fact and where one side of the case clearly has no real prospect of success. Thus, for certain types of disputes, the availability of summary determination may be a key factor tending to favour litigation over arbitration.

In the context of carve-out disputes, the ability to obtain summary judgment in a national court may be an effective deterrent to opportunistic attempts by a remorseful buyer to expand the scope of the assets subject to the carve-out (for example, on the basis of

---

4 CPR r 3.4(2)(a).
5 CPR r 24.2.

an alleged nexus to the business unit being divested) or to seek to expand the scope of the transitional services that the seller is obliged to provide following the sale. If a buyer is aware that summary judgement is unlikely because the parties must arbitrate such disputes (rather than litigate in the national courts), the buyer may be encouraged to lodge an arbitration claim in order to press its position and potentially re-open the deal. On the other hand, if the jurisdiction clause requires the dispute to be heard in for example, the English Commercial Court, then the buyer may be less inclined to press its claims knowing that such claims may be quickly disposed of by the court (with cost consequences – see section 6 below).

2.4 Disclosure

The extent to which the parties are required to disclose documents as part of any dispute can vary significantly depending on whether they have agreed to submit their dispute to litigation or arbitration. For example, litigants in the English courts are generally required to provide 'standard disclosure', which requires a party to disclose not only the documents on which they rely, but also any documents which: adversely affect their own case; adversely affect another party's case; or support another party's case.[6] In complex and document-heavy cases, this can be a time-consuming and expensive task. Indeed, disclosure can be the single biggest driver of the cost of litigation and arbitration. Thus, careful thought should be given to this issue.

Disclosure in arbitration can take a number of forms, and will depend on the procedural rules agreed upon by the parties. However, it is generally more limited than the disclosure found in common law jurisdictions such as the United States or the United Kingdom. Typically, disclosure in arbitration is request-based: the parties will submit requests for categories of documents that they believe are relevant to the issues in dispute. Most institutional rules provide that arbitral tribunals shall have the power to order the parties to give disclosure.[7]

The question for parties is: if a dispute arises under the contract, will broad disclosure be helpful? In cases where fraud or misrepresentation is alleged, or where the true state of affairs may have been concealed, more extensive disclosure may be beneficial. On

6 CPR r 31.6.

7 See, for example, Article 22.1(v) of the LCIA Rules 2014, which provides that the tribunal shall have the power "to order any party to produce to the Arbitral Tribunal and to other parties documents or copies of documents in their possession, custody or power which the Arbitral Tribunal decides to be relevant".

the other hand, if the dispute is likely to concern a straightforward matter of contractual construction, the parties are unlikely to benefit from having to undergo an extensive and costly disclosure exercise.

In the context of carve-out disputes, the ability to secure broad disclosure is more likely to benefit the buyer. By their very nature, carve-out transactions involve a high level of asymmetry of information between buyers and sellers. A seller will have all relevant business information about the assets being divested and the ongoing support that those assets may require, whereas a buyer will only have access to such information that the seller chooses to disclose as part of the transaction (leaving the buyer to seek protection through warranties and indemnities). Thus, a buyer may wish to provide additional protection by ensuring that it will have access to broad disclosure should a dispute arise.

Ultimately, the decision as to whether a jurisdiction clause should favour a forum that provides broad disclosure will come down to a cost/benefit analysis. Whilst access to broad disclosure may seem advantageous in certain contexts, it is important that the parties understand that it will likely come at a significant cost when the dispute arises.

2.5 Multi-party disputes

If it is anticipated that future disputes may involve third parties to the contract in question, litigation may be more advantageous. Because arbitration is a consensual process, third parties cannot be joined to proceedings without their consent (which is often not provided once a dispute arises). For similar reasons, it can often be cumbersome to consolidate existing arbitral proceedings even if consent is provided.

Courts, on the other hand, tend to have broad powers to add third parties to existing proceedings so that all the matters in dispute can be resolved.[8] For cases where it is important that multiple parties are bound by the same decision, litigation may be more appropriate.

Those drafting jurisdiction clauses should be alive to this risk particularly in complex M&A disputes where there may be multiple

8 For example, see CPR r 19.2.

contracts with multiple different parties being negotiated. This factor may be less important in carve-out disputes where all critical transactional documents tend to be between the seller and buyer (or their respective corporate groups) only. However, even in such cases, it is still important to ensure the same jurisdiction clause is used across the full suite of transaction documents. The failure to ensure consistency across the transaction documents could result in parallel proceedings in different forums involving the same parties.

2.6 Privacy and confidentiality

The general rule, at least in most common law jurisdictions, is that court proceedings are to take place in public. Some jurisdictions also allow the public to access documents on the court file.[9] Judgments of the court are also generally published.

On the other hand, arbitral proceedings are generally private (and it is of course possible to impose the terms of confidentiality as part of a jurisdiction clause that provides for arbitration). Generally speaking, arbitral awards are not published without consent. This 'default rule' is reflected in most institutional rules. For example, Article 30 of the LCIA Rules 2014 provides:

> *30.1 The parties undertake as a general principle to keep confidential all awards in the arbitration, together with all materials in the arbitration created for the purpose of the arbitration and all other documents produced by another party in the proceedings not otherwise in the public domain, save and to the extent that disclosure may be required of a party by legal duty, to protect or pursue a legal right, or to enforce or challenge an award in legal proceedings before a state court or other legal authority.*
>
> *30.2 The deliberations of the Arbitral Tribunal shall remain confidential to its members, save as required by any applicable law and to the extent that disclosure of an arbitrator's refusal to participate in the arbitration is required of the other members of the Arbitral Tribunal under Articles 10, 12, 26 and 27.*
>
> *30.3 The LCIA does not publish any award or any part of an award without the prior written consent of all parties and the Arbitral Tribunal.*

This approach is reflected in the laws of a number of jurisdictions. For example, the English Court of Appeal has said that:

---

9 For example, see CPR r 5.4C.

> *...[t]he uncontroversial starting point is that in English law arbitration is a private process;*
>
> *...[p]arties who arbitrate in England expect that the hearing will be in private, and that is an important advantage for commercial people as compared with litigation in court;*

and that:

> *...in England...there is, separate from confidentiality an implied obligation (arising out of the nature of arbitration itself) on both parties not to disclose or use for any other purpose any documents prepared for and used in the arbitration, or disclosed or produced in the course of the arbitration, or transcripts or notes of the evidence in the arbitration or the award, and not to disclose in any other way what evidence has been given by any witness in the arbitration, save with the consent of the other party, or pursuant to an order or leave of the court.*[10]

Parties should give thought to the nature of any potential dispute that might arise under a contract. If any dispute is likely to give rise to reputational concerns, or if there is a concern that publicity of a particular claim might attract further claims, the privacy of an arbitration may be more appropriate. However, if it is important that the outcome of a dispute be capable of creating precedent that can be used against third parties, or if there are matters of public or industry importance that might arise, litigation may be the more appropriate choice.

3. Substantive issues

3.1 Governing law

Generally speaking, parties to a contract may choose the law in accordance with which they would like disputes under their agreement to be resolved, regardless of whether they opt for those disputes to be determined by litigation or arbitration. In both cases, governing law is a distinct issue.

If the parties choose to litigate their disputes, their choice of jurisdiction will be important as under some national laws an express choice of law will not always be decisive. For example, even in commercial disputes that fall within the scope of the Rome I Regulation,

---

10 *Emmott v Michael Wilson & Partners Limited* [2008] EWCA Civ 184 at [60], [62] and [81].

an express choice of law is subject to some qualifications.[11] Arbitral tribunals, on the other hand, will generally abide by the parties' express choice of law. This is codified in a number of countries' arbitration laws, including the English Arbitration Act 1996.[12]

The outcome of any dispute may be more 'predictable' (by which it is meant that there may be less litigation risk) depending on the law by which the parties choose to have their disputes determined. For example, jurisdictions such as England and Wales, Delaware and New York all have well-developed case law on M&A disputes. In these jurisdictions, there may even be case law interpreting the typical contractual provisions found in carve-out agreements. Thus, choosing a governing law in such a jurisdiction will provide more certainty as to how a court or tribunal applying those laws will decide a particular point.

3.2 Precedent

Related to the previous point on governing law, lawyers should also consider the different approach taken to precedent by common law jurisdictions such as the United States and England and Wales, and the approach taken by arbitral tribunals.

In the former, the doctrine of *stare decisis* means that lower courts will be bound by the decisions of higher courts on the same points of law. This provides further predictability and, thus, less litigation risk.

On the other hand, the decisions of arbitral tribunals, because they are creatures of the parties' consent, cannot bind third parties. The corollary of that is that arbitral tribunals are not bound by the decisions of other tribunals or of national courts, even on the same or similar points, although such decisions will be of persuasive value.

As a result, the choice of governing law and the choice of forum for disputes (ie, court litigation or arbitration) are interrelated. Even if the parties choose a governing law with well-developed legal principles on M&A disputes (such as English law), an arbitral tribunal will have more flexibility in how it applies that law.

4. Enforcement

In cases with an international dimension it may be of particular importance that any decision of a court of tribunal be easily capable of enforcement in a number of jurisdictions. There is no

---

11 See Article 3(4) of the Rome I Regulation No 593/2008.

12 Arbitration Act 1996, s 46(1).

comprehensive regime for the enforcement of court judgments abroad. For example, whether or not an English judgment can be enforced abroad will depend, ultimately, on local law (particularly the private international law) of the country in which the judgment is sought to be enforced. This process may be more straightforward in those jurisdictions where there is a multilateral treaty (eg, EU or EFTA countries, which are parties to the regime in the Recast Brussels Regulation and the 2007 Lugano Convention respectively) or a bilateral treaty (as exists between the United Kingdom and a number of Commonwealth countries).

On the other hand, the 1958 New York Convention on the Recognition and Enforcement of Foreign Arbitral Awards (the New York Convention), which currently has 159 signatories, provides a relatively straightforward regime for enforcing arbitral awards in Contracting States. Each Contracting State is obliged to give effect to an international arbitration award, and to recognise and enforce those awards made in other states, subject to specific limited exceptions. Where a challenge has been made to an award before the courts of the seat of the arbitration, the court before which the enforcement application is made can adjourn its decision on enforcement.[13] The result is a much more certain enforcement regime.

The ability to enforce with ease in multiple jurisdictions can be an important consideration in the context of carve-out disputes, where the underlying transaction may involve the transfer (or purported transfer) of assets and liabilities from multiple sellers to multiple buyers, not all of whom may be located in jurisdictions where local law is enforcement-friendly. In those circumstances, arbitration likely will have an advantage over court litigation given the broad coverage of the New York Convention. It is therefore worth considering potential enforcement jurisdictions at the drafting stage to determine where enforcement may be necessary should a dispute arise. If the parties and assets subject to the carve-out are all located in a single jurisdiction, then court litigation may be appropriate from an enforcement perspective. However, if it may be necessary to enforce in multiple jurisdictions, then arbitration may be the better option.

13 The New York Convention, Article VI (codified in the United Kingdom in section 103(5) of the Arbitration Act 1996).

5. Finality

It is common for the procedural rules of national courts to provide that a judgment may be appealed once or more (whether as of right or with permission). These may, depending on the jurisdiction, mean that an appellate court reviews a lower court's decision for errors, or conducts a re-hearing and considers the matter afresh. This can be time-consuming and is one of the main reasons why it can take several years until a final decision is obtained.

In arbitration, however, the general principle is that the award of a tribunal is final. Awards can usually only be challenged on limited grounds, in accordance with the law of the seat of the arbitration. Where an arbitration is seated in London, a challenge is only permitted under the three limited grounds set out in the Arbitration Act 1996: firstly, the tribunal lacked jurisdiction; secondly, serious irregularity affecting the tribunal, the proceedings or the award; or thirdly, appeal on a point of law (unless the parties have contracted out of this right),[14] if all the parties agree or with the leave of the court.

6. Cost

A consideration that will be important for all commercial parties is cost. Whilst arbitration can result in a more streamlined (and possibly shorter) procedural timetable, with more limited disclosure, parties to an arbitration will still need to pay both the fees of the arbitral institution (sometimes a percentage of the value of the claim) and the fees of the arbitrators. This is in distinction to litigation, where often all that has to be paid is a court fee (which in some countries will be a nominal sum).

If the parties choose to litigate then, depending on their jurisdiction of choice, there may be cost shifting rules that apply. In England and Wales, the general rule is that costs follow the event (ie, the party that succeeds on its claim recovers its cost). Courts tend to have very defined rules governing when costs can be recovered and in what amount. Whilst arbitral tribunals also tend to follow the 'costs follow the event' rule in general terms, they tend to retain far more discretion as to the amount of costs to be awarded.

---

14 Waiver may take place through the provisions of institutional rules. For example, the right to appeal an award on a point of law is waived by Article 26.8 of the LCIA Rules 2014.

7. Practical points

It is important that those advising parties to M&A transactions consider the above points in good time. Drafting the jurisdiction clause will often require careful consideration of the types of disputes likely to arise out of the substantive content of the deal, and whether a client is likely to obtain a strategic advantage by having that dispute heard in a particular forum or in accordance with a particular procedure. It is also important to ensure that in cases where there are a 'suite' of contracts that a consistent approach is taken throughout. The importance of these issues means that jurisdiction clauses are best not left to be considered as an afterthought.

Carve-out issues for private equity sponsors

Katie Peek
Huw Thomas
Latham & Watkins

1. Introduction

This chapter is intended to provide an overview of the particular issues faced by private equity sponsors on carve-out transactions. It is hoped that this will provide insights not just for those sponsors and their deal counsel but also for corporate sellers and their advisers that are hoping to capitalise on private equity interest in carve-out transactions.

2. Private equity interest in carve-out transactions

Previous chapters touch upon the rise in the number of carve-out transactions, resulting from corporate divestments of non-core assets, merger authority mandated disposals, the decline of old business models, the rise of disruptive new technologies and various other factors. In recent years, private equity sponsors have taken an increasing interest in these transactions and that may in turn have helped to fuel their growth in popularity. The interest from private equity sponsors has been driven by a number of factors:

- the number of private equity sponsors has increased (with a new record of 3,921 private equity sponsors in the market as at the start of Q4 2018)[1] and the level of 'dry powder' (ie, capital committed but not yet deployed) has reached a record high (passing $1.2 trillion in 2018).[2] Sponsors have a mandate, and a limited time period, to invest that capital;
- alternative investors such as sovereign wealth funds, pension funds and family offices have become more active in the

1 Available at http://docs.preqin.com/quarterly/pe/Preqin-Quarterly-Update-Private-Equity-Venture-Capital-Q3-2018.pdf.

2 Available at www.preqin.com/insights/blogs/alternatives-in-2019-private-capital-dry-powder-reaches-2tn/25289.

private markets, increasingly competing with private equity sponsors for investment opportunities;
- since the global financial crisis, we have been living through an era of record low interest rates (averaging 0.49%[3] in the United Kingdom since January 2009), which has reduced the cost of the leverage that private equity sponsors depend upon;
- at the same time, the rise of the alternative (non-bank) lenders, US-style financing (high yield bonds, Term Loan B, etc), new forms of fund and 'holdco' finance and 'covenant light' terms mean that private equity sponsors have been able to achieve better terms and higher leverage; and
- the market has matured and many businesses have already transitioned through a number of phases of private equity ownership leaving limited scope for further operational improvement.

Together, these factors have resulted in a greater number of market participants and a greater volume of money pursuing every investment opportunity. That has pushed up valuations, making it harder for private equity sponsors to achieve their target returns and a number of sponsors have now started to raise longer duration funds with lower target returns.

Against that backdrop, carve-out transactions are perceived to offer opportunities to acquire and nurture unloved, under-managed and/or undervalued assets lacking focus and capital, and to bring to bear financial and operational expertise to unlock value and deliver greater returns. In addition, there may be the opportunity for synergies with existing portfolio companies or for future 'bolt-on'/'tuck-in' acquisitions.

For most private equity sponsors, carve-out transactions are just one type of transaction that they will look at in sourcing new deal opportunities. However, there are some private equity sponsors that have a particular focus on carve-out transactions and have developed their own 'playbooks' that they use to plan and execute the separation of carve-out businesses.

From the perspective of corporate sellers the increased interest from private equity sponsors is a welcome development. Not only does it increase competition (and, in theory, therefore, the price

---

3 Official Bank of England Base Rate, Bank of England Database.

likely to be achieved) for carve-out businesses, but private equity sponsors often come with reduced antitrust risk and greater deal execution expertise as compared with potential corporate purchasers, meaning greater speed and certainty of execution.

However, for corporate sellers that want to realise the benefits of this increased interest and for private equity sponsors that wish to maximise value from carve-out transactions, there are traps for the unwary. It is those 'traps' that are the subject of the remainder of this chapter.

3. Transaction perimeter and structuring

As noted in previous chapters, defining the transaction perimeter is critical: ie, identifying the assets and liabilities that together comprise the carve-out business and determining which of those assets and liabilities will transfer to the purchaser and which will be retained by the seller.

Only once the transaction perimeter is understood can the seller begin to consider the transaction structure, ie:

- how the assets and liabilities that are to transfer will be packaged for sale and the steps required to ensure that the assets and liabilities that are to be retained do not transfer; and
- how each party will continue to obtain the benefit of any assets and liabilities relevant to its business and transferred to or retained by the other party.

Although these are the fundamental building blocks of any carve-out transaction, this exercise is arguably particularly important for private equity sponsors (for reasons set out in the remainder of this chapter). As such, private equity sponsors will typically expect to see evidence of extensive preparatory work, including:

- thorough legal, financial, tax and (depending on the business) environmental due diligence commissioned by the corporate seller and conducted by reputable professional advisers to identify the transaction perimeter; and
- a detailed carve-out steps paper outlining the legal, financial and tax consequences of the proposed structuring steps and the costs involved.

4. Transitional services

Any purchaser of a carve-out business needs to give careful consideration as to how, and the terms on which, it will continue to obtain the benefit of any assets required for the continuation of the carve-out business post-closing but which are to be retained by the corporate seller. However, these concerns are amplified for private equity sponsors given the following.

- In contrast to corporate purchasers and unless the transaction is a 'bolt-on'/'tuck-in' transaction for an existing portfolio company, a private equity sponsor is unlikely to be in a position to provide critical 'group'/'HQ'-functions such as legal, regulatory, financial, tax, human resources (HR) and treasury and may not have any alternative to continuing use of the existing brand (which may require a fairly long-term brand licence arrangement).
- The financial impact of, firstly, the ongoing interdependencies (for example, if a service was previously provided to the carve-out business by the corporate seller at below market rates and will in future be provided on market terms); and, secondly, go-forward stand-alone costs (for example, costs relating to new employees, real estate, financial systems, insurance policies and perhaps the loss of any bulk buying or other contractual discounts), will need to be reflected in any *pro forma* accounts required for the purposes of securing debt finance and taken into account in modelling future debt service capacity (see comments below). This is an area of financial diligence that is sometimes overlooked and which needs to be considered at an early stage in the transaction given the knock-on implications for other aspects of the overall process.
- The leverage that private equity sponsors use, and the fact that each portfolio company is held separately and that there is therefore no scope (other than in the case of a 'bolt-on'/'tuck-in' transaction for an existing portfolio company) for cross-subsidy from other business lines, may make them particularly sensitive to unforeseen carve-out/transitional support costs.
- In the most complex carve-outs, transitional support may be required for longer than the private equity sponsor's anticipated hold period.

Private equity sponsors may therefore prove more demanding than potential corporate purchasers (that may perhaps have greater margin for error) in wanting to develop a detailed understanding of:

- the scope of the transitional support that may be required, which will typically require access to management; and
- the scope of the transitional support that the corporate seller is prepared to offer, the duration of that support and the relevant costs and other terms.

This can often become a key area of tension with a less well-prepared corporate seller that is keen to sign a transaction and pushing the private equity sponsor to 'trust us' to work out the details of the transitional support after signing. A well-advised corporate seller will seek to anticipate these issues and to present alongside the vendor due diligence, carve-out steps paper and sale and purchase agreement, a comprehensive proposal on transitional support.

5. Financing

Private equity sponsors are reliant on debt finance; this is fundamental to the concept of the leveraged buyout. Occasionally, perhaps in a very hotly contested auction, a private equity sponsor may sign a transaction without debt finance in place and then look to put in place the debt finance between signing and closing, or to refinance its equity investment shortly post-closing; but this is rare.

From the perspective of the corporate seller, this means that (in addition to being prepared for the detailed financial due diligence that private equity sponsors will want to conduct in order to understand the level of debt that the carve-out business can support) consideration needs to be given to the requirements of the lenders that will provide that debt finance. Specifically, these requirements may include the following.

- *Pro forma* accounts for the carve-out business – these are potentially audited and for a number of prior years. Typically, these will not have been prepared previously and will take time to prepare; and, in order to prepare them, the accountants will need to have clarity on the transaction perimeter, the financial impact of any carve-out costs and/or transitional support arrangements as well as additional costs required for the business to operate on a stand-alone basis. Careful consideration may need to be given as to how shared contracts, central costs or complex transfer pricing arrangements are treated in the *pro forma* accounts.
- Formal due diligence reports – typically, these cover legal, financial, tax and (depending on the business) environmental matters on which the lenders will be granted reliance. It is

therefore worth understanding in detail the lenders' likely diligence requirements (which, depending on the nature and jurisdiction of the financing, may be limited to more informal question and answer sessions), how long the lenders will require to review the relevant diligence materials, etc.

- A detailed understanding of anticipated post-closing cost savings that the private equity sponsor may be seeking to 'add back' as EBITDA adjustments in order to justify higher leverage.

There is often a significant lead time for some of these items and this will need to be taken into account when considering the overall transaction timeline.

6. Implementation

From the perspective of the private equity sponsor, fund performance and the compensation of the individual deal team members are typically calculated by reference to the internal rate of return realised on the investment. As such, they are incentivised not just to deliver a return on invested capital or multiple of money, but to do so as quickly as possible.

Private equity sponsors are therefore often particularly keen to ensure that they hit the ground running immediately on closing and will usually look to develop a robust implementation plan that addresses the key value creation initiatives underpinning their investment thesis, as well as the steps required to enable the carve-out business to operate independently of the corporate seller. Amongst other things, this may involve:

- the private equity sponsor seconding its own operations personnel to the carve-out business, or having third-party strategy consultants start work in the carve-out business, prior to closing;
- the acquisition of similar businesses as part of a 'buy and build' strategy or the disposal of non-core assets (and the private equity sponsor may want to begin discussions in relation to any such acquisitions or disposals prior to closing – or, in extremis, even to have the corporate seller start making those acquisitions or disposals prior to closing); and/or
- significant changes to the current financial reporting practices of the carve-out businesses – most private equity sponsors will have a clear view regarding how they want their portfolio companies to report.

To the extent that the private equity sponsor wishes to make progress on implementing its plan prior to closing, gun-jumping issues should be carefully considered by deal counsel and (assuming such measures are permissible) provisions should be included in the transaction documents to regulate these matters.

In addition, the plan should be carefully reviewed by (or at least understood in outline by) the private equity sponsor's legal, tax and accounting advisers so that they are able to identify any legal, tax or accounting issues that may hinder or prevent the implementation of the plan as part of the general due diligence process.

7. Management

Private equity sponsors tend to back existing management teams so, unless the transaction is a 'bolt-on'/'tuck-in' transaction for an existing portfolio company with a trusted management team, a private equity sponsor is likely to be particularly keen to understand which managers will transfer with the carve-out business, and to meet with and conduct their own due diligence on those managers. If the management team that will transfer with the carve-out business is not considered to be capable of delivering on the private equity sponsor's value creation plan then the private equity sponsor may need or want to bring in additional or replacement hires.

Generous management incentivisation packages that are intended to reward outperformance and align the interests of the management team with the interests of the private equity sponsor are another key feature of the private equity business model. As such, managers that transfer to the carve-out business and win the backing of the private equity sponsor may be well-rewarded if the investment performs. An industry of 'management advisers' has grown up on the back of this: legal, financial and tax advisers that specialise in helping management teams to secure the most advantageous terms from their private equity sponsor backers.

From the perspective of either the corporate seller or the private equity sponsor, it is therefore worth considering whether the management team of the carve-out business have or should have management advisers instructed in order to smooth the process of negotiating the management incentive arrangements and ensure that this does not become a gating item later on.

8. Conclusion

A huge amount of planning goes into any successful carve-out transaction. However, from the perspective of the corporate seller, attracting and capitalising on the interest of the private equity sponsor community requires an even greater level of preparatory work.

Even where a corporate seller is thoroughly prepared there remains a large amount of work to be carried out by the private equity sponsor and its advisers to ensure that they fully understand the transaction perimeter and the implications of that with respect to separation, transitional support and implementation. Thorough diligence, high-quality carve-out financial statements and a clear and open dialogue between the corporate seller, the private equity sponsor, management and their respective advisers on issues such as transitional support are critical.

Key differences between UK and US practice

Edward Barnett
Terry Charalambous
Scott Shean
Latham & Watkins

1. Introduction

This chapter focuses on the key differences between UK and US practice with respect to the preparation of sale documents for a carve-out transaction.

While the difference between the United Kingdom and United States is being narrowed as a result of transactions becoming more international and the recent influx of US bidders entering the European legal market, key differences relating to conditionality, disclosure and remedies still remain due to the historical differences in the development of the mergers and acquisitions (M&A) markets either side of the Atlantic.

At the heart of this issue is who the market is seeking to protect. The general perception is that a UK-style agreement is seller-friendly, with the principle of *caveat emptor* (buyer beware) running through case law; whereas a US-style agreement is perceived as being more buyer-friendly.

2. Conditionality

2.1 Overview

Conditionality in sale agreements causes uncertainty for both parties as to whether or not completion shall occur. From a seller's perspective, this transfers transactional risk to the seller, while for a buyer it provides a means of terminating the agreement often without paying any costs. Given UK practice is generally more pro-seller and US practice is generally more pro-buyer, there is a difference in approach to the scope of conditions precedent which are seen as 'market'.

2.2 Conditions

UK-style agreements generally include only mandatory antitrust or other regulatory approvals, on the basis that economic risk transfers to the buyer on signing;[1] any other conditions create deal uncertainty and risk for the seller. Indeed, in our experience, only a small proportion of UK deals included conditions relating to a material adverse change, financing or a material breach of a covenant or warranty in the interim period prior to completion.

In comparison, US-style agreements often permit a greater array of conditions, from financing to absence of material adverse change, on the premise that economic risk transfers to the buyer on completion.[2] Unlike the UK approach regarding certainty of funds,[3] a limited financing condition is often included in US-style agreements. To balance the competing interests of the seller, the buyer and the lender, so-called 'SunGard' provisions[4] are included within:

- the sale agreement relating to, among others, the capacity and authority of the seller, the seller's title to the assets and any other representations and warranties which would be in the interests of the lenders; and

---

1 In the United Kingdom, locked-box mechanisms are currently the preferred consideration mechanism, which reflects the seller-friendly approach in UK M&A. In a locked-box deal, economic risk passes to the buyer at signing; the consideration is set at signing by reference to a set of locked-box accounts which reflect the target's balance sheet as at a certain date (the 'locked-box date'), with no subsequent price adjustment (save for any 'leakage'). Accordingly, the buyer bears the risk of any downturn in the economic performance of the target since the locked-box date, but also enjoys any upside. As discussed further in this book, in a carve-out, completion accounts are, however, likely to be the preferred approach as the entity is unlikely to have stand-alone accounts and the ability to prepare a set of these from which the buyer can receive sufficient comfort is likely to be challenging.

2 In contrast to the UK approach, completion accounts are the preferred consideration mechanism in the United States. Completion accounts are viewed as being more buyer-friendly as the buyer pays the 'true' value of the target as at the date of completion, rather than by reference to a set of historical accounts. Here, the parties agree an initial purchase price which then gets adjusted pound-for-pound (or dollar-for-dollar) upwards or downwards depending on whether the actual levels of net debt, net working capital and/or net assets is greater or lower than the targeted/estimated levels.

3 In UK-style agreements, the expectation is that buyers will have certainty of funds to pay the consideration in full on completion, which might comprise a debt commitment letter, a bridge loan or full form facility documentation entered into at the time of signing of the sale and purchase agreement.

4 Following the acquisition of SunGard Data Systems by a private equity consortium in 2005.

- the debt commitment letters relating to the buyer's capacity and authority among others, which, in each case, if untrue at closing would permit the lender to not fund the debt and, in turn, permit the buyer not to proceed with the proposed acquisition (although the buyer might be required to pay a reverse break fee to the seller).[5]

2.3 Material adverse change

Where there is a split signing and completion, there is a risk for the buyer that, during this interim period (or between the date of the last audited accounts of the target and completion), the prevailing economic situation of the target or the industry in which it operates changes to such an extent that the transaction is no longer an attractive proposition for the buyer. In order to counter this risk, a buyer might seek to include a termination right in the event of a material adverse change in the target.

A material adverse change provision in an agreement can take one of two forms:

- as a condition precedent to completion (which is satisfied immediately prior to completion); or
- as a warranty which is repeated at completion.

As noted above in section 2.2, in UK private M&A, a material adverse condition is rarely included,[6] stemming from the underlying principle that risk transfers to the buyer at signing. In recent years, however, there has been a slow increase in the number of UK transactions which include a (often limited and specific) material adverse change provision (although they are still uncommon in general), partly due to volatile market conditions and also a steady influx of US buyers who are accustomed to such provisions.

To the extent such a condition is included in the sale agreement in a UK transaction, a well-advised seller should seek to:

---

5 In the United Kingdom, in our experience, the inclusion of any reverse break fee is very uncommon in private M&A deals. In the public M&A sector, there is a general prohibition on break fees payable by the target company to which the City Code on Takeovers and Mergers applies, although there are limited situations in which break fees can be paid by the target company to an offeror.

6 In contrast, such provisions are common place in UK public M&A transactions, however, they are also subject to a high bar; the circumstances must be of "material significance to the offeror in the context of the offer" (rule 13.5 of The City Code on Takeovers and Mergers) and must strike at the heart of the purposes of the transaction (Practice Statement 5 issued by The Panel on Takeovers and Mergers).

- define what amounts to a 'material adverse change' (for example, by reference to a drop in revenue or production, or an increase in liabilities), while any such criteria should be objective (as, where the criteria is subject to the buyer's opinion, a buyer need only prove to the court that their opinion that a material adverse change had occurred is "honest and rational",[7] which is a lower threshold); and
- exclude certain events such as changes in the macroeconomic environment which do not disproportionately affect the target. In the absence of a definition of what constitutes a material adverse change, it will be left to the courts to assess whether a material adverse change has occurred.

In the United States, the Delaware courts have held that the threshold for a buyer to rely on a material adverse change provision to terminate an agreement is high and that the adverse effect must be material when viewed in the long-term rather than the short-term (to be measured in years, rather than months); reliance on the provision should be seen as a 'backstop' for the buyer and a "short-term hiccup in earnings should not suffice".[8] In October 2018, the Delaware Court of Chancery[9] found in favour of a buyer who sought to rely on its termination right on the occurrence of a material adverse effect; it was found that the decline in business was "durationally significant" and was disproportionate compared to its competitors within the industry. Although the first of its kind under Delaware law (all previous judgements required the buyer to close despite the target's value diminishing), this decision is fact-specific and the bar to relying on a material adverse change in the United States remains a high one. The United Kingdom adopts a similar approach when construing such provisions and the underlying interpretation principles of the English courts apply[10] but, where unambiguous language is used, the court must apply such

7 *Cukurova Finance International Limited and another v Alfa Telecom Turkey Ltd* [2013] UKPC 25. Although this is a Privy Council decision and, therefore, not binding on English courts, it is likely to be considered by English courts in cases of a similar nature as instructive.

8 *IBP Shareholders Litigation v Tyson Foods, Inc.* (789 A.2d 14 (Del Ch 2001)).

9 *Akorn v Fresensius Kabi AG*, 2018 WL 4719347 (Del Ch 1 October 2018), Akorn intends to appeal to the Delaware Supreme Court.

10 The English courts will seek to apply a construction which is reasonable and which "is consistent with business common sense" (*Rainy Sky SA v Kookmion Bank* [2011] 1 WLR 2900).

unambiguous language.[11] The English courts have held that it is for the party seeking to rely on the provision to prove that such circumstances exist, such change must not be temporary and it must be material[12] (it must be "substantial" or "significant"[13]). In *Grupo Hotelero Urvasco*, it was also held that for the party relying on the material adverse change provision, it must prove that it was not aware of the circumstances that could lead to the change; it must be an unknown event which brings about the change (which is also aligned to the Delaware courts' position in *IBP Shareholders Litigation*[14]) and such change must cause the adversity.[15]

Although the bar for relying on a material adverse change provision is high and, therefore, a buyer might choose not to pursue its right to terminate, a well-advised seller should still be reluctant to accept such a provision due to the possibility that an adverse event could provide the buyer with strong leverage to renegotiate the price should it threaten to invoke its termination right.

3. Disclosure

3.1 Overview

The underlying principle that matters disclosed to a buyer qualify any warranty given by a seller is a common concept between the United Kingdom and the United States. In the United Kingdom, such matters are disclosed by way of a separate disclosure letter, which contains general disclosures (these are, typically, publicly available documents or information available at public registries which seek to qualify all warranties) and specific disclosures (being statements which seek to qualify the specific warranties they are disclosed against); while in the United States, specific disclosures are made in a disclosure schedule or disclosure letter. Beyond such similarities, the approach to disclosure varies between the United Kingdom and the United States.

The disclosure letter or disclosure schedule is an important document for both the seller and buyer. For the seller, the

---

11 *Rainy Sky SA v Kookmion Bank* [2011] 1 WLR 2900.

12 *Grupo Hotelero Urvasco SA v Carey Value Added SL* [2013] EWHC 1039.

13 The principle established in *Grupo Hotelero Urvasco SA v Carey Value Added SL* was applied in *Decura IM Investments v UBS* [2015] EWHC 171.

14 Although the court in *Akorn* held that the scope of the material adverse change was to be referenced by the explicit drafting of the provision rather than to risks which may or may not be within the buyer's knowledge at the time of signing.

15 *Ipsos SA v Dentsu Aegis Network Ltd* [2015] EWHC 1726.

disclosures bring to the buyer's attention certain matters, facts or circumstances which qualify the warranties and, thereby, absolve the seller from liability for the matters disclosed. For the buyer, the disclosures provide it with critical due diligence information, especially where previously unknown issues are disclosed and, depending on the nature and extent of the disclosure, the ability to renegotiate price, seek additional indemnities or walk away from the deal.

3.2 Standard of disclosure

The standard of disclosure is an important consideration in sale agreements as it determines the threshold to be met in order for any disclosures to qualify the warranties and, therefore, avoid any liability for the seller in respect of such matter, fact or circumstance.

In both the United Kingdom and the United States, the standard to be met is as set out in the sale agreement.[16] In the United Kingdom, the standard is usually 'fair' disclosure, with the concept of 'fair' being a well-established principle of UK common law: it is the requirement for the seller to set out the "facts and circumstances sufficient in detail to identify the nature and scope of the matter disclosed and to enable the purchaser to form a view whether to exercise any of the rights conferred on him by the contract."[17] A disclosure which is merely a reference to a source of information from which a diligent enquirer might be able to determine the extent of the issue risks the possibility that such disclosure is not 'fair',[18] while inferences a buyer might make from the documents provided could be deemed disclosed if the standard of disclosure includes "all matters to be inferred" from the documents.[19] It has also been held that fair disclosure requires some positive statement and not merely the omission of information.[20]

In comparison, in US transactions, the parties often negotiate the standard of disclosure in the sale agreement or in the introductory language of the disclosure schedule or disclosure letter.

---

16 *Infiniteland Ltd v Artisan Contracting Ltd* [2005] EWCA Civ 758 (for the United Kingdom).

17 *Edward Prentice v Scottish Power* [1997] 2 BCLC 264.

18 *New Hearts v Cosmopolitan Investments* [1997] 2 BCLC 249.

19 Obiter comments in *MAN Nutzfarhrzeuge AG and others v Freightliner Limited* [2005] EWHC 2347 (Comm).

20 *Daniel Reeds Ltd v EM ESS Chemists Ltd* [1995] CLC 1405.

3.3 Buyer's knowledge

If the buyer has conducted a thorough due diligence exercise (covering legal, financial, tax and commercial matters), there is a possibility that the buyer is aware of matters which the sell-side deal team were unaware of as they are too far removed from the day-to-day operations. Sellers will argue that the buyer should be prevented from being able to bring a breach of warranty claim for matters of which it was aware as a result of its due diligence investigations. The inclusion of such provision in a sale agreement is known as an 'anti-sandbagging' clause, in other words, lifting the blindfold of the buyer and making it aware of its surroundings. Buyers, on the other hand, would prefer not to be prevented from bringing a claim in respect of matters which they might have knowledge of as they cannot control who the seller has given information to and, more importantly, buyers are unable to determine whether a person in one of their business divisions is fully aware of the impact of the information on another business division; for this reason, buyers prefer to include a 'pro-sandbagging' clause.

In the United Kingdom, in *Infiniteland*, it was commented in the Court of Appeal that where the buyer had actual knowledge of the matter giving rise to the warranty claim, it would be precluded from bringing a claim even where there was a pro-sandbagging clause which referred to the actual knowledge of the buyer, whereas the buyer's constructive knowledge (knowledge which the buyer ought to have) would not. The construct of the buyer's imputed knowledge (being the knowledge the buyer would have through the knowledge of its advisers (even if such advisers did not make the buyer aware of such information)) was also discussed in *Infiniteland* and it was held that if imputed knowledge was to also be captured by such clause then it should be expressly referred to. The underlying theme in the case law is that if the buyer was aware of an issue but nonetheless entered into the transaction, the consideration paid for the target was the 'bargain' made with the seller in light of all the information the buyer had available; if the buyer knew of a matter which could have affected the consideration paid, the buyer should have requested a reduction in the consideration or sought a specific indemnity in respect of that matter. A common compromise is for the parties to specify the relevant individuals whose knowledge would constitute the actual knowledge of the buyer.

In the United States, the inclusion of pro-sandbagging clauses is more common than anti-sandbagging clauses, however, sale agreements are often silent on this point and leave it to be determined by the governing state law of the agreement, which can lead to differing conclusions; for example, some states[21] require reliance upon a warranty in order to bring a claim, while others[22] simply require an untrue statement with the buyer's knowledge not affecting such claim.

3.4 Disclosure of the data room

In a transaction, it is commonplace for documents which are to be reviewed for the purposes of due diligence to be hosted in a virtual data room. Depending on the nature of the target being sold and its history, the data room can be heavily populated. Reviewing the data room can often be a burdensome task for the buyer and requires appropriate scoping and materiality discussions with advisers to ensure an efficient and effective review is undertaken.

In the United Kingdom, it is commonplace (and, in our experience, in the vast majority of deals) for the entire contents of the data room to be deemed generally disclosed to the buyer (including those documents which the buyer or its advisers have not reviewed), stemming from the *caveat emptor* principle that the buyer should be aware of what it is buying. A well-advised buyer should have its advisers confirm which documents have been reviewed enabling the buyer to understand where the gaps lie and possible risks associated with accepting the general disclosure of the contents of the data room.

Where a buyer accepts the general disclosure of the contents of the data room, a well-advised buyer should seek to qualify the contents of the data room to the extent it is 'disclosed' (referencing the agreed upon standard of disclosure in the sale agreement). By doing so, the buyer is afforded some protection if the nature, scope and extent of the relevant matter, fact or circumstance is not adequately summarised or apparent in the relevant document within the data room or is buried in a footnote; while a well-advised seller should ensure that its data room is well organised to avoid the risk of falling short of the required disclosure standard.

---

21 For example, California, Colorado and Texas.

22 For example, Delaware, Florida, Illinois and New York (in New York, if the source of the buyer's knowledge is from the seller, this will prevent the buyer from bringing a claim; if, however, the knowledge is from third parties, this will not defeat a breach of warranty claim).

In contrast, in the United States, it is market practice for the seller to be required to disclose each and every document it is seeking to rely on for the purposes of qualifying the relevant warranty, rather than relying on a general disclosure of all documents in the data room. In addition, sellers will often be required to specifically reference each warranty to which the specific disclosure applies to, with agreements often containing a provision that a disclosure against one warranty will not apply to all other warranties unless they are specifically cross-referenced.

4. Remedies

4.1 Basis of recovery

One of the most significant differences between the United Kingdom and United States is in respect of the approach to remedies for a breach of warranty or representation.

In the United States, warranties and representations are often treated as the same, with no distinction between the two. The remedy, therefore, for a breach of warranty or representation, in the United States, is negotiated between the parties but, in our experience, is often on an indemnity basis, entitling the buyer to recover for the loss suffered or incurred by the buyer in remedying the defect (there is no reference to the actual loss suffered by the target), subject to negotiated limitations. Any requirement on the buyer to mitigate its losses is also subject to negotiation between the parties.

In contrast, in the United Kingdom, there is a real distinction between warranties and representations and the remedies for a breach. Warranties are statements of fact given by the seller as at a certain date, whereas representations are statements which, but for the representation, induce the other party to enter into a contract.

Remedies for a breach of warranty under English law are subject to the usual contractual principles for damages, to put the claimant (the buyer) in the position they would have been in had the warranty been true. In order to be able to recover damages:

- there must be legal causation between the breach and the loss;
- the loss must have been foreseeable at the time the parties entered into the sale agreement; and
- the buyer must seek to mitigate its losses.

For a breach of a representation, a misrepresentation, damages are available to claimants (subject to similar principles as for a breach of warranty), however, the award of damages is calculated differently; they seek to put the claimant in the position they were in prior to entering into the sale agreement. The difference in the award of damages under contract (for a breach of warranty) and tort (for a misrepresentation) is ultimately whether or not the price paid by the buyer represents poor value. For a breach of warranty, the assessment of damages is determined by reference to the loss of value of the shares (the difference between the true value of the target (and not the price paid by the buyer) and the value of the target accounting for the breach), whereas for a misrepresentation, the assessment of damages is calculated by reference to the value paid by the buyer and the value of the target accounting for the breach. More importantly for the buyer, a misrepresentation also provides an alternative equitable remedy of rescinding the sale agreement[23] (where this is possible), restoring the parties to the position they were in prior to entering into the sale agreement, which effectively means consideration flows back to the buyer and the assets are transferred back to the vendor.[24]

For these reasons, in UK-style sale agreements a well-advised seller should seek to exclude all representations (howsoever made) previously given in the course of negotiations or other documents entered into prior to the entry into the agreement through entire agreement clauses (and any reference in the agreement that representations are given).[25] In addition, express provisions excluding the right of rescission should also be included, with damages stated as being the sole remedy of the buyer in the event of any breach of warranty or representation.[26]

4.2 Limitations

Financial and time limitations on remedies on both sides of the Atlantic are generally aligned. In our experience, in the United

23 Depending on the type of misrepresentation, the award of damages and rescission may not be available. For example, courts can exercise discretion and award damages in lieu of rescission for negligent and innocent misrepresentation and for negligent misstatement only damages are available.

24 The effect of rescission is different to that of termination; termination releases the parties from the performance of their future obligations, whereas rescission restores the parties to their original position as far as possible.

25 In *Idemitsu Kosan Co Ltd v Sumitomo Corp* [2016] EWHC 1909 (Comm) it was held that a warranty will not be considered a representation unless expressly stated to be so, on the basis that if that was the parties' intention then the drafting would reflect that.

26 The remedy of rescission is also available in US-style agreements for misrepresentations and so a well-advised US seller should bear these exclusions too.

States, caps for business warranties tend to be in the range of 10% to 15% of the consideration paid, while fundamental warranties[27] and representations are capped up to 100% of the consideration paid; in the United Kingdom, business warranties are typically capped up to 30% of the consideration paid, with fundamental warranties capped at 100% of the consideration paid. In both jurisdictions, the aggregate liability of the seller for all claims under the sale agreement is also typically capped at 100% of the consideration.

In respect of time limits, in our experience, across both jurisdictions commercial warranties tend to survive for a period of either 18 months or two years, tax warranties between four to seven years (or in accordance with the relevant statute of limitations) and fundamental warranties up to a period of six years (or in accordance with the relevant statute of limitations).

Notwithstanding the above, the principle difference between UK and US approaches with respect to limitations is the basis of recovery. In the United States, the remedy for a breach of warranty or representation is on an indemnity basis (and so on a dollar-for-dollar recovery), whereas for the United Kingdom the remedy is based in damages; indemnities in UK agreements are only provided for specific identified liabilities (for example, environmental liabilities or current litigation matters) and, in our experience, capped up to a specified sum.

4.3 Insurance

During negotiations, one point of contention between the buyer and the seller is the recoverability under the warranties (and their scope). The parties' positions may be at opposite extremes and could lead to a deadlock in negotiations. One method of cutting through this is by one of the parties taking out a warranty and indemnity insurance policy (or sometimes referred to as a representation and warranty insurance policy). In addition to breaking the deadlock, the other benefits of taking out such a policy include, for the buyer, the possibility of extending the time limitations of the warranties and reducing the credit risk of relying upon the seller for a pay-out and, for the seller, giving the seller a clean exit and not having to hold back any proportion of the consideration in the event of a claim in the future.

27 Fundamental warranties are usually warranties which cover the seller's title to the assets and capacity and authority to enter into the sale documentation (others might be included within the scope such as warranties relating to insolvency matters).

Although this is a relatively new insurance product, the insurance market has rapidly become well developed and competitive, with policies able to be incepted within a matter of weeks. Historically, the UK insurance market has been more mature than the US market, possibly due to the fact that the scope of warranties and representations in US-style agreements are broader (and, therefore, represent an increase in the risk of a breach) and the fact that recovery under US-style agreements are typically on a dollar-for-dollar basis (rather than in the United Kingdom, where recovery is typically limited to damages).

Given the competitive nature of the insurance market, there has been a decline in the premiums attaching to such insurance. In our experience, in the United Kingdom, the premium is generally between 0.5% to 1% of the cover sought and, in the United States, generally between 2.5% to 3.5% of the cover sought; excess also varies, with an excess of between 0% to 0.5% of the enterprise value in the United Kingdom and between 0.5% to 1% of enterprise value in the United States. These limits vary depending on the target and the industry and jurisdictions in which it operates.

5. Conclusion

Parties seeking to conclude a transaction governed by the relevant laws of the United Kingdom or United States should be aware of the differences in approaches to conditionality, disclosure and remedies between the two jurisdictions. US buyers might be viewed as unfavourable in the United Kingdom if they do not familiarise themselves with such differences and submit 'off market' offers (especially in a competitive auction process), while UK sellers might be subject to more onerous disclosure requirements in the United States.

Restructuring

Neil McFerran
Sean O'Flynn
Mark Veldon
Julia Windsor
AlixPartners

1. Overview

For reasons explained elsewhere in this book, in recent years there has been an increase in corporate carve-out activity, driven by a need for focus on core business operations and funding targeted mergers and acquisitions (M&A).

Consequently, successful planning and delivery of any resulting business carve-out has taken on huge importance to avoid leaving 'value on the table' for both purchasers and vendors. In our experience, there are five key steps that any business contemplating a divestment should follow to ensure a successful separation that delivers value both in terms of sales price, as well as ensuring strong retained business performance post-divestment. We discuss each of these key steps in detail below.

2. Define the strategy

In its essence the decision to proceed to a divestment is made in the determination of a target EBITDA and cash flow for the stand-alone asset. EBITDA is used as a simple measure of the underlying earnings of a company as it is calculated as revenue minus expenses (before deducting tax and interest which are affected by the level of debt in the company and depreciation and amortisation which can be affected by the stock, property, equipment and intellectual property (IP) owned by a company) and allows investors to quickly compare opportunities. Cash flow is important in that it allows purchasers to calculate the level of debt that can be used to acquire a company, as cash flow will be used to repay any debt. Failure to correctly anticipate the drivers that contribute to EBITDA and cash flow is the main reason for value destruction. Set out below in Figure 1 is a representation of these drivers and how a clearly defined carve-out strategy can help identify a realistic and

Figure 1. Business case for carve-out entity

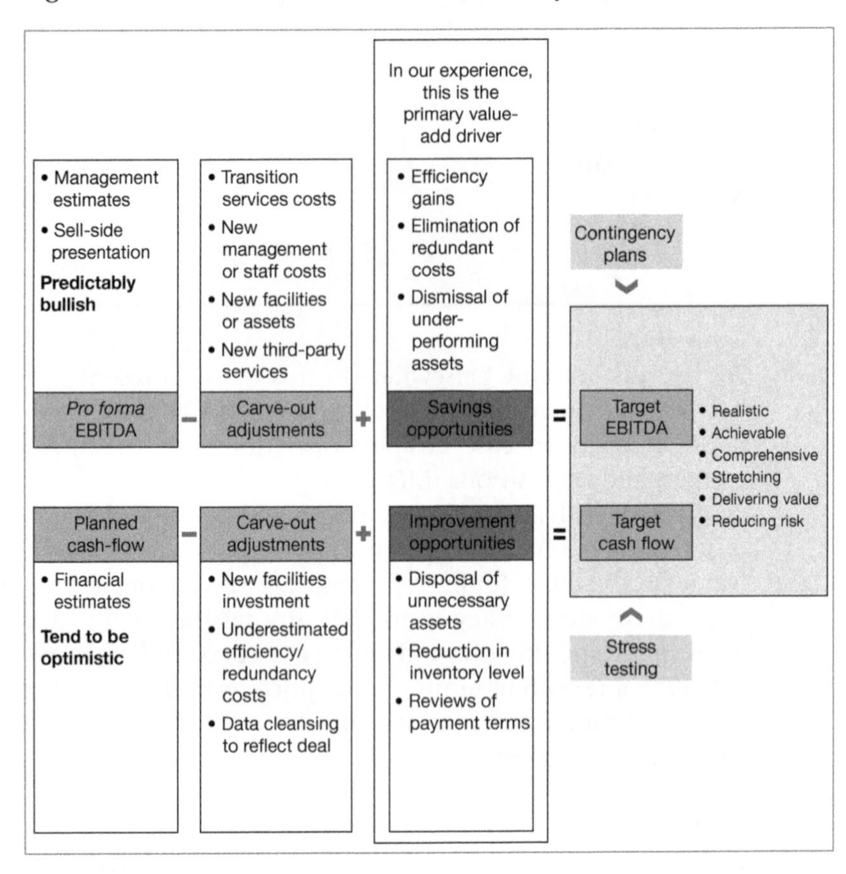

achievable target EBITDA and cash flow as well as strengthen the business case for the carve-out entity.

The success of a carve-out is measured, firstly, against the ability of the carved-out business (NewCo) to have all the parts and features necessary to operate following legal divestment and financial close of the M&A transaction known as 'Day 1' (as distinct from being an 'inert aggregation of assets') and, secondly, against NewCo's parent's ability to remain a strong trading entity with its key stakeholders retained. A thorough Day 1 plan and early organisational alignment are key factors in preparing for the separation.

As discussed above, a successful carve-out starts with defining the overall strategy for the separation to clarify the 'must have' requirements for the parent. Once the baseline cost, revenue and headcount for the parent and NewCo have been established, the process of preparing a Day 1 plan can begin. This process involves examining the cross-functional and cross-business interdependencies as well as the risk points and areas that need to be prioritised. Drafting the Day 1 plan helps ensure that every detail is thought through as NewCo is prepared for separation and allows for performance metrics to be collected and tracked.

Key learnings that we have observed from previous carve-outs suggest a number of pitfalls that organisations fall into by not adequately setting a clear strategy early on, namely:

- the failure to seize opportunities to start from a 'blank sheet of paper' and instead replicating the existing team's structure, reporting lines and key performance indicators (KPIs). Wherever possible, the day-to day tasks of individuals within an organisation should be mapped to understand the tremendous opportunities that might exist to simplify and reduce overheads as well as increase productivity;
- the failure to give adequate consideration to critical deal considerations, like information technology (IT) architecture, pension liabilities and possible trapped cash in challenging geographies;
- the willingness to compromise on Day 1 readiness and to not simplify as much as possible from the start by relying on the first 100 days following close to remedy any unresolved items such as stranded assets, orphaned roles with no clear reporting lines and undefined performance goals;
- the failure to establish a clear understanding of 'who's doing what and where' early on, which will be critical to understanding TSA requirements and designing the new organisation to ensure that all cross-functional and cross-business interdependencies are superseded; and
- the failure to orient as quickly as possible towards the 'end game' solution which can amplify the uncertainty within the organisation, making it harder to win support to implement the change management process and risk attrition of key personnel.

3. Separation objectives

Once the strategy has been defined and approved by the parent, establishing and resourcing the Separation Management Office (SMO) is a critical step to maintaining momentum in the process. Successful carve-outs require alignment of all impacted parties and the process should begin around six to 12 months before Day 1

Figure 2. Definition of separation objectives

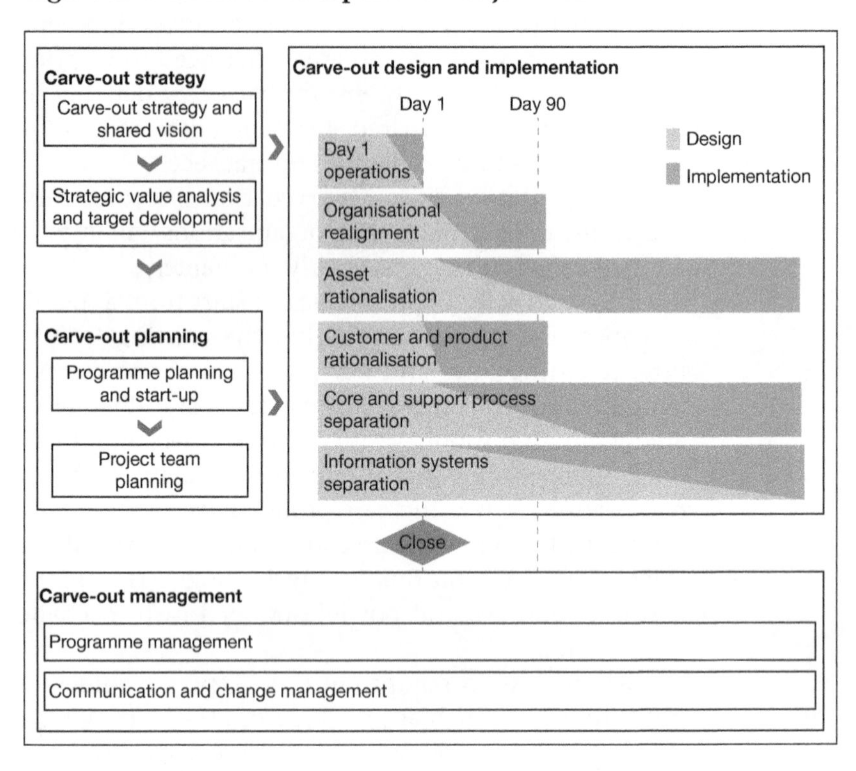

based on the complexity of the proposed carve-out. Figure 2, above, provides an overview of this process.

Best practice delivery always keeps ensuring independent Day 1 operations are at its core and ensuring the delivery workstreams reflect this accordingly.

Failure to anticipate and mitigate for many of the common pitfalls of carving-out assets can significantly erode deal value. Table 1 summarises this across five key aspects of the transaction. As discussed above, the SMO with executive level sponsorship will be accountable to deliver the preparation required for Day 1 readiness.

Regardless of the previous experience of the organisation of M&A transactions, it is always best to assume an organisation that is unprepared for the change it is due to face. Hence communication as the process evolves is critical to maintain engagement of the business at large and ensuring that conjecture does not impact

Table 1. Risks to deal value

Area	Risk	Risk to deal value
Stand-alone costs	• Lack of clarity in historical cost allocations • Separation of joint contracts • Incremental stand-alone costs not understood	• Failing to anticipate dis-synergy of stand-alone cost base negatively impacting EBITDA • Underestimated one-off and incremental separation costs could impact the stand-alone business cash flow
Transitional support	• Definition of services required from parent on Day 1 through to full separation	• Cost and potential legal liability questions for services provided outside of formal TSA contracts • Business disruption if any parent provided services have not been identified pre-Day 1
Deal perimeter definition	• Understanding which assets are in or out of the transaction • Agreements for sharing or transition from combined operational footprints	• Liabilities resulting from shared systems, processes and assets, and potential disruption to business continuity
Stakeholder separation	• Transaction impact and change of control on combined supplier or customer contracts	• Lack of clarity in communication leading to opportunistic competitor behaviours • Loss of scale leading to price and value erosion in supplier and customer contracts • Risk of continuity disruption in critical third-party services/relationships

continued on next page

Area	Risk	Risk to deal value
Project management	• Failure to deliver Day 1, transitional and end state stand-alone operations	• Excess double running costs associated with poorly defined transitional solutions post-Day 1 • Risks to staff retention if communication and Transfer of Undertakings (Protection of Employment) Regulations (TUPE) arrangements not adequately handled • Loss of control over costs and delivery of carve-out initiatives required for Day 1 and beyond

business as usual considerations. Figure 3, below, sets out the multiple steps required to ready an organisation for Day 1.

Key learnings that we have observed from previous carve-outs suggest a number of failings that organisations fall into by not adequately setting separation objectives to address the following points.

- Short-term carve-out actions at closing, which include:
  - security and logical data segregation issues;
  - business continuity topics such as management reporting (eg, cash flow reporting); and
  - other potential closing topics (eg, certification and compliance requirements may need to be re-established on separation which can be time consuming, expensive and difficult to achieve).
- Coordination with other streams (eg, work council, antitrust etc) and the management of interdependencies to have a realistic plan.
- Ensuring that the technical carve-out is kept simple with a 'lift and shift' approach favoured if possible. Platform renewal can be achieved incrementally once separation is complete.

Figure 3. Best practice Day 1 readiness planning

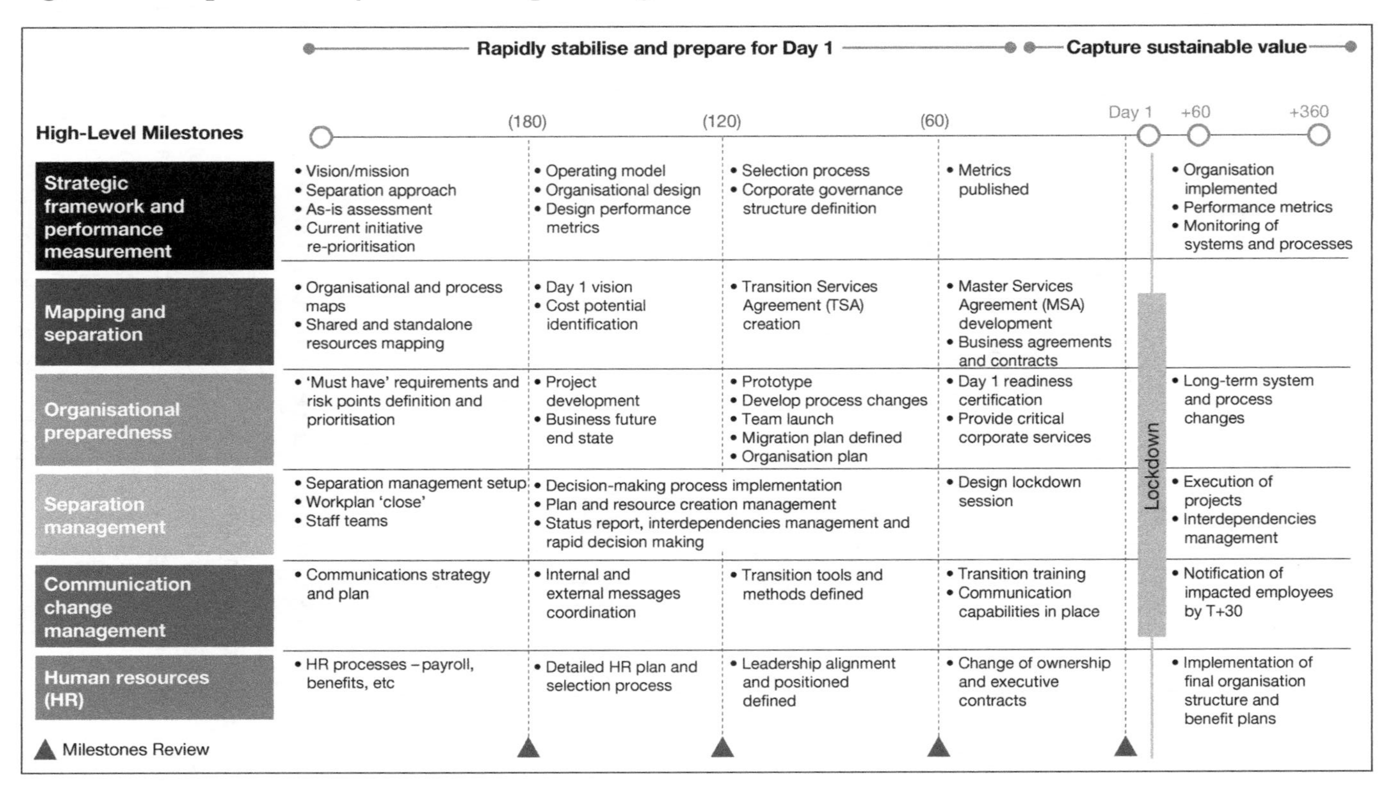

4. Preparing the organisation for separation

An important part of Day 1 planning is the mapping of ownership of the assets, resources, licences and material contracts needed by NewCo to run its business so that provisions can be made for NewCo to take legal ownership of certain assets or arrange for the assignment or novation of material licences, leases and contracts (as detailed elsewhere in this book). Another element of Day 1 planning is examining the tax, legal and financing structure for NewCo. This allows the parent to simplify the holding structure of NewCo to make it easier for multiple layers of debt to be used in the acquisition of NewCo (if required) and for the reliance on group funding to be determined. This process also highlights any risk points that might be identified as part of future vendor due diligence that could either delay divestment or have an impact on the purchase price.

Finally, the parent should consider whether it can undertake an organisational realignment under separate management prior to close. An early organisation realignment allows for buy-in across the organisation and can assist with the identification of any stranded roles, costs and Day 1 checklist items before close.

By way of example, by mapping the roles of individuals within the organisation at a day-to-day task level and not by merely aligning their title or place in a team, we were able to identify personnel integral to the running of NewCo sitting outside of the traditional teams. By mapping the overall organisational efficiency and effectiveness of the parent, we were able to identify stranded costs that were attributable to NewCo. Through establishing a new division representing the proposed NewCo 12 months prior to close, the new division was already established and working as a team as the due diligence process kicked off. This assisted the vendor in establishing a clearer financial baseline for the division and negated accusations of talent being cherry picked prior to close as it was clear who was part of the team.

5. Evaluating TSA architecture to be offered as part of the separation

While the vendor and purchaser will inevitably spend the most time and energy evaluating the purchase price and negotiating the terms of the sale and purchase agreement (SPA), the importance and value derived from a well thought out TSA is often overlooked.

The TSA provides the framework for support following the separation of the organisations and will typically set out the services, fees, warranties and personnel who will manage the relationship and time frame during which services will be provided by the parent company to NewCo. Typically, the TSA covers finance and accounting, human resources (HR), information technology (IT) and procurement services but is also an invaluable framework for communication post-acquisition to assist with resolving issues that may arise in the physical separation period. Spending time on identifying the systems, processes and people that NewCo may require on Day 1, and a clearly established basis on how service costs are derived on a time, task and personnel basis, greatly assists with negotiating the TSA.

Regardless of prior history between the parent and any purchaser, during an acquisition the nature of the relationship will become more vendor/customer focused. Following separation, it is imperative that the TSA clearly provides for defined channels of communication (preferably through a single point of communication within management), designated roles and responsibilities and the fees that will be charged for those roles, payment terms (which often are the most controversial term to negotiate), a clear escalation path to resolve issues and a defined timeframe for the agreement. Winding down the services is important and a process that is often overlooked when negotiating the TSA.

While the baselining of the organisation and the Day 1 plan will identify which systems, processes and people NewCo will need to acquire post separation, the nature of the acquiring organisation will inform whether NewCo will establish these capabilities internally following separation or transition these services to a third-party vendor. By way of example, a private equity sponsor acquiring NewCo through a new vehicle would not necessarily have an existing accounting team and software and would require assistance with general ledger accounting until it establishes its own accounting team (either internally or through a third-party vendor), whereas an existing corporate would be looking for cover for a short period of time while it migrates invoicing, accruals and account reconciliation onto its own system.

To ensure that the right services are included in the TSA, and consistency is maintained in managing day-to-day activities, the managers involved in overseeing the TSA should also be involved in drafting the TSA. Consistency across the TSA, SPA and keyman contracts is also important to ensure that all material assets, systems and personnel are accounted for as part of the separation. To ensure a timely migration of services, performance metrics should be collected and tracked, and incorporated into the reporting requirements of all parties. While the TSA should be as specific as possible, and all arrangements made should be documented, it is also invaluable for both parties to specify catch-all provisions that outline what assistance, information and clarification the parent is obliged to provide. This will hopefully ensure a smooth transition of outstanding matters such as tax, asset and contractual consent that have been identified during the Day 1 planning process and which can only be finalised following close.

6. Driving the change management process

Driving a successful change management process is about managing the complexity risk of the carve-out and the business risk involved with any change scenario while at the same time guiding the transformation journey. Complexity risk is driven by the number of stakeholders involved (eg profit and loss (P&L) units), number of employees affected, number of locations, number of affected business units, different legal frameworks involved, the type of measures to be undertaken at the same time (reorganisation, reduction, closures), interdependencies of measures and geographies and organisational history – the 'here we go again' mentality. Business risk is driven by any delay in separation affecting the long-term growth strategy of NewCo, customer defections due to unsubstantiated rumours, the one-time cost of undertaking a carve-out, loss of trust with stakeholders and the attrition of key staff. For this reason, internal and external messaging that is honest, complete, rapid and frequent is critical, as is training and coaching change agents and leaders to drive the process and reach all audiences.

In order to implement effectively the changes required for the carve-out, all individuals – executives, management and the workforce – must undertake the transformation journey, each at their own pace. Without buy-in, the process will be more fragmented and there is a greater risk of losing the trust of key stakeholders and staff and that individuals move through the stages of the transformation journey at markedly different paces, which can create frustration. Behavioural change consequently moves the lever on cultural change. For these reasons, to be successful, change management needs to start with a clear statement of direction and purpose from senior leadership. Then management must: *believe* the change will take place, *agree* that it should take place and *commit* to being a part of the change. The last stage is achieved through championing, when individuals start to influence the transformation journey of others. Strategic communication and ongoing leadership support is necessary to maintain change momentum and guard against recidivism, as individuals can waver between the stages of belief, agreement, commitment and championing.

7. Conclusion

As non-core asset divestments become increasingly present in the M&A landscape to restructure portfolios on core business investors and sellers are becoming more aware of the pitfalls of poor carve-out execution and its impact on value creation. A successfully planned and delivered carve-out process is increasingly being built into the purchase price, hence vendors are taking the carve-out process more seriously and planning in a much more robust and execution focused way. Purchasers are also spending more time evaluating whether the divested entity has all the parts and features necessary to operate on Day 1 as part of their due diligence process, ensuring a business that can run seamlessly on Day 1, but more importantly has a medium-term plan to operate fully independently from the parent.

If due diligence uncovers assets that will not be transferred to NewCo but which are required for it to operate, that key personnel are being cherry picked to remain with the parent or that there is no clear transition planned for IT and accounting processes, purchasers will penalise vendors with respect to the purchase price that they offer as well as the terms and conditions, warranties and clean up provisions expected in the SPA. To ensure that vendors do not leave value on the table, a well thought through carve-out strategy is key to securing a higher purchase price. While a successful carve-out process can take up to 12 months from engagement of consultants to close, with purchase price multiples continuing to rise in most industries, the cost of implementing a strategic carve-out can be recouped in the value of the M&A transaction multiple times.

As more organisations contemplate the value of their core and non-core assets, being carve-out ready is an increasing trend with many organisations redesigning along profit reporting lines well before any carve-out and sale is anticipated. Some funds are structuring acquisitions through multiple holding companies or including an organisational redesign in their post-merger integration strategy with a view to being able to quickly carve-out businesses in the future.

Appendix 1: Carve-out checklist*

The checklist below sets out some of the key considerations for buyers and sellers in the various stages of a carve-out.

1. Early stage preparation

Estimated time: three to six months

No.	Consideration	Comment
1.	The seller should identify the key commercial drivers for the separation so all stakeholders are aligned, while simultaneously exploring alternative structures to achieve the desired outcome.	
2.	The seller should establish a dedicated separation team, whose remit should include the following. • Establishing the nature of assets to be included within the transaction perimeter. • Conducting diligence on the services and service levels currently provided by the seller's group to the divestment business, to identify the true cost of providing such services and the ability of the seller's retained group to provide these services post-completion at a satisfactory level. Process mapping will be essential to identify current dependencies and areas of support likely to be required post-completion.	

* Appendix 1 is reproduced with the kind permission of Latham & Watkins.

continued on next page

No.	Consideration	Comment
	• Reviewing the immediate and long-term impact on the continuity of the seller's retained business, including the effect any reduced buying power might have going forwards and whether any existing costs should be reduced (eg, software licensing) to reflect the group's structure post-completion. • Monitoring progress on the separation plan through regular updates/meetings. This team will also prove invaluable to potential buyers later in the process in providing clear and consistent messaging and being a central point of contact. They will also serve as the 'first responders' in the event of any significant interruptions to the operation of the divested business on Day 1.	
3.	An initial tax analysis to identify the most tax efficient structure (eg, by transferring those assets which are to be retained by the seller out of the target business and to the seller's group to avoid a de-grouping tax charge arising on completion) and any adverse tax consequences of the divestment (both in respect of the seller's retained group and the transaction itself) should be conducted. Addressing tax consequences early on will enable the seller to discuss the most tax efficient structure with potential buyers.	
4.	The legal form the divestment is to take should also be considered, together with the means to extract excess cash and/or retained assets from the business which is to be divested (eg dividends, return of capital, intra-group asset transfers etc).	

No.	Consideration	Comment
5.	To assist the seller and its separation team, external consultants may also be engaged. This reduces the risk of a leak within the organisation of the divestment as it limits the number of internal resources required at this early stage.	

2. Commencing the sale process

Estimated time: two months

No.	Consideration	Comment
1.	The seller should: • prepare a sell-side financial due diligence report and also consider whether any other sell-side due diligence reports (eg, legal and tax) should be prepared, especially where the carve-out is likely to be complex; and • consider producing comprehensive financial statements for the carve-out business (which may or may not be audited). The seller should factor into its initial timeline how long it will take to complete this exercise as, depending on the nature of the business and its complexity, this can take longer than anticipated. Where the buyer finances the transaction, in whole or in part, with debt financing, its lenders will require these financial statements to be produced and reviewed. By taking the time to produce comprehensive due diligence reports and financial statements, this will provide potential buyers with a better understanding of the carve-out business, instil confidence and possibly increase interest in and the price achieved in the transaction.	

continued on next page

No.	Consideration	Comment
2.	The separation team should prepare a comprehensive information memorandum for potential buyers. This information memorandum should be relatively detailed in setting out how the anticipated divestiture is to be structured and what, if any, transitional services are likely to be required. The more detailed the information memorandum is, the more confidence this will give potential buyers that initial considerations have been carefully considered, which ultimately impacts deal value. In preparing the information memorandum, the seller should also consider the intended recipients and the pool of potential buyers. If trade buyers are likely to be interested, they might not have a need for an extensive scope of transitional services, whereas private equity buyers will not have the support functions necessary so they are likely to be more dependent on transitional services. To maximise value, the seller should have a flexible deal structure to accommodate as wide a pool of interested parties as possible.	

3. Buyer due diligence

Estimated time: three months

No.	Consideration	Comment
1.	Both parties will need to ensure that they keep the management teams involved in the divestment business on side; the sellers will need to keep management engaged and focused on delivering the divestment, while buyers will not want to burden management with onerous and unnecessary requests prior to working alongside them.	

No.	Consideration	Comment
2.	The buyer should review the seller's due diligence reports (to the extent available) and, if they are comprehensive, then limited 'top up' diligence should be conducted by the buyer and its advisers, otherwise a fully scoped due diligence exercise should be considered. On a carve-out, it is recommended that the following areas are subject to due diligence at a minimum (other areas are subject to the type of business being acquired, the industry in which it operates and the risk appetite of the buyer).	
	Corporate: • Review the terms of any intra-group agreements transferring assets in/out of the divestment business and, to the extent necessary, the incorporation of the new entities comprising the divestment business.	
	Finance: • Review terms of any banking arrangements and/or guarantees (whether provided by, or in favour of, the divestment business), eg, cash pool arrangements and cross-group guarantees, to ensure the divestment business is released from any obligations and security thereunder. • Review all intra-group indebtedness owed by or to the business which is to be divested to ensure such amounts are repaid in full on completion.	

continued on next page

No.	Consideration	Comment
	Contracts: • Review the material customer and supplier contracts, in particular, to determine whether there are: • any restrictions on assignment and change of control provisions which might be triggered, either as a result of any sell-side internal reorganisations or as a result of the proposed transaction; and • any shared contracts, ie, they are not exclusive to the divestment business and cover other products/services, and will, therefore, need to be separated. To the extent required, the parties should factor into their timetable the need to obtain third party consents from material customers and suppliers. • Review the standard terms and conditions of order, sale, supply or purchase. • Review any sales, agency, distribution, franchise or other similar agreements with third parties.	
	Intellectual property: • The buyer will need to be confident that the business to be divested owns and/or has the necessary licences for the intellectual property (IP) which is required to continue the business. • An exercise will need to be undertaken to determine whether the IP relating to the divestment business is exclusively used by such business, or whether IP is used across the seller's group in other business divisions.	

No.	Consideration	Comment
	• Where IP rights relate exclusively to the divestment business, these should ordinarily be assigned to the buyer; whereas those which predominantly relate to the divestment business may either be assigned or licensed to the buyer and this will need to be a negotiation between the parties (the seller may want to retain ownership and control of the IP and its use so it does not cause harm or damage to the seller's retained IP rights). • Where IP rights are acquired, the scope (eg, geography) will need to be carefully negotiated, whereas in the event a licence is granted to the buyer, care will need to be given as to the terms of such licence (in particular the termination provisions where IP is later sold by the seller to a third party). • Where IP rights are assigned to the buyer, the parties will also need to determine whether any IP rights need to be licensed back to the seller, eg, to enable the seller to perform services under the transitional services agreement. The parties will also need to consider whether the buyer should be granted a limited licence to use the IP rights of the seller's retained group until it has, for example, rebranded the products with its own marks or until it has sold off remaining inventory bearing such marks. • Review the employees who are to transfer (if any) to determine whether those who contribute to the development of any IP and/or have know-how relating to the divested business are transferring.	

continued on next page

No.	Consideration	Comment
	Information technology: • Review the information technology (IT) services of the seller's group to determine whether there are any shared services which need to be separated and whether those services which are to transfer satisfy the business' needs (taking into account the number of users and scope of intended activities). • Review the software licensing arrangements to determine if the business will be able to use such software post-completion, either on a stand-alone basis or if they can be licensed by the seller under the transitional services agreement; if not, the buyer will need to factor into its timetable negotiations with the software supplier (to the extent the buyer's existing software platform cannot provide the required support) and any associated costs in obtaining such software or consents. • Review the process of any electronic data transfer, eg, the nature of information which is to be transferred, how it is to be transferred to the buyer and stored and in what format. The parties should be aware of obligations imposed on them under data privacy laws. • Review whether any open source software is used in the technology platforms and services to be acquired and if they can be easily replaced. • Review back office functionality to ensure payments can be made on Day 1, eg, payroll.	

No.	Consideration	Comment

	Employees:
	• Review the process for employees to transfer, whether by operation of law (for example, automatically under the Transfers of Undertakings Directive as implemented locally by member states in the European Union) or otherwise.
	• Consider whether the key employees of the divestment business will transfer and whether any other employees (who might provide services to other business divisions within the seller's group) should also transfer.
	• Consider whether any consultation periods with employees and/or employee representative bodies or works councils are required.
	• Review contracts of key employees and contractors (if any) and the standard terms and conditions of employees and contractors.
	• Review pension arrangements and other benefits provided to employees to determine:
	  • the minimum level of pension arrangements to provide employees who automatically transfer over and what other benefits should be provided to employees after completion; and
	  • whether there are any liabilities for the carve-out business in relation to any defined benefit pension schemes operated by the seller and, to the extent there are, whether the Pensions Regulator should be consulted in advance of completion and the inclusion of contractual remedies for the buyer in the sale documentation.	

continued on next page

No.	Consideration	Comment
	Real estate: • Review the real estate portfolio of the divestment business to determine whether any sub-licence from the seller's group is required in respect of any shared occupation or whether consent from a landlord is required to assign a lease.	
	Regulatory: • Review all licences, permissions, authorisations, registrations and consents required for the divested business to continue to operate, in particular to determine whether any third party consents are required for, or if any will terminate as a result of, any sell-side internal reorganisations or as a result of the proposed transaction.	
	Litigation: • Review all litigation which is ongoing, pending or threatened against the divestment business, whether as claimant or defendant, including employment- and IP-related disputes and to determine whether the buyer should receive the benefit of any such litigation.	
3.	As well as conducting thorough due diligence, the buyer is also likely to require a substantial set of warranties from the seller in relation to the sufficiency of assets which comprise the divestment business, together with a tax covenant for all pre-completion tax liabilities and any liabilities arising as a result of any sell-side reorganisation to effect the divestment.	

No.	Consideration	Comment
4.	The parties should hold regular separation and integration meetings/workshops to identify the dependencies the carve-out business will require and ensure that any sell-side pre-completion restructuring steps are achieved on time.	
5.	To the extent possible, 'dummy runs' of information transfer should be conducted prior to completion to ensure that any issues which might arise on Day 1 are discovered in advance to ensure a smoother transition on completion.	

4. Buyer considerations

No.	Consideration	Comment
1.	Potential buyers should be encouraged to explain the rationale for the transaction, the synergies which are likely to be achieved as a result of the transaction and any transitional services they would expect to be provided based on the limited due diligence available and their own capabilities. This will enable: • the seller to better understand the extent of transitional services it will be required to provide post-completion; and • the buyer to identify its long term integration plan and identify synergies.	
2.	Potential buyers should factor in any synergies which might be achieved post-completion in an attempt to make its offer more competitive; however, these should also be balanced against any anticipated costs for transitional services and potential closures post-completion (which might be subject to regulation).	

continued on next page

No.	Consideration	Comment
3.	Although price is a main factor for sellers in determining which bidder to put through to the final stages, a potential transaction which is of a lower value but which represents a clean break (or one which requires a limited scope of transitional services to be provided by the seller) and a quick execution are also very attractive to sellers.	

5. Post-completion integration

Estimated time: six to 12 months

No.	Consideration	Comment
1.	The buyer should put in place an effective communication strategy with all key stakeholders affected by the transaction, including employees and counterparties, with a comprehensive Q&A fact sheet to address common queries which they might face.	
2.	The buyer should consider whether the terms of the transitional services agreement is sufficiently flexible to enable it to: • remove services (and associated costs) where the buyer is able to take over such service earlier than anticipated; and • add additional services as might be required from time to time.	
3.	The seller should also devise its own post-completion separation plan to eliminate stranded costs (being costs incurred in serving the divested business).	

No.	Consideration	Comment
4.	The parties should continue to meet regularly to ensure that the post-completion integration is being conducted efficiently and in line with any agreed upon timelines and service levels.	
5.	The buyer should ensure its own integration timetable is implemented quickly so as to avoid a lengthy and inefficient integration process post-completion.	

Appendix 2: Carve-out strategy, planning and management**

Successful carve-outs require alignment of all impacted parties and should be focused around the Day 1 close

Detailed approach

Carve-out strategy

- Carve-out strategy and shared vision
- Strategic value analysis and target development

Carve-out planning

- Programme planning and start-up
- Project team planning

Carve-out design and implementation

Day 1 — Day 90

- Day 1 operations
- Organisational realignment
- Asset rationalisation
- Customer and product rationalisation
- Core and support process separation
- Information systems separation

Close

Design
Implementation

Carve-out management

- Programme management
- Communication and change management

*Carve-out strategy is often developed as part of the valuation/due diligence/negotiation process. Our carve-out approach includes it for completeness.

** Appendix 2 is reproduced with the kind permission of AlixPartners. © AlixPartners.

A clear vision, operating model and targets must be defined along with sufficient resources and a specific work plan

Detailed approach

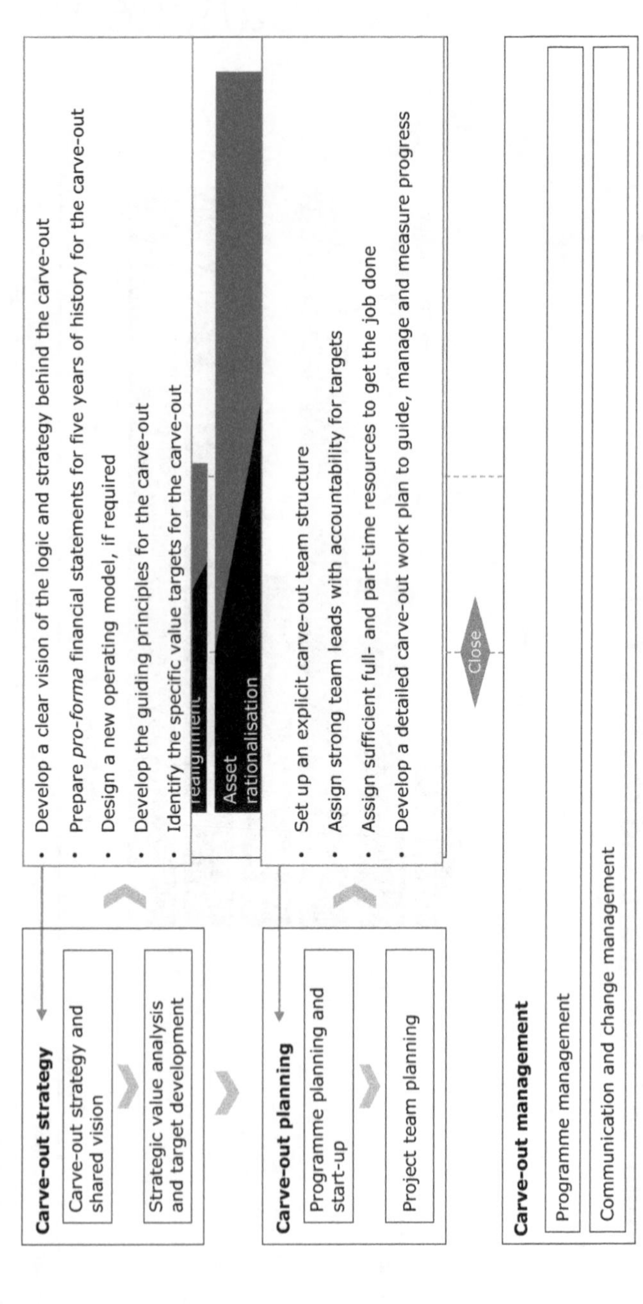

*Carve-out strategy is often developed as part of the valuation/due diligence/negotiation process. Our carve-out approach includes it for completeness.

A carve-out is a huge, complex programme that must be proactively managed as such

Detailed approach

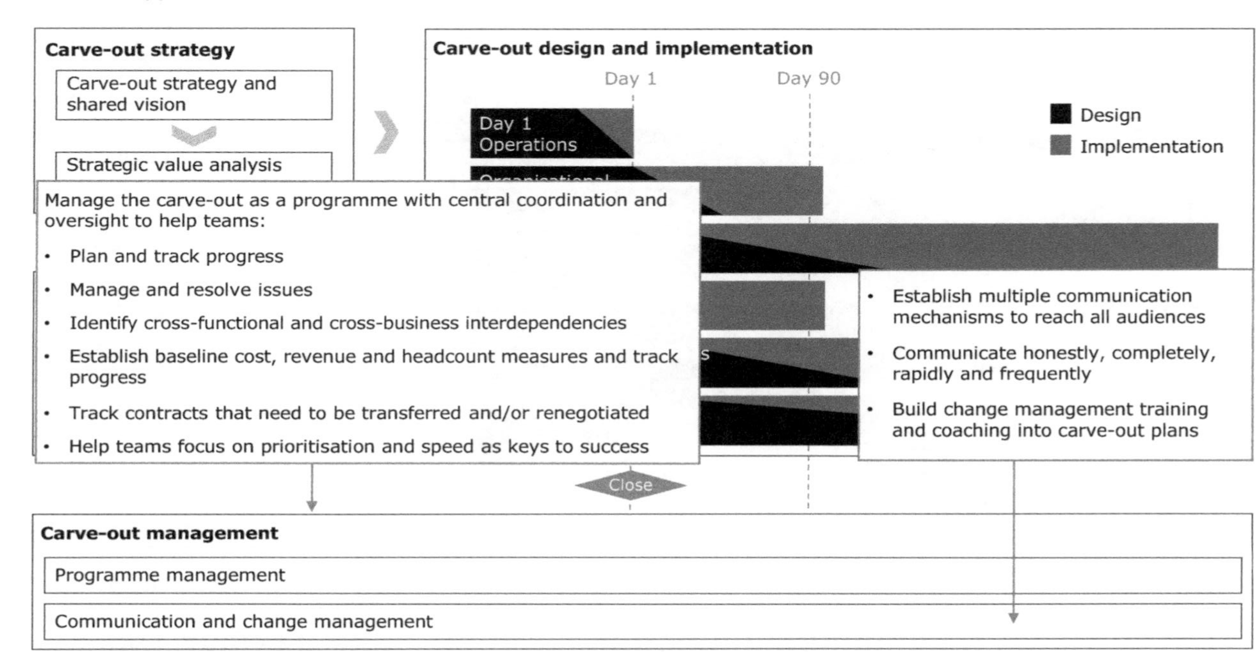

*Carve-out strategy is often developed as part of the valuation/due diligence/negotiation process. Our carve-out approach includes it for completeness.

Thorough preparation is required to be ready to conduct business the day after close

Detailed approach

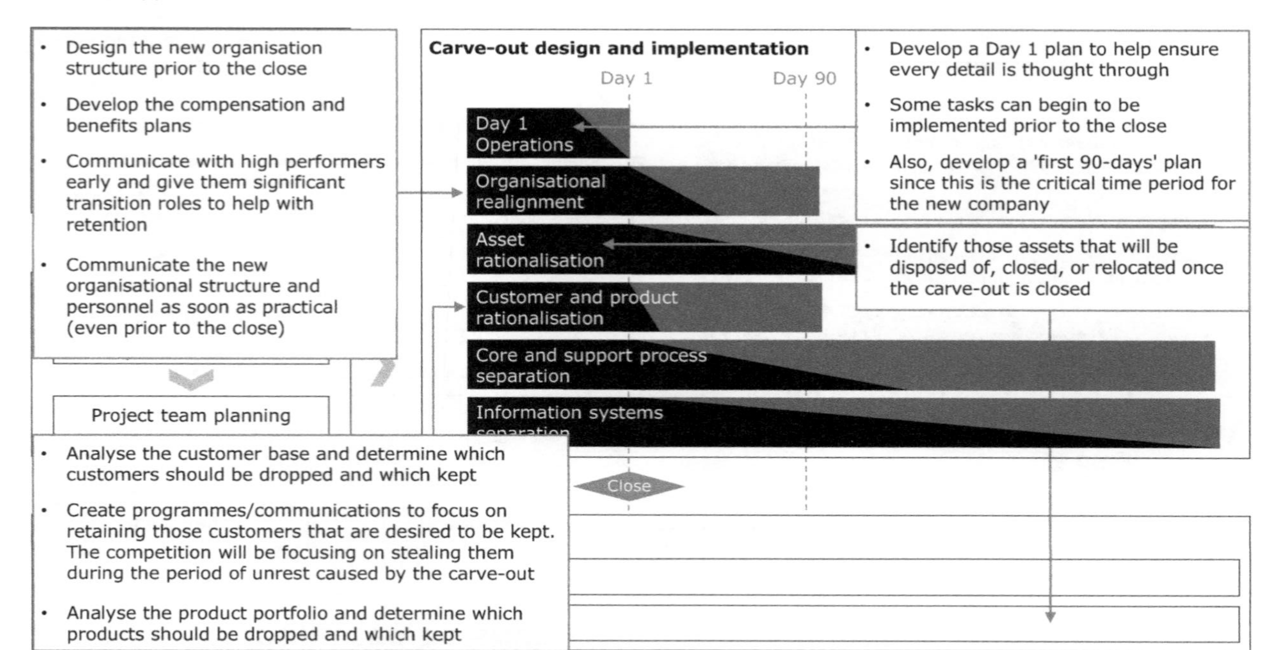

*Carve-out strategy is often developed as part of the valuation/due diligence/negotiation process. Our carve-out approach includes it for completeness.

Thorough preparation is required to be ready to conduct business the day after close (cont.)

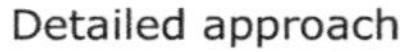

Detailed approach

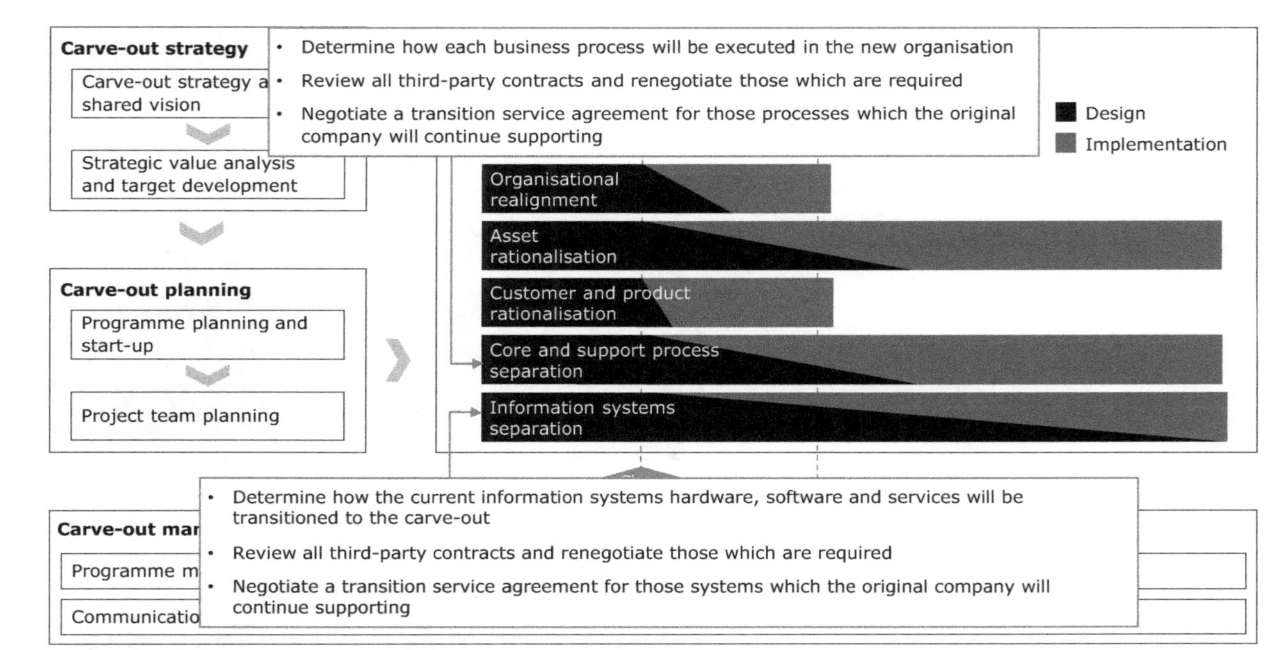

*Carve-out strategy is often developed as part of the valuation/due diligence/negotiation process. Our carve-out approach includes it for completeness.

Day 1 readiness plan ensures the two businesses can work independently on Day 1 (and after)

Detailed approach

Rapidly stabilise and prepare for Day 1 — Capture sustainable value

High-Level Milestones		(180)	(120)	(60)	Day 1	+60 / +360
Strategic Framework and Performance Measurement	• Vision/mission • Separation approach • As-is assessment • Current initiative re-prioritisation	• Operating model • Organisational design • Design performance metrics	• Selection process • Corporate governance structure definition	• Metrics published		• Organisation implemented • Performance metrics • Monitoring of systems and processes
Mapping and Separation	• Organisational and process maps • Shared and standalone resources mapping	• Day 1 vision • Cost potential identification	• Transition Services Agreement (TSA) creation	• Master Services Agreement (MSA) development • Business agreements and contracts	Lockdown	
Organisational Preparedness	• 'Must have' requirements and risk points definition and prioritisation	• Project development • Business future end state	• Prototype • Develop process changes • Team launch • Migration plan defined • Organisation plan	• Day 1 readiness certification • Provide critical corporate services	Lockdown	• Long-term system and process changes
Separation Management	• Separation management setup • Workplan 'close' • Staff teams	• FastTrack™ decision-making process implementation • Plan and resource creation management • Status report, interdependencies management and rapid decision making		• Design lockdown session	Lockdown	• Execution of projects • Interdependencies management
Communication Change Management	• Communications strategy and plan	• Internal and external messages coordination	• Transition tools and methods defined	• Transition training • Communication capabilities in place	Lockdown	• Notification of impacted employees by T+30
Human Resources (HR)	• HR processes – payroll, benefits, etc	• Detailed HR plan and selection process	• Leadership alignment and positioned defined	• Change of ownership and executive contracts		• Implementation of final organisation structure and benefit plans

▲ Milestones Review

The Business Separation Agreement (BSA) defines the key legal arrangements of the separation

Detailed approach

BSA guiding principles

The BSA is a legally binding document.

The separation of both businesses requires the legal resolution of eight topics, for each topic a detailed contract defines the legal terms.

Any of these agreements will be subject to each of the following conditions precedent being fulfilled or waived:

- Consent of majority lenders
- Consent of security agent
- Approval by the original equipment manufacturer (OEM) of transfer of key customer contracts and rights to use customer owned tools
- Approval of the supervisory board of the company to the BSA and the transactions contemplated by it
- Approval of the board of the company to the BSA and the transactions contemplated by it
- Other customary conditions precedent, if any, which are necessary to complete, perfect and execute the agreements set out hereunder

Business Separation Agreement

1. Patents purchase contract
2. Adjustment of real estate lease contract
3. New real estate lease contract
4. Machinery lease contract
5. Transfer of business contracts
6. Supply agreements
7. Trademark agreements
8. Labour union and contracts

Once carve-out principles are agreed in the BSA, details are defined in TSA

Detailed approach

	Content	Creation	Delivery	Payment
Activities	• Understand the type and duration of the services • Determine if services under the TSA are provided by an outside vendor • Understand past history between the organisations and how the relationship may change under a TSA	• Establish a TSA management structure and processes • Define and communicate TSA management roles and responsibilities • Develop the structure and elements of the TSA and ensure consistency among all TSA-related documents	• Develop a master agreement to explain certain issues that are common to all processes • Deliver shared services according to terms and conditions detailed in the TSA • Establish TSA performance metrics, penalties, incentives and issue resolution processes	• Define financial arrangements and payment terms and processes • Develop and communicate process to track and review costs • Define the basis on which costs are derived and record nature of cost basis
Key learnings	• The relationship, regardless of past history, will become much more vendor/customer focused • A 'back channel' of communication can prove very valuable in getting issues resolved • An informal process of communicating will be developed between companies • Insight will be gained on each company's respective position on certain issues	• One point of contact is most efficient to manage the overall TSA process for each organisation • A clear escalation path should be created to resolve issues • Performance metrics should be collected and tracked, and incorporated into the reporting requirements of all parties • Periodic TSA reviews are essential to address performance issues to help maintain the overall relationship	• The people involved in managing the TSA should also write the TSA to ensure that the right services are included, and consistency is maintained in managing day-to-day activities • A realistic time frame should be allowed to complete the TSA generation process • Inconsistent language between agreements should be avoided as vague language creates potential areas of dispute • Terms in the TSA should be as articulate as possible, and all arrangements made should be documented	• The payment terms for the TSA should be spelt out as they are the most controversial • Performance metrics and expectations/baseline should be defined for both parties • Agreements should be structured to help align incentives for TSA managers

Selected TSAs will need to be in place on Day 1 to support the buyer during the transition process

Detailed approach

TSA example – client case

TRANSITION SERVICES AGREEMENT ORDER
Schedule [A or B]
This Transition Services Order is subject to the terms and conditions of the Transition Services Agreement

Functional Team:	
TSA Order #:	
TSA Order Rev:	

TSA Title:	

A) Description of Services

B) Service Provider

C) Service Receiver

D) Deliverables

E) Terms of Service

F) Cost Methodology

G) Special Terms and Conditions

H) Functional Contacts

	Levi Strauss & Co.	*Buyer*
Name		
Title		
Phone Number		
Email Address		

Levi Strauss & Co.
By: ____________
(Authorised Signature)
Name:
Title:
Date:

Buyer
By: ____________
(Authorised Signature)
Name:
Title:
Date:

TSA guiding principles

- TSAs should be as short in duration as possible and will typically not extend beyond 12 months past the closing date
- Transition as many services as possible prior to the closing date (this includes contracts with third-party providers)
- If services need to be provided for only a short period of time (less than one month), consider whether a TSA is necessary
- Provide services that are 'consistent in all material respects' with existing ones. Enhancements are considered outside the scope
- Strive for fast and simple solutions
- Group-related services should be put together under a single TSA if the term of the service, the functional contacts and the service providers/receivers are identical

Appendix 3: Transitional service conditions*

This appendix sets out certain issues for consideration in connection with the separation of a business from a retained business. This can be completed by a Seller or a Purchaser as part of its separation planning efforts in connection with its divestment or acquisition (as applicable) of a business.

Part 1 of the appendix lists questions to be considered in connection with separation and the development of a transitional services agreement, which will help to define key terms of the transitional services agreement and identify the transitional services required and the period for which they will be provided (the Service Term).

Part 2 of the appendix is a detailed service provision breakdown and is split into two parts: 1) Services to be provided by the seller and 2) Services to be provided by the purchaser (if applicable) and consists of a table for the parties to complete with columns for: a description of the services to be provided, the proposed Service Term, the historic costs of service delivery, any underlying third-party contracts and details of a contact(s) within the Seller who would be best placed to discuss any comments or questions in relation to a particular service. This detailed information can be used as the starting point to develop schedules of services to be included in the transitional services agreement itself.

Part 1: Overview of considerations for separation

1. Services provided
   (a) What services will be covered by the agreement?
   See Part 2, below, for examples of types of services that may need to be included.

* Appendix 3 is reproduced with the kind permission of Latham & Watkins.

(b) Who will bear financial and administrative responsibility for third-party contracts?
(c) If responsibilities for any aspect of the services or separation activities will be shared, a 'responsibility matrix' defining the points at which each party's responsibilities begin and end is a useful tool.

2. Service Recipients
   (a) Will the recipients of each service (Service Recipients) be limited to the acquired entities?
   (b) For reverse transitional services agreement services, will the services be provided to the Seller group as a whole or just specific entities?
   (c) Will the services be limited to specific locations?

3. Term of service provision and termination
   (a) How long will each of the services be provided?
   (b) Will separation have occurred or a standalone agreement be put in place by closing?
   (c) Will a transitional period of post-closing service provision be required?
   (d) Will the relevant Service Recipient have the right to extend the services or agreement?
   (e) Will the Service Recipient have the right to terminate the services or agreement early without cause?
   (f) Will the Service Recipient need the right to terminate portions of the services at different times?

4. Charges
   (a) If the services will be provided at cost, can the Seller provide visibility over costs, eg, cost over last 12 months? This information needs collating to assist negotiations.
   (b) If the services will be charged on some basis other than cost, can visibility on the rationale for the charging mechanic be provided? This information will assist negotiations.

5. Changes
   (a) Will it be necessary to include a change proposal and approval mechanism?
   (b) Will it be possible for the Service Recipient to add or request to add new or omitted services?
   (c) What is the mechanism for determining price for new or omitted services?

6. Consents
   (a) Are third-party consents needed under third-party contracts for shared usage of services or for shared access to leased facilities?
   (b) Consents may be required for Service Recipients to utilise items licensed or leased to the service provider and for the service provider to utilise items licensed or leased to the Service Recipient on the Service Recipient's behalf.
   (c) Who bears the cost of obtaining the consents?

7. Performance standards
   (a) Will the agreement specify that the services will be performed to the same level as in the [x] month period prior to signing/completion?
   If not already measured, the Services Recipient should start documenting current levels of service in advance, to form the basis of performance standards under the agreement.
   (b) Will there be a service credit mechanism for failures?

8. Intellectual property
   (a) If any intellectual property (IP) is developed under the agreement, who owns it?
   If the Service Recipient does not have ownership rights, the Service Recipient may need a licence to use the IP after the agreement terminates.

9. Confidentiality, data privacy and security
   (a) The transitional services agreement should identify confidential information of each party, require protection of confidentiality and require each party to use reasonable efforts to limit exposure by its personnel to confidential information of the other.
   (b) Will a party be acting as a data processor on behalf of the other in respect of such party's personal data? If so, General Data Protection Regulation (GDPR) compliant processing clauses may need to be included.
   (c) Where will data be stored and accessed, by whom and for what purposes?
   (d) How often should data be backed up and how should it be archived?
   (e) How will errors in data be corrected and who is responsible for the cost?

10. Liability and indemnification
    (a) Will liability be capped per service at the service charges or in aggregate?
    (b) Will liability for loss of profits, loss of data and any other indirect and consequential losses be excluded?
    (c) Will a liability cap in respect of any breaches of confidentiality and data privacy provisions be included?
    (d) Will indemnities be subject to any overall liability cap?

Part 2: Detailed service provision breakdown

Part A: Services to be provided by the Seller						
	Service	**Description of service**	**Service Term/ any renewal permitted?**	**Cost of service delivery in last 12 months/ monthly charge**	**Any underlying third-party contract(s)?**	**Responsibility**
	Property and Facilities Management					
1.	For example, access and use of specified facilities and associated services, including building security and safety, parking, janitorial and grounds maintenance, HVAC, utilities, mailroom, office equipment and supplies, office furniture, trash and recycling, loading dock, safety services, storage.	*[Complete with detailed description of specific service to be provided including proposed service provider(s) and Service Recipient(s).]*	*[Complete with detailed description of proposed Service Term.]*	*[Complete with details of internal costs of service delivery in last 12 months or proposed charging mechanism.]*	*[Complete with detailed description of any third-party contracts required for the provision or receipt of the relevant Service and any requirement thereunder for obtaining consent.]*	*[Complete with details of an individual within the Seller who will make themselves available to answer Purchaser's questions in relation to a specific service line.]*
	Financial Services					
2.	Financial, accounting and tax services.	*[Complete with detailed description of specific service to be provided including proposed service provider(s) and Service Recipient(s).]*	*[Complete with detailed description of proposed Service Term.]*	*[Complete with details of internal costs of service delivery in last 12 months or proposed charging mechanism.]*	*[Complete with detailed description of any third-party contracts required for the provision or receipt of the relevant Service and any requirement thereunder for obtaining consent.]*	*[Complete with details of an individual within the Seller who will make themselves available to answer Purchaser's questions in relation to a specific service line.]*

Part A: Services to be provided by the Seller						
	Human Resources (HR) Services					
3.	Payroll and benefits services.	*[Complete with detailed description of specific service to be provided including proposed service provider(s) and Service Recipient(s).]*	*[Complete with detailed description of proposed Service Term.]*	*[Complete with details of internal costs of service delivery in last 12 months or proposed charging mechanism.]*	*[Complete with detailed description of any third-party contracts required for the provision or receipt of the relevant Service and any requirement thereunder for obtaining consent.]*	*[Complete with details of an individual within the Seller who will make themselves available to answer Purchaser's questions in relation to a specific service line.]*
4.	HR services.	*[Complete with detailed description of specific service to be provided including proposed service provider(s) and Service Recipient(s).]*	*[Complete with detailed description of proposed Service Term.]*	*[Complete with details of internal costs of service delivery in last 12 months or proposed charging mechanism.]*	*[Complete with detailed description of any third-party contracts required for the provision or receipt of the relevant Service and any requirement thereunder for obtaining consent.]*	*[Complete with details of an individual within the Seller who will make themselves available to answer Purchaser's questions in relation to a specific service line.]*

	Back Office Services					
5.	Procurement services.	*[Complete with detailed description of specific service to be provided including proposed service provider(s) and Service Recipient(s).]*	*[Complete with detailed description of proposed Service Term.]*	*[Complete with details of internal costs of service delivery in last 12 months or proposed charging mechanism.]*	*[Complete with detailed description of any third-party contracts required for the provision or receipt of the relevant Service and any requirement thereunder for obtaining consent.]*	*[Complete with details of an individual within the Seller who will make themselves available to answer Purchaser's questions in relation to a specific service line.]*
6.	Legal, government relations, regulatory/compliance services.	*[Complete with detailed description of specific service to be provided including proposed service provider(s) and Service Recipient(s).]*	*[Complete with detailed description of proposed Service Term.]*	*[Complete with details of internal costs of service delivery in last 12 months or proposed charging mechanism.]*	*[Complete with detailed description of any third-party contracts required for the provision or receipt of the relevant Service and any requirement thereunder for obtaining consent.]*	*[Complete with details of an individual within the Seller who will make themselves available to answer Purchaser's questions in relation to a specific service line.]*
7.	Insurance.	*[Complete with detailed description of specific service to be provided including proposed service provider(s) and Service Recipient(s).]*	*[Complete with detailed description of proposed Service Term.]*	*[Complete with details of internal costs of service delivery in last 12 months or proposed charging mechanism.]*	*[Complete with detailed description of any third-party contracts required for the provision or receipt of the relevant Service and any requirement thereunder for obtaining consent.]*	*[Complete with details of an individual within the Seller who will make themselves available to answer Purchaser's questions in relation to a specific service line.]*

Part A: Services to be provided by the Seller						
	IT Services					
8.	IT services (eg, data centre operation; help desk; software support and maintenance; application development and maintenance; LAN/WAN management and monitoring; email; website hosting and monitoring; hardware and software moves, adds, and changes; data security and disaster recovery).	*[Complete with detailed description of specific service to be provided including proposed service provider(s) and Service Recipient(s).]*	*[Complete with detailed description of proposed Service Term.]*	*[Complete with details of internal costs of service delivery in last 12 months or proposed charging mechanism.]*	*[Complete with detailed description of any third-party contracts required for the provision or receipt of the relevant Service and any requirement thereunder for obtaining consent.]*	*[Complete with details of an individual within the Seller who will make themselves available to answer Purchaser's questions in relation to a specific service line.]*
9.	Telecommunications services (eg, voice (local and long distance); data (intranet, internet, frame relay, etc); pagers; mobile phones; equipment; directories; voicemail; operators; equipment moves, adds and changes).	*[Complete with detailed description of specific service to be provided including proposed service provider(s) and Service Recipient(s).]*	*[Complete with detailed description of proposed Service Term.]*	*[Complete with details of internal costs of service delivery in last 12 months or proposed charging mechanism.]*	*[Complete with detailed description of any third-party contracts required for the provision or receipt of the relevant Service and any requirement thereunder for obtaining consent.]*	*[Complete with details of an individual within the Seller who will make themselves available to answer Purchaser's questions in relation to a specific service line.]*

10.	Use of hardware (eg, servers, desktops, laptops, printers and peripherals).	*[Complete with detailed description of specific service to be provided including proposed service provider(s) and Service Recipient(s).]*	*[Complete with detailed description of proposed Service Term.]*	*[Complete with details of internal costs of service delivery in last 12 months or proposed charging mechanism.]*	*[Complete with detailed description of any third-party contracts required for the provision or receipt of the relevant Service and any requirement thereunder for obtaining consent.]*	*[Complete with details of an individual within the Seller who will make themselves available to answer Purchaser's questions in relation to a specific service line.]*
11.	Use of software and databases (eg, systems software, applications software, tools).	*[Complete with detailed description of specific service to be provided including proposed service provider(s) and Service Recipient(s).]*	*[Complete with detailed description of proposed Service Term.]*	*[Complete with details of internal costs of service delivery in last 12 months or proposed charging mechanism.]*	*[Complete with detailed description of any third-party contracts required for the provision or receipt of the relevant Service and any requirement thereunder for obtaining consent.]*	*[Complete with details of an individual within the Seller who will make themselves available to answer Purchaser's questions in relation to a specific service line.]*
	Regulatory Services					
12.	For example, preparation and submission of any applications to transfer/vary any regulatory authorisations or licences, provision of required documentation, forwarding of correspondence, etc.	*[Complete with detailed description of specific service to be provided including proposed service provider(s) and Service Recipient(s).]*	*[Complete with detailed description of proposed Service Term.]*	*[Complete with details of internal costs of service delivery in last 12 months or proposed charging mechanism.]*	*[Complete with detailed description of any third-party contracts required for the provision or receipt of the relevant Service and any requirement thereunder for obtaining consent.]*	*[Complete with details of an individual within the Seller who will make themselves available to answer Purchaser's questions in relation to a specific service line.]*

Part A: Services to be provided by the Seller						
	Research and Development (R&D) Services					
13.	For example, provision of R&D services, market or product research, provision of reports and documentation, etc.	*[Complete with detailed description of specific service to be provided including proposed service provider(s) and Service Recipient(s).]*	*[Complete with detailed description of proposed Service Term.]*	*[Complete with details of internal costs of service delivery in last 12 months or proposed charging mechanism.]*	*[Complete with detailed description of any third-party contracts required for the provision or receipt of the relevant Service and any requirement thereunder for obtaining consent.]*	*[Complete with details of an individual within the Seller who will make themselves available to answer Purchaser's questions in relation to a specific service line.]*
	Distribution Services					
14.	For example, distribution of products, etc.	*[Complete with detailed description of specific service to be provided including proposed service provider(s) and Service Recipient(s).]*	*[Complete with detailed description of proposed Service Term.]*	*[Complete with details of internal costs of service delivery in last 12 months or proposed charging mechanism.]*	*[Complete with detailed description of any third-party contracts required for the provision or receipt of the relevant Service and any requirement thereunder for obtaining consent.]*	*[Complete with details of an individual within the Seller who will make themselves available to answer Purchaser's questions in relation to a specific service line.]*

	Warehousing Services					
15.	For example, provision of warehouse space, inventory management, etc.	*[Complete with detailed description of specific service to be provided including proposed service provider(s) and Service Recipient(s).]*	*[Complete with detailed description of proposed Service Term.]*	*[Complete with details of internal costs of service delivery in last 12 months or proposed charging mechanism.]*	*[Complete with detailed description of any third-party contracts required for the provision or receipt of the relevant Service and any requirement thereunder for obtaining consent.]*	*[Complete with details of an individual within the Seller who will make themselves available to answer Purchaser's questions in relation to a specific service line.]*
	Logistical Services					
16.	For example, provision of logistics management and services, etc.	*[Complete with detailed description of specific service to be provided including proposed service provider(s) and Service Recipient(s).]*	*[Complete with detailed description of proposed Service Term.]*	*[Complete with details of internal costs of service delivery in last 12 months or proposed charging mechanism.]*	*[Complete with detailed description of any third-party contracts required for the provision or receipt of the relevant Service and any requirement thereunder for obtaining consent.]*	*[Complete with details of an individual within the Seller who will make themselves available to answer Purchaser's questions in relation to a specific service line.]*

Part A: Services to be provided by the Seller						
	Manufacturing Services					
17.	For example, production of products or specific components, etc. This may also be dealt with separately in a manufacturing and supply agreement providing full details of the relevant technical and quality obligations.	*[Complete with detailed description of specific service to be provided including proposed service provider(s) and Service Recipient(s).]*	*[Complete with detailed description of proposed Service Term.]*	*[Complete with details of internal costs of service delivery in last 12 months or proposed charging mechanism.]*	*[Complete with detailed description of any third-party contracts required for the provision or receipt of the relevant Service and any requirement thereunder for obtaining consent.]*	*[Complete with details of an individual within the Seller who will make themselves available to answer Purchaser's questions in relation to a specific service line.]*
	Services Related to Separation					
18.	Regulatory, ie, services related to the transfer and variation of regulatory authorisations, licences, consents, etc.	*[Complete with detailed description of specific service to be provided including proposed service provider(s) and Service Recipient(s).]*	*[Complete with detailed description of proposed Service Term.]*	*[Complete with details of internal costs of service delivery in last 12 months or proposed charging mechanism.]*	*[Complete with detailed description of any third-party contracts required for the provision or receipt of the relevant Service and any requirement thereunder for obtaining consent.]*	*[Complete with details of an individual within the Seller who will make themselves available to answer Purchaser's questions in relation to a specific service line.]*

19.	IP, ie, services related to the identification, transfer and registration of IP rights.	*[Complete with detailed description of specific service to be provided including proposed service provider(s) and Service Recipient(s).]*	*[Complete with detailed description of proposed Service Term.]*	*[Complete with details of internal costs of service delivery in last 12 months or proposed charging mechanism.]*	*[Complete with detailed description of any third-party contracts required for the provision or receipt of the relevant Service and any requirement thereunder for obtaining consent.]*	*[Complete with details of an individual within the Seller who will make themselves available to answer Purchaser's questions in relation to a specific service line.]*
20.	Contracts, ie services related to the novation/transfer of contracts.	*[Complete with detailed description of specific service to be provided including proposed service provider(s) and Service Recipient(s).]*	*[Complete with detailed description of proposed Service Term.]*	*[Complete with details of internal costs of service delivery in last 12 months or proposed charging mechanism.]*	*[Complete with detailed description of any third-party contracts required for the provision or receipt of the relevant Service and any requirement thereunder for obtaining consent.]*	*[Complete with details of an individual within the Seller who will make themselves available to answer Purchaser's questions in relation to a specific service line.]*

Part B: Services to be provided by the Purchaser, if any

	Service	Description of service	Service Term/ any renewal permitted?	Cost of service delivery in last 12 months/ monthly charge	Any underlying third-party contract(s)?	Responsibility
	Property and Facilities Management					
1.	For example, access and use of specified facilities and associated services, including building security and safety, parking, janitorial and grounds maintenance, HVAC, utilities, mailroom, office equipment and supplies, office furniture, trash and recycling, loading dock, safety services, storage.	*[Complete with detailed description of specific service to be provided including proposed service provider(s) and Service Recipient(s).]*	*[Complete with detailed description of proposed Service Term.]*	*[Complete with details of internal costs of service delivery in last 12 months or proposed charging mechanism.]*	*[Complete with detailed description of any third-party contracts required for the provision or receipt of the relevant Service and any requirement thereunder for obtaining consent.]*	*[Complete with details of an individual within the Purchaser who will make themselves available to answer Seller's questions in relation to a specific service line.]*
	Financial Services					
2.	Financial, accounting and tax services.	*[Complete with detailed description of specific service to be provided including proposed service provider(s) and Service Recipient(s).]*	*[Complete with detailed description of proposed Service Term.]*	*[Complete with details of internal costs of service delivery in last 12 months or proposed charging mechanism.]*	*[Complete with detailed description of any third-party contracts required for the provision or receipt of the relevant Service and any requirement thereunder for obtaining consent.]*	*[Complete with details of an individual within the Purchaser who will make themselves available to answer Seller's questions in relation to a specific service line.]*

	Human Resources (HR) Services					
3.	Payroll and benefits services.	*[Complete with detailed description of specific service to be provided including proposed service provider(s) and Service Recipient(s).]*	*[Complete with detailed description of proposed Service Term.]*	*[Complete with details of internal costs of service delivery in last 12 months or proposed charging mechanism.]*	*[Complete with detailed description of any third-party contracts required for the provision or receipt of the relevant Service and any requirement thereunder for obtaining consent.]*	*[Complete with details of an individual within the Purchaser who will make themselves available to answer Seller's questions in relation to a specific service line.]*
4.	HR services.	*[Complete with detailed description of specific service to be provided including proposed service provider(s) and Service Recipient(s).]*	*[Complete with detailed description of proposed Service Term.]*	*[Complete with details of internal costs of service delivery in last 12 months or proposed charging mechanism.]*	*[Complete with detailed description of any third-party contracts required for the provision or receipt of the relevant Service and any requirement thereunder for obtaining consent.]*	*[Complete with details of an individual within the Purchaser who will make themselves available to answer Seller's questions in relation to a specific service line.]*
	Back Office Services					
5.	Procurement services.	*[Complete with detailed description of specific service to be provided including proposed service provider(s) and Service Recipient(s).]*	*[Complete with detailed description of proposed Service Term.]*	*[Complete with details of internal costs of service delivery in last 12 months or proposed charging mechanism.]*	*[Complete with detailed description of any third-party contracts required for the provision or receipt of the relevant Service and any requirement thereunder for obtaining consent.]*	*[Complete with details of an individual within the Purchaser who will make themselves available to answer Seller's questions in relation to a specific service line.]*

Part B: Services to be provided by the Purchaser, if any						
6.	Legal, government relations, regulatory/compliance services.	*[Complete with detailed description of specific service to be provided including proposed service provider(s) and Service Recipient(s).]*	*[Complete with detailed description of proposed Service Term.]*	*[Complete with details of internal costs of service delivery in last 12 months or proposed charging mechanism.]*	*[Complete with detailed description of any third-party contracts required for the provision or receipt of the relevant Service and any requirement thereunder for obtaining consent.]*	*[Complete with details of an individual within the Purchaser who will make themselves available to answer Seller's questions in relation to a specific service line.]*
7.	Insurance.	*[Complete with detailed description of specific service to be provided including proposed service provider(s) and Service Recipient(s).]*	*[Complete with detailed description of proposed Service Term.]*	*[Complete with details of internal costs of service delivery in last 12 months or proposed charging mechanism.]*	*[Complete with detailed description of any third-party contracts required for the provision or receipt of the relevant Service and any requirement thereunder for obtaining consent.]*	*[Complete with details of an individual within the Purchaser who will make themselves available to answer Seller's questions in relation to a specific service line.]*
	IT Services					
8.	IT services (eg, data centre operation; help desk; software support and maintenance; application development and maintenance; LAN/WAN management and monitoring; email; website hosting and monitoring; hardware and software moves, adds, and changes; data security and disaster recovery).	*[Complete with detailed description of specific service to be provided including proposed service provider(s) and Service Recipient(s).]*	*[Complete with detailed description of proposed Service Term.]*	*[Complete with details of internal costs of service delivery in last 12 months or proposed charging mechanism.]*	*[Complete with detailed description of any third-party contracts required for the provision or receipt of the relevant Service and any requirement thereunder for obtaining consent.]*	*[Complete with details of an individual within the Purchaser who will make themselves available to answer Seller's questions in relation to a specific service line.]*

9.	Telecommunications services (eg, voice (local and long distance); data (intranet, internet, frame relay, etc); pagers; mobile phones; equipment; directories; voice-mail; operators; equipment moves, adds and changes).	*[Complete with detailed description of specific service to be provided including proposed service provider(s) and Service Recipient(s).]*	*[Complete with detailed description of proposed Service Term.]*	*[Complete with details of internal costs of service delivery in last 12 months or proposed charging mechanism.]*	*[Complete with detailed description of any third-party contracts required for the provision or receipt of the relevant Service and any requirement thereunder for obtaining consent.]*	*[Complete with details of an individual within the Purchaser who will make themselves available to answer Seller's questions in relation to a specific service line.]*
10.	Use of hardware (eg, servers, desktops, laptops, printers and peripherals).	*[Complete with detailed description of specific service to be provided including proposed service provider(s) and Service Recipient(s).]*	*[Complete with detailed description of proposed Service Term.]*	*[Complete with details of internal costs of service delivery in last 12 months or proposed charging mechanism.]*	*[Complete with detailed description of any third-party contracts required for the provision or receipt of the relevant Service and any requirement thereunder for obtaining consent.]*	*[Complete with details of an individual within the Purchaser who will make themselves available to answer Seller's questions in relation to a specific service line.]*
11.	Use of software and databases (eg, systems software, applications software, tools).	*[Complete with detailed description of specific service to be provided including proposed service provider(s) and Service Recipient(s).]*	*[Complete with detailed description of proposed Service Term.]*	*[Complete with details of internal costs of service delivery in last 12 months or proposed charging mechanism.]*	*[Complete with detailed description of any third-party contracts required for the provision or receipt of the relevant Service and any requirement thereunder for obtaining consent.]*	*[Complete with details of an individual within the Purchaser who will make themselves available to answer Seller's questions in relation to a specific service line.]*

Part B: Services to be provided by the Purchaser, if any						
	Regulatory Services					
12.	For example, preparation and submission of any applications to transfer/vary any regulatory authorisations or licences, portfolio services, provision of required documentation, forwarding of correspondence, etc.	*[Complete with detailed description of specific service to be provided including proposed service provider(s) and Service Recipient(s).]*	*[Complete with detailed description of proposed Service Term.]*	*[Complete with details of internal costs of service delivery in last 12 months or proposed charging mechanism.]*	*[Complete with detailed description of any third-party contracts required for the provision or receipt of the relevant Service and any requirement thereunder for obtaining consent.]*	*[Complete with details of an individual within the Purchaser who will make themselves available to answer Seller's questions in relation to a specific service line.]*
	Research and Development (R&D) Services					
13.	For example, provision of R&D services, market or product research, provision of reports and documentation, etc.	*[Complete with detailed description of specific service to be provided including proposed service provider(s) and Service Recipient(s).]*	*[Complete with detailed description of proposed Service Term.]*	*[Complete with details of internal costs of service delivery in last 12 months or proposed charging mechanism.]*	*[Complete with detailed description of any third-party contracts required for the provision or receipt of the relevant Service and any requirement thereunder for obtaining consent.]*	*[Complete with details of an individual within the Purchaser who will make themselves available to answer Seller's questions in relation to a specific service line.]*

	Distribution Services					
14.	For example, distribution of products, etc.	*[Complete with detailed description of specific service to be provided including proposed service provider(s) and Service Recipient(s).]*	*[Complete with detailed description of proposed Service Term.]*	*[Complete with details of internal costs of service delivery in last 12 months or proposed charging mechanism.]*	*[Complete with detailed description of any third-party contracts required for the provision or receipt of the relevant Service and any requirement thereunder for obtaining consent.]*	*[Complete with details of an individual within the Purchaser who will make themselves available to answer Seller's questions in relation to a specific service line.]*
	Warehousing Services					
15.	For example, provision of warehouse space, inventory management, etc.	*[Complete with detailed description of specific service to be provided including proposed service provider(s) and Service Recipient(s).]*	*[Complete with detailed description of proposed Service Term.]*	*[Complete with details of internal costs of service delivery in last 12 months or proposed charging mechanism.]*	*[Complete with detailed description of any third-party contracts required for the provision or receipt of the relevant Service and any requirement thereunder for obtaining consent.]*	*[Complete with details of an individual within the Purchaser who will make themselves available to answer Seller's questions in relation to a specific service line.]*

Part B: Services to be provided by the Purchaser, if any						
	Logistical Services					
16.	For example, provision of logistics management and services, etc.	*[Complete with detailed description of specific service to be provided including proposed service provider(s) and Service Recipient(s).]*	*[Complete with detailed description of proposed Service Term.]*	*[Complete with details of internal costs of service delivery in last 12 months or proposed charging mechanism.]*	*[Complete with detailed description of any third-party contracts required for the provision or receipt of the relevant Service and any requirement thereunder for obtaining consent.]*	*[Complete with details of an individual within the Purchaser who will make themselves available to answer Seller's questions in relation to a specific service line.]*
	Manufacturing Services					
17.	For example, production of products or specific components, etc. This may also be dealt with separately in a manufacturing and supply agreement providing full details of the relevant technical and quality obligations.	*[Complete with detailed description of specific service to be provided including proposed service provider(s) and Service Recipient(s).]*	*[Complete with detailed description of proposed Service Term.]*	*[Complete with details of internal costs of service delivery in last 12 months or proposed charging mechanism.]*	*[Complete with detailed description of any third-party contracts required for the provision or receipt of the relevant Service and any requirement thereunder for obtaining consent.]*	*[Complete with details of an individual within the Purchaser who will make themselves available to answer Seller's questions in relation to a specific service line.]*

	Services Related to Separation					
18.	Regulatory, ie, services related to the transfer and variation of regulatory authorisations, licences, consents, etc.	*[Complete with detailed description of specific service to be provided including proposed service provider(s) and Service Recipient(s).]*	*[Complete with detailed description of proposed Service Term.]*	*[Complete with details of internal costs of service delivery in last 12 months or proposed charging mechanism.]*	*[Complete with detailed description of any third-party contracts required for the provision or receipt of the relevant Service and any requirement thereunder for obtaining consent.]*	*[Complete with details of an individual within the Purchaser who will make themselves available to answer Seller's questions in relation to a specific service line.]*
19.	IP, ie, services related to the identification, transfer and registration of IP rights.	*[Complete with detailed description of specific service to be provided including proposed service provider(s) and Service Recipient(s).]*	*[Complete with detailed description of proposed Service Term.]*	*[Complete with details of internal costs of service delivery in last 12 months or proposed charging mechanism.]*	*[Complete with detailed description of any third-party contracts required for the provision or receipt of the relevant Service and any requirement thereunder for obtaining consent.]*	*[Complete with details of an individual within the Purchaser who will make themselves available to answer Seller's questions in relation to a specific service line.]*
20.	Contracts, ie, services related to the novation/transfer of contracts.	*[Complete with detailed description of specific service to be provided including proposed service provider(s) and Service Recipient(s).]*	*[Complete with detailed description of proposed Service Term.]*	*[Complete with details of internal costs of service delivery in last 12 months or proposed charging mechanism.]*	*[Complete with detailed description of any third-party contracts required for the provision or receipt of the relevant Service and any requirement thereunder for obtaining consent.]*	*[Complete with details of an individual within the Purchaser who will make themselves available to answer Seller's questions in relation to a specific service line.]*

About the authors

Edward Barnett
Partner, Latham & Watkins
edward.barnett@lw.com

Edward Barnett is a partner in the Corporate Department of the London office of Latham & Watkins, co-chair of the firm's Global Mergers & Acquisitions practice and former co-chair of the firm's Global Public Company Representation practice.

Mr Barnett's practice spans a variety of cross-border mergers and acquisitions and corporate finance transactions, including public takeovers, takeover defence, joint ventures, and private company and business acquisitions and divestments, with a particular focus in the consumer, technology, pharmaceuticals, entertainment, media and sports sectors.

His practice also focuses on company representation work, including advising on a range of corporate governance matters.

Gregory Bonné
Associate, Latham & Watkins
greg.bonne@lw.com

Greg Bonné is an associate at Latham & Watkins and a member of the global Antitrust and Competition team based in London, practising UK and EU competition law.

Prior to joining Latham & Watkins, Mr Bonné worked as assistant director of mergers at the UK Competition and Markets Authority (CMA). During this period, he coordinated over 100 Phase I merger investigations for the CMA and was an active member of the Mergers Intelligence Committee. Mr Bonné also acted as a project director and he led a Phase 2 merger investigation. In addition to merger control work, he has worked on cartel investigations, UK market investigations, judicial review proceedings before the Competition Appeal Tribunal and on price control appeals in regulated sectors.

Prior to his time at the CMA, Mr Bonné worked in private practice at a global law firm in London and in Brussels.

Jennifer Cadet
Associate, Latham & Watkins
jennifer.cadet@lw.com

Jennifer Cadet is an associate in the London office of Latham & Watkins and a member of the firm's Corporate Department. Ms Cadet's transactional practice includes representation of public and private companies in mergers, acquisitions and divestitures. She also advises companies and underwriters in connection with public offerings and general corporate governance.

In addition to her legal practice, Ms Cadet is a local leader of Latham

& Watkins' Black Lawyers Group and has served on the firm's Recruiting Committee.

Terry Charalambous
Associate, Latham & Watkins
terry.charalambous@lw.com

Terry Charalambous is an associate in the Corporate Department of the London office of Latham & Watkins, having qualified in 2014. Mr Charalambous' practice focuses on mergers and acquisitions, private equity (PE) and general corporate matters.

He has experience in various industries, including healthcare, consumer products, leisure and technology, and has advised both corporates and PE firms on a range of transactions.

Nick Cline
Partner, Latham & Watkins
nick.cline@lw.com

Nick Cline is a partner and co-chair of the Corporate Department in the London Office of Latham & Watkins. Mr Cline is a mergers and acquisitions (M&A) lawyer with more than 20 years of experience focusing on UK and international, cross-border M&A, private equity investments and joint ventures.

He has represented, among others, Qatar Investment Authority, Thomas Cook Group plc, VEON, Emerson Electric Co, Aon plc, Mattel Inc, Yahoo! Inc, Virgin Media Inc, ACCO Brands, Global Infrastructure Partners and Human Rights Watch.

Clients describe Mr Cline as "very pragmatic, responsive and easy to deal with" (*Chambers UK*, 2018).

Gail Crawford
Partner, Latham & Watkins
gail.crawford@lw.com

Gail Crawford is a partner in the London office of Latham & Watkins, chair of the Data Privacy Committee and co-chair of the Technology Transactions Group. Ms Crawford advises clients – from start-ups to multinationals, across all industries – on technology, intellectual property and commercial law. She has experience advising on the technology and data aspects of complex commercial arrangements often driven by mergers and acquisitions and other corporate activity, including carve-out transactions in transitional services agreements, joint ventures, procurement and outsourcing.

Ms Crawford has particular expertise in data privacy and protection matters. Ms Crawford is recommended in *The Legal 500 UK* 2019 for commercial contracts, IT and telecoms and listed as a "leading individual" in data protection privacy and cybersecurity.

Commentators report that she is "a very thoughtful and friendly person" who is "accommodating from a time perspective, and she can get clients what they need, when they need it" (*Chambers UK*, 2019).

Emily Cridland
Associate, Latham & Watkins
emily.cridland@lw.com

Emily Cridland is an associate in the London office of Latham & Watkins and a member of the firm's Corporate Department. Ms Cridland's practice focuses on cross-border mergers and acquisitions for strategic corporate and private equity clients, joint ventures, reorganisations and general corporate matters. She trained in the London and Singapore offices of Latham & Watkins, qualifying in 2012.

Ms Cridland has previously spent time working in-house on secondment to IHS Markit and has recently served on the firm's Associates Committee.

Catherine Drinnan
Partner, Latham & Watkins
catherine.drinnan@lw.com

Catherine Drinnan is a partner in the London office of Latham & Watkins. Ms Drinnan's practice focuses on employment law, pensions law and the human resources and pensions aspects of corporate and finance deals, and has particular expertise in advising on transfers of undertakings, carve-outs and cross-border acquisitions.

Ms Drinnan advises on the full spectrum of employment and pensions issues including: TUPE, works council, trade union issues, executive and employee compensation, hiring and termination issues, UK Pensions Regulator clearance applications and pension plan de-risking.

Clients praise her "helpful professionalism" on substantial corporate transactions.

Moeiz Farhan
Associate, Gibson, Dunn & Crutcher
mfarhan@gibsondunn.com

Moeiz Farhan is an associate in the London office of Gibson, Dunn & Crutcher specialising in complex commercial litigation and international arbitration. Mr Farhan also acts as an advocate, having appeared as both sole and junior counsel in the English courts on a number of occasions.

Mr Farhan is qualified as a barrister, having been called to the Bar of England and Wales in 2014 by Lincoln's Inn. Before he was called to the Bar, Mr Farhan spent a year working as part of the Commercial and Common Law team at the Law Commission of England and Wales, and as a visiting tutor at King's College London.

Edward Heaton
In-house mergers and acquisitions lawyer, BT
edward.heaton@bt.com

Edward (Edd) Heaton is an experienced mergers and acquisitions (M&A) lawyer with a long track record of a wide variety of M&A. Mr Heaton gained this experience in private practice at Olswang (now CMS) and lately in an in-house M&A role at BT.

Mr Heaton has led the Corporate Transactions team at BT since 2018. Inherent in working in a large corporate like BT is dealing with complex carve-out issues, separating businesses from the connections that they have to group functions and resources. This, together with past experience in private practice, has given Mr Heaton experience dealing with the complexities that these issues can present to the smooth execution of successful M&A.

Claire Keast-Butler
Partner, Cooley
ckeastbutler@cooley.com

Claire Keast-Butler is a partner at Cooley specialising in equity capital markets transactions and public company representation.

Ms Keast-Butler has considerable experience representing issuers, investment banks and investors on initial public offerings and secondary offerings. In particular, she advises listed companies on a range of corporate and securities matters and corporate governance.

Deborah Kirk
Partner, Latham & Watkins
deborah.kirk@lw.com

Deborah Kirk is a partner in the Corporate Department of the London office of Latham & Watkins. Ms Kirk specialises in the operational aspects of carve-out transactions, including the intellectual property, information technology and data aspects of these deals. She guides clients through the process of carve-out deals, including preparatory steps on the sale side, diligence on the buy side and putting in place post-completion transitional and long-term arrangements (including licences and supply arrangements) to achieve full separation.

Ms Kirk has acted for numerous buyers and sellers, across a variety of industries including finance, pharma and medical devices, consumer goods, chemicals and the travel industry.

James Leslie
Associate, Latham & Watkins
james.leslie@lw.com

James Leslie is an associate in the Tax Department of the London office of Latham & Watkins. Mr Leslie is a transactional and advisory lawyer who focuses on the direct and indirect tax aspects of national and international transactions.

He advises on the tax aspects of a wide range of matters including banking, structured finance, capital markets issues, project finance, investment funds, mergers and acquisitions and corporate reorganisations.

Beatrice Lo
Senior associate, Latham & Watkins
beatrice.lo@lw.com

Beatrice Lo is a senior associate in the Corporate Department of the London office of Latham & Watkins. Ms Lo's practice covers a range of corporate and commercial matters, including mergers and acquisitions, carve-outs, joint ventures, reorganisations and general corporate advice.

Ms Lo has particular expertise in the energy, financial services and insurance sectors.

Karl Mah
Partner, Latham & Watkins
karl.mah@lw.com

Karl Mah is a partner in the Tax Department of the London office of Latham & Watkins. Mr Mah acts for a broad range of corporate and financial clients, and his practice area focuses on international and corporate tax matters.

He has particular expertise in advising on the tax aspects of mergers and acquisitions and private equity deals, capital markets offerings and finance transactions.

Neil McFerran
Director, AlixPartners
nmcferran@alixpartners.com

Dr Neil McFerran is currently the UK lead of the AlixPartners Private Equity (PE) practice. Neil is an experienced operations and transactions professional with strong delivery experience in complex assignments including business unit carve-outs, operational due diligence, post-merger integration and rapid post-deal value creation.

He has a broad range of mergers and acquisitions and corporate finance experience, having worked with PE and corporate clients in a range of high-profile cross-border deals with complex carve-out requirements.

Neil has deep experience in the specialty chemicals space and most notably has advised a private equity client on the acquisition of a c. $5bn revenue asset separated from a chemicals major with operational and carve-out due diligence.

Neil holds a PhD in mechanical engineering from Queen's University Belfast and an MBA from Cass Business School in London.

Robbie McLaren
Partner, Latham & Watkins
robbie.mclaren@lw.com

Robbie McLaren is a partner in the London office of Latham & Watkins and co-chair of the London Corporate Group. Mr McLaren specialises in cross-border private mergers and acquisitions (M&A) transactions for corporates and private equity, with a particular focus on clients who operate in the life sciences/healthcare and telecommunications, media and technology (TMT) sectors. He was recognised by *The Legal 500* in 2018 for his work in M&A: Upper Mid-Market and Premium Deals in 2018 with clients noting that he is a "pharmaceuticals sector expert".

Mr McLaren has advised on a number of significant carve-out M&A transactions, in particular those in highly regulated industries including: Allergan on the $40.5bn disposal of their global generics business to Teva; Actavis on the disposal of its Western European generics and OTC business to Aurobindo; Telenor on the €2.8bn disposal of its CEE mobile business to the PPF Group; Norsk Hydro on its $5bn acquisition of the aluminium business of Vale; and Theramex on its acquisition of the international women's health business from Teva.

Mr McLaren has contributed a number of chapters to books on M&A and has also authored a number of articles on M&A trends and the impact of new regulations on M&A.

Anna Ngo
Associate, Latham & Watkins
anna.ngo@lw.com

Anna Ngo is an English law qualified associate specialising in international capital market transactions, representing issuers, investment banks and investors on primary and secondary equity capital market transactions and general corporate matters. Ms Ngo regularly advises listed companies on corporate and securities law matters and corporate governance. She also has experience in both public and private mergers and acquisitions transactions.

In particular, Ms Ngo advised TI Fluid Systems plc on its £1.3 bn initial public offering on the London Stock Exchange and Applus Services SA and The Carlyle Group on the €1.2 bn initial public offering of Applus and its admission to the Spanish Stock Exchange. She has considerable experience advising on the corporate and capital markets aspects of complex cross-border transactions including FMC Technologies Inc, the subsea oil services group, on its US$17bn merger with Technip SA on the New York Stock

Exchange and Euronext Paris, and the dual listing of LivaNova plc on the London Stock Exchange and Nasdaq on the closing of the merger between Cyberonics Inc and Sorin SpA.

Farah O'Brien
Partner, Latham & Watkins
farah.o'brien@lw.com

Farah O'Brien is a partner in the London office of Latham & Watkins. Ms O'Brien specialises in cross-border private mergers and acquisitions (M&A) transactions for both private equity and strategic clients. She has experience across all aspects of corporate transactions, including in particular carve-outs, leveraged acquisitions and joint ventures.

She was recently featured in *Legal Week*'s 2018 Rising Stars in Private Equity and commended for her "depth of experience advising on some of the market's most significant transactions".

Ms O'Brien has advised on many carve-out M&A transactions. Her experience includes advising Norsk Hydro on the acquisition of an aluminium smelter and two metal supplying companies from Rio Tinto, the sale of Thomas Cook Airlines Belgium (TCAB), a Belgium-based leisure airline, to Brussels Airlines, a subsidiary of Lufthansa as well as the acquisition by Onex of SIG Combibloc Group from the Reynolds Group.

Sean O'Flynn
Director, AlixPartners
soflynn@alixpartners.com

Sean O'Flynn is an experienced transactions professional with more than 15 years' industry and advisory experience in the deal environment with a focus on automotive, industrial and consumer products across all stages of the deal lifecycle.

Prior to joining AlixPartners, Mr O'Flynn led engagements for both multinational corporate and private equity clients in carve-out, post-deal cost restructuring, performance improvement and integrations, as well as pre-deal due diligence and carve-outs.

He started his career in financial services working for both Barclays International and Deutsche Bank.

Jonathan Parker
Partner, Latham & Watkins
jonathan.parker@lw.com

Jonathan Parker is a partner in the Antitrust & Competition practice in the London office of Latham & Watkins. Mr Parker's practice focuses on European and UK competition law and he has considerable experience in merger control matters.

With nearly 20 years of experience in government and private practice, Mr Parker advises clients on a wide range of competition issues, including mergers and acquisitions, market studies, cartels/restrictive agreements and abuse of dominance cases before the European Commission and the UK Competition and Markets Authority (CMA), as well as in relation to appeals to the UK Competition Appeal Tribunal and the EU General Court.

Prior to joining Latham & Watkins, Mr Parker worked as director of mergers at the CMA.

Katie Peek
Associate, Latham & Watkins
katie.peek@lw.com

Katie Peek is an associate in the UK Corporate Department of the London office of Latham & Watkins, having trained in the firm's London and Singapore offices.

Her practice is focused on private equity, mergers and acquisitions, joint ventures, corporate restructurings and general corporate matters.

Niall Quinn
Associate, Latham & Watkins
niall.quinn@lw.com

Niall Quinn is an associate in the UK Corporate Department in the London office of Latham & Watkins. His practice focuses on private equity, mergers and acquisitions and general corporate matters.

Scott Shean
Partner, Latham & Watkins
scott.shean@lw.com

Scott Shean serves as primary outside counsel to several public and private companies in various industries, including healthcare, technology and real estate. Mr Shean's practice focuses on mergers and acquisitions (M&A), corporate governance and capital markets, and he has led the firm's representation on numerous high profile and complex transactions.

Mr Shean is the Orange County Corporate Department chair and a global co-chair of Latham's Healthcare and Life Sciences practice. He formerly served as the managing partner of the Orange County office from 2007 to 2014. Mr Shean has experience in M&A and capital markets transactions, representing both companies and investment banks.

He also provides corporate governance advice to several companies for which he serves as primary outside counsel.

Frances Stocks Allen
Associate, Latham & Watkins
frances.stocks.allen@lw.com

Frances Stocks Allen is a senior associate in the London office of Latham & Watkins. Ms Stocks Allen sits in the Technology Transactions Group and advises clients on intellectual property, commercial law and privacy matters for clients of all sizes and across all industries but with a particular focus on clients in the life sciences industry.

Ms Stocks Allen has experience advising on the short- and longer-term separation, transition, licensing and complex commercial arrangements resulting from mergers and acquisitions and strategic corporate activity, including a particular specialism in complex carve-outs.

Jeffrey Sullivan
Partner, Gibson, Dunn & Crutcher
jeffrey.sullivan@gibsondunn.com

Jeffrey Sullivan is a partner in the London office of Gibson, Dunn & Crutcher. Mr Sullivan is a member of the firm's International Arbitration Group. His practice has a particular focus on disputes arising in the energy, extractive industries and infrastructure sectors.

His experience includes handling post-mergers and acquisitions disputes as well as those arising out of long-term supply agreements, offtake agreements, concession agreements, production sharing and operating agreements, and joint venture agreements. He also has extensive experience acting for clients in the renewable energy sector, including advising numerous private equity, infrastructure and green energy funds.

Mr Sullivan is a dual-qualified lawyer, admitted to practice in Washington DC and England and Wales.

Huw Thomas
Partner, Latham & Watkins
huw.thomas@lw.com

Huw Thomas is a partner in the London office of Latham & Watkins. His practice is focused on cross-border mergers and acquisitions, joint ventures, corporate restructurings and general corporate matters across the investment lifecycle for private equity sponsors and their portfolio companies, as well as for strategic clients.

Mr Thomas has experience across a broad range of sectors (including energy and financial services) and has advised on a number of complex carve-out transactions, including multiple regulator-mandated disposals.

He has previously spent time on secondment to BP and Deutsche Bank, has contributed chapters to *Private Equity: A Transactional Analysis* and *Global Investment Funds: A Practical Guide to Structuring, Raising and Managing Funds* and has authored numerous articles on key M&A trends and developments.

Mark Veldon
Managing director, AlixPartners
mveldon@alixpartners.com

Mark Veldon leads AlixPartners' Private Equity (PE) practice in EMEA, where he works extensively in guiding companies through mergers and acquisitions transactions, and operational transformations.

Mr Veldon has two decades of experience in advising PE and corporate clients in due diligence, post-merger integration and carve-out, restructuring and operational performance improvement in manufacturing, procurement, and selling, general and administrative expenses (SG&A), along with undertaking interim management roles. He has a particular focus on large cross-border companies and has extensive experience across a range of sectors such as pharmaceutics, oil and gas, consumer goods and industrial products.

Mr Veldon holds a master's degree from Princeton University and degrees in business studies and operations management from Aberdeen University.

Julia Windsor
Consultant, AlixPartners
jwindsor@alixpartners.com

Julia Windsor has worked with private-equity firms, investment funds and pension boards for the last 12 years. She has primarily undertaken due diligence on target companies and assets, assisted with the financing of acquisitions and project finance for greenfield and brownfield developments and advised on the post-merger process, including organisational design and value creation.

Before joining AlixPartners, Ms Windsor worked as a finance lawyer at international law firms gaining experience across the real estate, infrastructure and resources sectors in Australia before moving to London to gain leverage finance experience in the telecommunications and energy sectors.

Ms Windsor holds an MBA from the University of Oxford's Saïd Business School and has degrees in law and economics from Murdoch University in Australia.

Index

Note: Page numbers in *italics* denote figures and tables.

About Globe Law and Business

Globe Law and Business was established in 2005, and from the very beginning, we set out to create law books which are sufficiently high level to be of real use to the experienced professional, yet still accessible and easy to navigate. Most of our authors are drawn from Magic Circle and other top commercial firms, both in the UK and internationally.

Our titles are carefully produced, with the utmost attention paid to editorial, design and production processes. We hope this results in high-quality books which are easy to read, and a pleasure to own. All our new books are also available as ebooks, which are compatible with most desktop, laptop and tablet devices.

We have recently expanded our portfolio to include a new range of journals, Special Reports and Good Practice Guides, available both digitally and in hard copy format, and produced to the same high standards as our books.

We'd very much like to hear from you with your thoughts and ideas for improving what we offer. Please do feel free to email me at sian@globelawandbusiness.com with your views.

Sian O'Neill
Managing director
Globe Law and Business
www.globelawandbusiness.com

Globe Law
and Business